WHO LEADS WHOM?

STUDIES IN COMMUNICATION, MEDIA, AND PUBLIC OPINION

A series edited by Susan Herbst and Benjamin I. Page

Who Leads Whom?

Presidents, Policy, and the Public

BRANDICE CANES-WRONE

THE UNIVERSITY OF CHICAGO PRESS   Chicago and London

BRANDICE CANES-WRONE is associate professor of politics and public affairs at
Princeton University.

The University of Chicago Press, Chicago 60637
The University of Chicago Press, Ltd., London
© 2006 by The University of Chicago
All rights reserved. Published 2006
Printed in the United States of America

15 14 13 12 11 10 09 08 07 06   1 2 3 4 5

ISBN: 0-226-09280-1 (cloth)
ISBN: 0-226-09282-8 (paper)

Library of Congress Cataloging-in-Publication Data

Canes-Wrone, Brandice.
    Who leads whom? : presidents, policy, and the public / Brandice Canes-Wrone.
        p.   cm.—(Studies in communication, media, and public opinion)
    Includes bibliographical references and index.
    ISBN 0-226-09280-1 (cloth : alk. paper)—ISBN 0-226-09282-8 (pbk. : alk. paper)
    1. Presidents—United States—Decision making. 2. Political leadership—United
States. 3. Public opinion—United States. I. Title. II. Series.
JK516.C37 2006
352.23'6'0973—dc22

                                                                2005008995

To David A. Wrone

Contents

List of Tables and Figures   ix
Preface   xi
Acknowledgments   xv

1. Presidents' Involvement of the Mass Public   1

PART ONE Public Appeals   15

2. A Theory of Public Appeals   19
3. Domestic Policy Appeals   51
4. Foreign Policy Appeals   83

PART TWO Policy Pandering and Leadership   103

5. Incentives for Policy Pandering   111
6. Examples of Policy Pandering and Leadership   131
7. Patterns of Presidential Decisions
   With Kenneth W. Shotts   157
8. Chief Executives, Policymaking, and the Public   185

References   193
Name Index   205
Subject Index   209

Tables and Figures

TABLES

3.1 Popularity of Initiatives in Domestic Policy Appeals, 1957–2000 55
3.2 Popularity of Initiatives in Domestic Policy Appeals, by President 56
3.3 Popularity of Initiatives in Domestic Policy Appeals, by Legislative
 Outcome 58
3.4 Determinants of Domestic Policy Appeals 71
3.5 Determinants of Domestic Policy Success 75
4.1 Popularity of Initiatives in Foreign Policy Appeals, 1957–2000 86
4.2 Popularity of Initiatives in Foreign Policy Appeals, by President 87
4.3 Popularity of Initiatives in Foreign Policy Appeals, by Legislative
 Outcome 88
4.4 Determinants of Foreign Policy Appeals and Legislative Success 93
4.5 Test of the Popularity of Foreign Positions Prediction 100
7.1 Competing Predictions on Policy Congruence 161
7.2 Proportion of Observations Reflecting Policy Congruence,
 by Key Theoretical Variables 167
7.3 Determinants of Policy Congruence, First-term Presidents 175
7.4 Determinants of Policy Congruence, Second-term Presidents 180

FIGURES

2.1 Effect of a Public Appeal on Congressional Preferences 24
2.2 Basic Results When President Lacks Veto Power 26
2.3 Basic Results When President Has Veto Power 27
2.4 Reagan's 1981 Tax Cuts 43
2.5 Reagan's Initiative to Abolish the Departments of Energy and
 Education 45
2.6 Clinton's Bosnia Mission 47
7.1 Conditional Pandering Theory Popularity Prediction 160

Preface

An ancient concern about democratic government is that it can encourage popularly elected leaders to incite the rule of the mob. Even Aristotle, who held that a multitude of people would generate more wisdom than any individual could, recognized this potential problem.[1] In the *Politics,* he observes that in democracies "where the laws are not supreme, there demagogues spring up . . . The demagogues make the decrees of the people override the laws, by referring all things to the popular assembly. And therefore they grow great, because the people have all things in their hands, and they [the demagogues] hold in their hands the votes of the people, who obey them" (Aristotle 1988 [350 B.C.E.], 89).

The Founders of the United States government sought to prevent this type of democracy through, among other mechanisms, the separation of powers. As Martin Diamond (1987, 671) observes, the forefathers hoped this separation would encourage some elected officials to "resist the wrong desires of the people to which other representatives are supinely yielding, or which they are even demagogically arousing." Notwithstanding these efforts of the forefathers, many students of the American presidency have observed that the institution encourages policymaking that yields to mass opinion. Writing in the early part of the nineteenth century, Alexis de Tocqueville (1945 [1835], 142–43) lamented that American chief executives are "an easy tool in the hands of the majority." John Stuart Mill expressed similar concern around that time in surmising, "every public question is discussed and decided with less reference to its merits than to its expected bearing on the presidential election" (1958 [1861], 201–2).

The institution of the American presidency has therefore long been perceived to encourage policymaking that caters to mass opinion,

---

1. For a discussion of Aristotle's beliefs about the wisdom of the multitude, see Waldron (1995).

potentially at the expense of societal welfare. Today this issue is as pertinent as ever. The two plebiscitary actions identified by Aristotle and Diamond—inciting and yielding to mass opinion—can be easily achieved by contemporary presidents. Mass communications afford a readily available means of appealing to the public. Polling is an integral component of White House operations. Thus to the extent that presidents' arousing and monitoring of public opinion do indeed induce policymaking that harms society, the detrimental impact should be as great as it ever has been.

This book analyzes how policymaking in Washington is in fact affected by these presidential activities. In particular, I examine the impact of presidents' public appeals and polling. Throughout the course of the text, I refer to these activities as presidents' *involvement of the mass public*. I assess both whether this involvement increases the impact of mass opinion on policymakers' decisions, as well as the degree to which any such impact entails presidents following mass opinion when they believe doing so is not in citizens' long-term interests.

The existing scholarly literature contains two recurring yet distinct themes about how presidents' involvement of the mass public influences policymaking. The first, perhaps surprising, theme is that the involvement does not necessarily move policy in the direction of public opinion. This theme emerges in a diverse body of work. For example, some research argues that the president employs polling and appeals to try to manipulate public opinion, thereby utilizing the activities to increase his influence but not that of the people.[2] Other studies suggest that presidents' appeals may be nothing more than grandstanding or credit-claiming. Yet other work finds that presidents are not substantively responsive to mass opinion.

A separate theme in the literature, and one more in keeping with the concerns of the Founders, Tocqueville, and Mill, is that presidents' arousing and monitoring of public opinion on balance harm society. Unlike the first theme, this one implies that plebiscitary activities grant the general populace significant policy influence. However, the influence ultimately harms citizens because presidents are more likely than they are to understand the long-term effects of policies and less likely to be swayed by emotional whims. A president's involvement of the mass public thus causes him to advance policies he believes are not in citizens' long-term interests.

The argument of this book diverges from each of these recurring themes. Specifically, I show that presidents' involvement of the public

---

2. Given that all American presidents have been male, I will typically employ the male pronoun when referring to the inhabitant of the office. This usage obviously does not imply a belief that the pattern will continue for the foreseeable future.

does move policy in the direction of majority opinion. Only under a limited set of circumstances, however, will the involvement encourage the president to advance a popular position he believes is likely to damage society. Thus presidents' arousing and monitoring of mass opinion substantially increase the influence of the people, and this influence does not entail presidents persistently ignoring societal welfare.

Before proceeding to the development of this argument, a few stylistic issues are worth noting. First, by studying the relationship among presidents, the mass public, and policymaking, the book bridges two areas of inquiry that the field of American politics typically separates: political institutions and behavior. Scholars of institutions tend to analyze political elites, leaving to scholars of mass behavior examination of the populace. Because readers immersed in one of these two subfields may not closely follow the other, I provide more detailed literature reviews than one might in a more narrow study.

Second, the chapters contain a mixture of formal, quantitative, and narrative analysis. The formal analysis serves to delineate the underlying theoretical assumptions, motivate the hypotheses, and structure the empirics. The empirical work centers on statistical tests, which facilitate the examination of broad patterns of presidential and legislative decisions. This formal and quantitative analysis is complemented by narrative evidence and case studies, which allow for more detailed examination of the particular circumstances surrounding individual policy decisions. Given this combination of methodological approaches, I have sectioned and layered the presentation so that audiences of various technical backgrounds may appreciate the core arguments without enduring material that they may find too detailed. The most technical material is reserved for the footnotes, tables, and figures.

Finally, it is worth noting that the analysis contains at least two potentially controversial choices of language. One is the term "current opinion," which I use to distinguish mass opinion at a particular time from what it might be in the future. Some readers may view the term as suggesting that mass opinion is ill-reasoned and/or ephemeral. The phrase, however, does not rest on any such assumptions. In fact, it is entirely consistent with the existence of a "rational electorate" or "rational public" as it incorporates the possibility that voters may learn new information about a particular proposal or policy issue.[3]

Another matter of semantics, and a potentially more controversial one, is that the analysis discusses presidents' beliefs about "societal welfare" or

3. The language is also consistent with V. O. Key's (1961) notion of "latent" opinion, which Key describes as opinion that may develop after a policy is enacted.

the "public interest." Many of the political scientists and philosophers (as well as pundits) who have lamented policymakers' attention to mass opinion have done so because they presume such attention causes leaders to disregard voters' long-term interests. Given that the book responds to these concerns, I utilize this language, acknowledging that it is exceedingly difficult, if not impossible, to prove that a given policy fulfills some sort of agreed-upon version of "the public interest." The purpose of the ensuing analysis is not to offer any such version. Instead, I am interested in whether presidents pursue the policies *they* believe are in voters' long-term interests. This is the primary practical concern that has long interested critics of plebiscitary politics.

In focusing on this concern, the book is attentive to the fact that when a leader claims to be acting in the public interest he or she is not necessarily doing anything remotely of the sort. Obviously, policy choices are affected by many factors that may not be associated with pursuing societal welfare. Parties, interest groups, and leaders' personal priorities are a few such important influences that the book will address through means such as including control variables (in the econometric analyses) and examining alternative explanations (in the case studies). Moreover, it is worth acknowledging at the outset that even when a president believes he is representing voters' interests, these beliefs may be influenced by his ideological leanings and other factors.

All of these complexities highlight the fact that responsiveness has many desirable qualities, such as accountability. Yet these qualities do not make the question of whether leaders will follow public opinion when they believe it is misguided any less interesting or important. Indeed, the complexities arguably help justify the need for scholarly work on the topic; if it were obvious that responsiveness to public opinion, or a lack thereof, were always desirable, then one would hardly need scholars to grapple with the subject.

Acknowledgments

Different components of the book have been developed at various points in my career; consequently, I have many to thank for their contributions. The foundations for two of the early chapters—chapters 2 and 3—derive from my dissertation at Stanford, where I benefited from the critical comments of numerous faculty. Keith Krehbiel, as my advisor, deserves enormous credit for overseeing a thesis somewhat distant from his core intellectual interests. The anticipation of his red pen continues to influence my research, even when I know he will not see it until after publication. Terry Moe helped spark an interest in studying the presidency and gave me confidence that such a research agenda could be fruitful for a young scholar. Doug Rivers naturally questioned this plan, as well as more specific aspects of the research, but in addition to this beneficial prodding offered much-needed encouragement at unexpected moments. Another colleague to whom I am grateful is John Cogan. I thank him for teaching me most of what I know about the budget and imparting an enthusiasm for relating events in Washington to more systematic analysis. Finally, David Brady's advice, while often buried in a string of profanities, was nonetheless invaluable. His willingness to relay a brilliant combination of knowledge about political science and politics has aided me enormously.

As indebted as I am to my core graduate advisors, had I simply planned to publish a "dissertation book," *Who Leads Whom* would have never been written. Most of the theory and empirical work was developed in my years on the faculties of MIT and Northwestern University, and several individuals deserve special mention for their contributions to this research. Steve Ansolabehere asked at the outset why anyone would want to analyze pandering with a rational choice framework (his words were something to the effect of "What's next? A rational choice theory of homelessness?"), but then, just as I was about to drop the project, he reminded me that often the most interesting research seems quirky when it commences. Jim Snyder and Charles Stewart also offered constructive feedback early on. Most significantly, Michael Herron and Ken Shotts invited me to collaborate on a formal theory of pandering, which drove me to work on a subject I had mulled over since the days of my dissertation but had never given serious attention to. This collaboration with Michael and Ken, as well as future collaborations with Ken, have been instrumental in my thinking. The influence of these partnerships should be apparent in part 2, not only in the chapter that Ken co-authored but elsewhere as well.

Once I had drafts of the various chapters, several people graciously read one or more. Craig Volden and Alan Wiseman are singled out for giving page-by-page comments on the entire manuscript before I submitted it for review. All scholars should be lucky enough to have such timely and helpful feedback. After incorporating it, I was privileged to have Jeff Cohen, William Howell, David Lewis, Nolan McCarty, and Bob Shapiro read the entire manuscript. The book is clearly the better for their criticisms. Ken Shotts perused several chapters, offering a good deal of thought-provoking feedback. Finally, I was fortunate to have two comparativists provide reactions. Chappell Lawson commented on the latter four chapters and Michael Wallerstein on the last one; their patience in helping an Americanist consider implications outside the American context is noteworthy.

A host of others have provided stimulating conservations on this research, including Mike Alvarez, David Austen-Smith, David Baron, Larry Bartels, Jenna Bednar, Jon Bendor, Dick Brody, Chuck Cameron, Dennis Chong, Josh Clinton, Josh Cohen, Scott de Marchi, Rui de Figueiredo, John Ferejohn, Mo Fiorina, Fred Greenstein, Susan Herbst, Bonnie Honig, Jeff Jenkins, Jonathan Katz, Bill Keech, Rod Kiewiet, Adam Meirowitz, Sara Monoson, Ben Page, Paul Quirk, Barry Weingast, and John Zaller. Stephanie Ng is acknowledged for more-than-able research assistance. Some of the research was conducted while on leave at the California Institute of Technology during 2001–2002, and I am grateful for all of the support that Caltech provided. The "finishing" touches were made at Princeton, where Chuck Cameron has supportively urged me to take whatever time needed in finalizing things and Larry Bartels has gently pushed in the opposite direction.

Credit is also due to the editorial team at the University of Chicago Press. Susan Herbst, Benjamin Page, and John Tryneski have provided an outstanding combination of encouragement and advice. Obviously, neither they nor anyone else can be held accountable for any remaining errors or limitations; these are exclusively mine.

Last, but far from least, are the family members who have supported this and other professional endeavors. I thank my parents Mary Pat and Michael Canes; my brothers David and Aran; my daughter Sarah, for providing a daily reminder of why understanding politics is so important; and my husband David Wrone, for his consistent support and confidence in me.

CHAPTER ONE

Presidents' Involvement of the Mass Public

On June 6 of 2002, President George W. Bush went on nationwide television to advocate adding a Department of Homeland Security to the executive cabinet. As Bush noted in the speech, he was promoting the largest restructuring of the federal government since 1947, when President Harry Truman moved the armed forces into the agency now called the Department of Defense. Bush's support for the new bureaucratic structure represented a departure from his previous position. For months, he had been claiming that internal security should be managed by an agency located within the Executive Office of the President. Indeed, the *Congressional Quarterly Weekly* referred to the switch in his stance as a "stunning turnabout."[1]

At the time of the speech, political pundits of various persuasions opined that the president had changed his position less because of a conversion in his beliefs and more out of a desire to placate mass opinion. For example, Representative Barney Frank (D-MA) conjectured that the administration had "gotten an indication from polling data that there's concern of their grip of the situation . . . They're doing this as a defensive reaction that they no longer look omnicompetent [sic] to the public."[2] Similarly, Ivan Eland of the libertarian Cato Institute opined that "the initiative is primarily designed to pretend that the administration is doing something, rather than administering much needed 'tough love' to the security bureaucracies."[3] Even the Republican membership of Congress expressed some doubt. Representative Adam Putnam (R-FL) complained "we can't afford to turn the federal government upside down through

---

1. Adriel Bettelheim and Jill Barshay, "Bush's Swift, Sweeping Plan Is Work Order for Congress," *Congressional Quarterly Weekly,* June 8, 2002, 1498–1504.

2. Ibid., 1501–2.

3. Ivan Eland, "Bush Plan Is Just 'Do Something,' " *Newsday,* June 10, 2002, A25.

rose-colored, daisy-sniffing marches toward group think."[4] Indeed, the idea of creating a Department of Homeland Security was quite popular with the public. In the weeks after Bush's address, surveys found that around 70 percent of the populace supported establishing a cabinet-level department responsible for internal security.[5]

As the legislative negotiations over Bush's initiative progressed, it faced the most serious resistance in the Senate, where the Democrats held a one-person majority.[6] The key point of contention concerned the personnel system of the prospective department. Bush wanted to limit the would-be employees' civil service protections and rights to join unions. The Senate leadership, headed by Majority Leader Tom Daschle (D-SD), opposed these provisions, claiming that the administration wanted to use the new agency to advance an anti-union agenda.[7] By the time Congress recessed for the 2002 elections, the Senate Democrats and President Bush had not been able to reach an agreement.

Republicans highlighted the disagreement in a number of senatorial races. For example, Saxby Chambliss, the Republican challenger to Democratic Senator Max Cleland of Georgia, released television advertisements that criticized the incumbent for failing to support the president's proposed Department of Homeland Security.[8] Jim Talent, the Republican challenger to Senator Jean Carnahan of Missouri, likewise stressed her

4. Susan Milligan, "Lawmakers Wary About Homeland Security Plan: Some Ask Whether to Include FBI, CIA," *Boston Globe,* June 12, 2002, A3.

5. In a CBS News poll conducted June 18–20, 2002, 70 percent of respondents replied affirmatively to the question, "Do you approve or disapprove of recent proposal to create the Department of Homeland Security, a cabinet department, which would unite a number of government agencies into one department?" In a Harris Interactive Poll conducted June 19–20, 69 percent of respondents replied affirmatively to the question, "Do you think the U.S. Congress should or should not pass legislation to create a new cabinet department of Homeland Security?" Finally, in a Gallup Organization survey conducted June 21–23, 73 percent of respondents replied affirmatively to the question, "As you may know, shortly after the September 11th (2001) terrorist attacks (on the World Trade Center and the Pentagon), President George W. Bush created the office of Homeland Security. Now, Bush is proposing that this office be combined with many existing government agencies to create a new cabinet level department. Do you think Congress should—or should not—pass legislation to create a new cabinet-level Department of Homeland Security?" All of the polls were conducted on the national adult population.

6. At that time, James Jefford of Vermont identified himself as an Independent but caucused with the Democrats.

7. Adriel Bettelheim, "Senate's Failure to Resolve Personnel Management Issue Stalls Homeland Security Bill," *Congressional Quarterly Weekly,* October 10, 2002, 2741.

8. Todd S. Purdum and David E. Rosenbaum, "The 2002 Elections: The Campaign; Bush's Stumping for Candidates Is Seen as a Critical Factor in Republican Victories," *New York Times,* Late Edition, November 7, 2002, B4.

opposition to the president's initiative.[9] Chambliss and Talent ultimately defeated their opponents, and observers cited the homeland security issue as contributing significantly to the victories. For instance, the *Financial Times* commented, "the lack of congressional approval for the new department was used effectively by Republicans in unseating two Democratic senators in Georgia and Missouri."[10] More dramatically, the *Congressional Quarterly Weekly* noted that Democrats "were pummeled in the fall campaigns by Republicans who said they had blocked the [president's Homeland Security] bill."[11]

Following these results, the Democrats yielded to the president on the issue of homeland security. On November 19, by a 90–9 vote, the Senate passed a bill creating a Department of Homeland Security with the personnel flexibility President Bush had requested. The House agreed to the Senate version by a voice vote on November 22, and the president signed the legislation into law three days later.

The events surrounding the creation of the Department of Homeland Security draw attention to several important ways in which policymaking in Washington may be affected by presidents' plebiscitary activities, such as polling and mass appeals. First, the pundits' claim that Bush championed the department in an effort to appease the electorate highlights that a president may support policies simply because they are popular, not because he believes in the merits. Second, Bush's appeal underscores that a president may employ the bully pulpit to pressure congressional members to enact his policy initiatives. These effects, in combination, suggest that a president may follow mass opinion when formulating a policy agenda and proceed to advance the agenda through the legislative process by rallying the public to support it.

Such behavior is precisely what architects of the United States Constitution feared. They did not want the populace directly involved in policymaking and were deeply skeptical of the citizenry's ability to participate in reasoned deliberation. The "masses" were perceived to be easily influenced by temporary passions. James Madison summarizes this viewpoint in Federalist Paper No. 49, proclaiming that "a nation of philosophers is as little to be expected as the philosophical race of kings wished for by Plato."[12] Indeed, as Ralph Ketcham (1986, 6) notes in his introduction

9. David Firestone, "The 2002 Campaign: Missouri; X-Factor May Provide the Edge in a Close Senate Race," *New York Times*, November 1, 2002, A26.

10. Deborah McGregor, "Bush Secures Breakthrough for Homeland Security Plan," *Financial Times*, November 13, 2002, 1.

11. Mary Dairymple, "Homeland Security Department another Victory for Administration," *Congressional Quarterly Weekly*, November 16, 2002, 3002–7.

12. *The Federalist Papers* 1987 [1788], No. 49, 314.

to the *Anti-Federalist Papers,* even statesmen who opposed the Constitution on certain grounds were generally anxious about "rule by the . . . demagogue-dominated 'voice of the people.'"

Consistent with this perspective, the *Federalist Papers* stipulate that elected officials should not involve the mass public in the policymaking process. For instance, in No. 71, Alexander Hamilton states that the president should not allow public opinion to guide his policy choices. Hamilton observes, "There are some who would be inclined to regard the servile pliancy of the Executive to a prevailing current . . . as its best recommendation. But such men entertain very crude notions . . . as of the true means by which the public happiness may be promoted."[13] Likewise, Madison in Federalist Paper No. 49 argues that regular mass appeals would not serve the national interest because they would cause "the *passions* . . . not the *reason,* of the public [to] sit in judgment."[14] As these statements suggest, the architects of the Constitution feared presidents' arousing and monitoring of public opinion could readily degenerate into demagoguery.[15]

To the extent that this fear has ever been relevant, it certainly should be today. As Eisinger (2003, 5) documents, polling has become "an integral part of [presidents'] White House modus operandi." Presidents, through their national party committees, spend millions of dollars on polls (Jacobs and Shapiro 2000, 367–68n). Likewise, televised appeals to the public are now commonplace; Ragsdale (1998) estimates that Presidents Richard Nixon through Bill Clinton gave a major address approximately five times every year. These days one simply cannot separate presidents' role in the policy process from their involvement of the mass public in the process.

The purpose of this book is to analyze how such plebiscitary activity affects the policy decisions of presidents and legislators. In particular, I examine how policymaking in Washington is influenced by presidents' appeals and attention to mass opinion. As mentioned in the preface, I refer to these actions jointly as presidents' *involvement of the mass public.* This book assesses whether this executive behavior in fact increases

13. *Federalist,* No. 71, 409.

14. *Federalist,* No. 49, 315.

15. It is worth highlighting that while a pure democracy was feared by most of the Founding Fathers, variation did exist among them. In particular, Thomas Jefferson (who did not attend the Constitutional Convention because during it he was the diplomatic representative to France) placed greater faith than many of his contemporaries in the wisdom of majority opinion (e.g., Sheldon 1991). As he wrote to John Breckenridge on January 29, 1800 with reference to political events in France, "we [American leaders] are sensible of the duty and expediency of submitting our opinions to the will of the majority" (*Papers of Thomas Jefferson, Volume 31,* 2004, 345).

the degree to which mass opinion guides policymaking and also the extent to which any such guidance indeed entails presidents disregarding societal welfare.[16]

The existing literature contains two recurring themes regarding the policy impact of presidents' involvement of the mass public. The first comports with the concerns voiced by the authors of the *Federalist*: namely, that the involvement encourages the enactment of policy that caters to transitory, ill-reasoned opinion at the expense of societal welfare. A separate, contrasting theme is that the involvement does not necessarily shift policy in the direction of existing opinion. This idea emerges in work that argues presidents use polls and public appeals to try to manipulate public opinion, in research that suggests congressional members do not alter their behavior in response to presidents' appeals, in studies that indicate the appeals are simply grandstanding, and in analyses that find presidents are unresponsive to public opinion.

In this book I argue against each of these perspectives. I find that presidents' involvement of the mass public does shift policy toward majority opinion. However, I also find that under most conditions a president will not endorse a popular policy he believes is contrary to the interest of society. In other words, under most conditions, the popular policies that the president takes to the airwaves are ones that he believes will improve societal welfare. Thus presidents' arousing and monitoring of public opinion increase the influence of the populace but not in a way that entails pervasive demagoguery.

The analysis is divided into two major parts. The first half focuses on presidents' appeals to the mass public, the second on presidents' incentives to pander to "current opinion," or the opinion that exists at the time the president is making his policy decision.[17] The earlier part shows why, at first glance, presidents may appear to be plebiscites to those believing pervasive responsiveness likely reflects demagogic behavior. When a chief executive selects among proposals to publicize over the airwaves, the decision is not independent of how popular each proposal is. On the

---

16. As discussed in detail in the preface, I use the term societal welfare (as well as public interest) because I am responding to the concern that a president's attention to mass opinion may cause him to disregard voters' longer-term interests. I am obviously not claiming that it is straightforward to ascertain an objective version of societal welfare. Instead, I am interested in examining the extent to which presidents are willing to disregard voters' longer-term interests when they believe public opinion is misinformed or misguided.

17. As discussed in the preface, the use of the term current opinion is not meant to imply that mass opinion is necessarily ill-reasoned or ephemeral, just that it may change in the future due to factors such as new information.

whole, presidents are more likely to issue appeals about initiatives that comport with citizens' policy preferences. This effect is stronger in the domain of domestic than foreign affairs, but even in the latter case, a president's selection of issues to take to the public is strategic in that he tends to avoid publicizing initiatives that face strong popular opposition.

The second half of the book shows that this behavior does not imply presidents take popular stances whenever citizens are likely to be attentive. Instead, depending on the president's personal popularity and the electoral cycle, his policy choices may be driven by concern about anticipated public reaction to the policy results or even by a desire to create good public policy. For example, when a president's personal approval is either high or low, he does not support popular policies that he believes will be detrimental to society. Likewise, when the next election is distant or he is not running for reelection, he does not cater to the mass citizenry unless he agrees with their preferred course of action. Only when a president is marginally popular and soon faces an electoral contest does he pander to public opinion by supporting a popular policy that he believes will not advance citizens' interests.

The book therefore finds that presidents strategically focus their public appeals on policies consistent with mass opinion but often would have supported the policies even if the public had not. Appealing to the populace simply increases a president's ability to achieve legislative success on policies that, for the most part, he and the people support. More generally, the analysis demonstrates that presidents' involvement of the public increases the likelihood popular initiatives are enacted and, at the same time, does not pervasively alter executive decision making. In other words, the involvement augments the influence of majority opinion but does not generally produce demagogic leadership.

OVERVIEW OF THE LITERATURE

Presidential Power

During the past fifty years, research on presidents' policy influence has primarily focused on topics other than the involvement of the mass public. For instance, a great deal of work examines how formal powers, such as the veto and executive orders, influence policymaking.[18] A literature also exists on how presidents' policy influence differs between foreign and

18. See, for example, Brady and Volden (1998), Cameron (2000), Kiewiet and McCubbins (1988), Krehbiel (1998), McCarty (1997), and McCarty and Poole (1995) on the veto; and Howell (2003), Mayer (2001), and Moe and Howell (1999) on unilateral action.

domestic affairs; on the whole, this research suggests that chief executives have particular advantages in foreign affairs.[19] Finally, following Richard Neustadt (1990 [1960]), scholars have examined how policymaking is affected by a president's public standing and dealings with other elites in Washington.[20] Obviously, the subject of personal standing or popularity is somewhat related to the topic at hand in that each concerns public opinion. It is therefore worth noting that most work on presidents' personal approval allows that mass appeals may not affect policymaking.

Neustadt (1990 [1960], 269) does recognize President Ronald Reagan's use of television to mobilize the public and acknowledges future presidents may similarly try to exploit the medium. He views the possibility cautiously, however, and does not assess public appeals to be a key component of executive power. Likewise, George Edwards (2003) argues that appeals typically fail to aid presidents' legislative efforts. Edwards bases this argument on evidence that presidents are unable to alter citizens' dispositions about policy issues.

Perhaps surprisingly, the strongest indication that presidents' appeals might engender policy influence comes from work focused less on executive power than on historical development. In particular, a number of studies document that over the past one hundred years chief executives have increasingly employed a strategy of "going public," to use Samuel Kernell's (1997) famous language.[21] While some of these studies are more optimistic (e.g., Kernell 1997) than others (e.g., Bessette 1994; Tulis 1987) about the prospects for systematic influence from the strategy, on the whole the historical works suggest it is effective at least rarely.

Only a few studies, both from within and outside this historical tradition, actually grapple with the question of why appeals might regularly aid presidents in the legislative process. The explanations that these analyses provide vary greatly, but all imply the action may not augment the degree to which citizens' policy positions guide policymakers' decisions.

19. E.g., Huntington (1961), Peterson (1994), Shull (1991) and Wildavsky (1966; but cf. Oldfield and Wildavsky 1991).

20. Research on how a president's standing in society affects his legislative influence includes Brace and Hinckley (1992), Canes-Wrone and de Marchi (2002), Ostrom and Simon (1985), and Rivers and Rose (1985). On the topic of presidential bargaining with other policy elites, see, for instance, Sullivan (1990) and de Marchi and Sullivan (1997).

21. Cornwell (1965), Gamm and Smith (1998), Hager and Sullivan (1994), Kernell (1997), Lowi (1985), Milkis (1998), Polsby (1978), Skowronek (1993), Tulis (1987). See also Ellis's edited volume (1998), which includes a number of pieces on the historical development of presidential speechmaking.

For instance, Gary Miller (1993) argues that appeals move legislation from the committee stage to the floor, Calvin Mouw and Michael MacKuen (1992) find they moderate the positions of congressional agenda setters, and Kernell (1997) contends that going public allows popular presidents to garner support for their positions. It also has been argued that the strategy can increase executive influence by enabling presidents to commit to vetoing legislation they actually prefer to the status quo (Ingberman and Yao 1991a; 1991b). Notably, in none of these accounts are the policy preferences of the mass public a central component.

The role of these preferences is actually strongest in research that argues presidential appeals only rarely affect congressional behavior. Specifically, Jeffrey Tulis (1987; 1998) and Joseph Bessette (1994) contend that appealing to the public will seldom aid a president but that when the action does so the impact is detrimental because it entails politicians giving more deference to the ill-informed views of the public.[22] Tulis (1998, 111–13), for example, stresses the difficulty in permitting rhetorical leadership without simultaneously encouraging leaders to cater to a mass opinion that he characterizes as transitory and ill-reasoned. Likewise, Bessette (1994, 212) suggests that presidents' mobilizing of public opinion can encourage congressional members to pass legislation they would not support "given a fuller consideration of information and arguments."

In sum, the literature on presidential power suggests three schools of thought about public appeals. The first, dominant perspective is that they are not a significant component of executive power. A second perspective is that they are indeed a significant component of executive power but do not necessarily increase the degree to citizens' policy preferences guide policymaking. Finally, a third school of thought suggests that appeals increase the influence of presidents as well as the mass public but then only on rare occasion and at the expense of societal welfare.

Presidential Decision Making

The literature has long maintained that public opinion affects the policy decisions of elected officials such as presidents (e.g., Downs 1957; Key 1961; Monroe 1979; Page and Shapiro 1983). Recently, a number of studies have examined whether presidents are indeed "responsive" to public

---

22. Indeed, Bessette (1994, 193) surmises that "successful efforts by presidents to move Congress, or even some significant part of Congress, by generating public pressure are relatively rare phenomena in American political history and indeed are noteworthy precisely because of their rarity."

opinion, in the sense of enacting policies currently favored by the populace, and several suggest that the overall level of presidential responsiveness is actually quite low. For instance, Jeffrey Cohen (1997) demonstrates that the level of ideological liberalism in society does not consistently influence presidents' stances in State of the Union addresses. Consistent with this finding, Lawrence Jacobs and Robert Shapiro (2000, 2002a) argue that presidents have recently employed polls and other public relations tools to try to shape public opinion rather than cater to it.[23]

A separate group of studies indicates presidents are in fact quite responsive to mass opinion. One such study is by John Geer (1996), who finds that polling has encouraged and enabled presidents to become more responsive to popular opinion. Consistent with this argument, analyses by Robert Erikson, Michael MacKuen, and James Stimson show that recent presidents' positions on roll call votes are highly responsive to changes in the liberalism of the public mood (Erikson, MacKuen, and Stimson 2002a, 2002b; Stimson, MacKuen and Erikson 1995). The literature thus provides two starkly distinct perspectives regarding the impact of current opinion on presidential policymaking.

In debating whether executive policy decisions follow mass opinion, research on responsiveness has not evaluated the extent to which presidents are taking popular stances independently of their merits. In other words, existing studies leave open the possibility that presidents are unwilling to cater to public opinion when they believe it is misguided or that presidents cater to current opinion at the expense of what they perceive to be the national interest. This latter prospect has been a recurring concern of political scientists and analysts. Walter Lippmann (1922), George F. Kennan (1951), and Hans Morgenthau (1948) each argued over a half-century ago that presidents should not follow public opinion because they are more likely than the mass public to know which policies will ultimately benefit society. More recently, Paul Quirk and Joseph Hinchliffe (1998, 21) have observed that "powerful mass opinion can lead to policies that are reckless, irresponsible, or ill-suited to their purposes." Consistent with this argument, Robert Weissberg (2001, 14) has forcefully contended that "under no circumstances should [polls] inform policy making or determine policy choices."

The literature on presidential decision making thus contains a great deal of uncertainty as to whether presidents' monitoring of opinion

---

23. Jacobs and Shapiro (2000, 2002a) argue that politicians other than presidents have also become likely to try to craft public opinion in recent years. In support of this argument, they present data that suggest policy congruence between public opinion and overall government policy has declined since the 1970s.

encourages them to follow it, particularly when doing so counters their information about the optimal course of action.

Perspectives of Representation

While this book focuses on the institution of the presidency, it contributes as well to the understanding of representation in American democracy. In important ways, the work builds on, and yet repudiates, archetypal perspectives of representation. Specifically, in keeping with E. E. Schattschneider (1960) and V. O. Key (1961), and in contrast to the traditional pluralist perspective in which competition among groups largely determines policymaking (e.g., Dahl 1961; Truman 1951), the analysis here grants mass opinion a central role in the policy process. Also like Schattschneider and Key, this study does not grant a deterministic role to mass opinion; neither the president nor Congress follows it universally. Still, the role of mass opinion differs from each of these classic perspectives.

In Schattschneider's analysis of democracy in America, the impact of popular opinion depends on the scope of conflict. When this scope is large, the general public strongly influences policymakers' decisions; otherwise, specialized interests dominate the process. Schattschneider recognizes the president to be a critical figure in increasing the scope of conflict and thus, as in this study, presidents' public appeals may increase the influence of the mass citizenry. Yet, unlike the ensuing analysis, Schattschneider does not delve into the question of how citizens' policy preferences may affect a president's incentives to broaden the scope of conflict. Correspondingly, he does not examine whether the influence that presidents obtain from appeals comes at the expense of policymaking that gives precedence to current opinion over citizens' long-term interests.

Key's perspective of American democracy better lends itself to analyzing differences between citizens' short-term inclinations and long-term interests. In particular, Key argues that policy elites respond not only to current opinion but also to the "latent opinion" that is expected to develop as a function of the policies chosen. Thus, consistent with the perspective of this study, a politician may forsake a popular course of action if it is likely to produce an outcome that citizens will not like. Key does not, however, attempt to identify circumstances under which a politician's concern about current opinion will drive his policy decisions. Indeed, he argues that leaders have a great deal of discretion within basic limits, which he terms "opinion dikes," to choose whatever policies they see fit. In contrast, this book identifies circumstances under which current opinion will guide presidential decision making. In specifying these conditions where classics like Key have avoided doing so, I offer a partial response to John Zaller's (1992, 273–74) call for such analysis of representation: "the question is not whether elites lead or follow, but *how much* and *which elites* lead rather than follow mass opinion, and *under what circumstances* they do so" [emphasis in the original].

THEORY TO TESTING

The book specifies circumstances under which mass opinion will guide presidential policymaking by testing theoretically derived predictions. In each part of the book, I derive a theory that generates hypotheses, and these predictions are subjected to empirical analysis.[24] This methodological approach offers numerous benefits. First, the explicit specification of assumptions provides a transparent motivation for the hypotheses and, in doing so, a foundation for future analysis of similar questions. Thus readers who wish to examine, say, the policy effects of presidents' speeches to citizens in other countries could build on the study presented here. Second, the theory suggests how the testing should be structured. For instance, the theory highlights that the relationship between a president's personal popularity and responsiveness to mass opinion may be nonmonotonic, with highly popular and unpopular presidents each being less likely than marginally popular ones to follow public opinion. The empirical analysis consequently takes account of the fact that this relationship may (or may not) be nonmonotonic.

In developing the theory, I use assumptions from the perspective commonly referred to as "rational choice." In particular, I assume that agents behave as if they are maximizing their interests given their preferences, beliefs, and available options. While the perspective has been employed to study a variety of questions about the presidency over the past decade,[25] its usage in presidential studies has been somewhat controversial. A key component of the controversy, not only in the area of study but also more generally, has been the question of whether the paradigm is a realistic psychological theory and therefore a good predictor of individual behavior.[26] In response to this concern, several scholars have argued that the assump-

---

24. I am by no means the first to use this approach to study presidential policymaking. See, for instance, Cameron (2000), Howell (2003), Krehbiel (1998), and Lewis (2003).

25. See, for example, Brady and Volden (1998), Cameron (2000), Chang (2003), Conley (2001), de Marchi and Sullivan (1997), Epstein and O'Halloran (2000), Geer (1996), Hammond and Knott (1996), Howell (2003), Kiewiet and McCubbins (1988), Krehbiel (1998), Lewis (2003), Matthews (1989), McCarty (1997), McCarty and Poole (1995), Miller (1993), Sullivan (1990), and Volden (2002).

26. See Cameron (2000, chap. 3) and Miller (1993) for a review of this debate.

tions of rational choice are most appropriate for contexts in which competitive forces influence the agents under examination and, correspondingly, where these agents face substantial benefits from optimal behavior as well as substantial costs from suboptimal behavior (Cameron 2000, chap. 3; Ferejohn and Satz 1995). The contexts I examine fit these criteria as they concern situations in which presidents and congressional members face pressures for their own reelection or, in the case of second-term presidents, for favorable historical evaluations and the reelection of their party (e.g., Moe 1985). Even given this suitable context, however, it is worth emphasizing that I do not need, or even want, to make the argument that the perspective of rational choice can explain *all* of the individual actions a president might take.[27] Instead, I am interested in understanding the broad *patterns* of behavior or, in other words, empirical regularities.

A separate critique of the rational choice paradigm is that it is often used to produce models that are disconnected from empirical analysis (e.g., Green and Shapiro 1994). Here, the primary purpose of developing theory is to generate predictions that are then evaluated empirically. This testing has the additional benefit of addressing the first concern in that the data should provide insight into whether the assumptions of the paradigm are appropriate for the context examined; to the extent they are not suitable, the empirical analysis should not support the theory.[28]

HISTORICAL CONTEXT

When Madison argued in the *Federalist* that public appeals would not serve the public interest, he thought they would only rarely increase presidents' influence in Washington. He believed that most public debates would alter the balance of power in favor of congressional members, who had more "connections of blood, of friendship and of acquaintance."[29] Research in American political development suggests that since

27. A separate but related issue is the suitability of assuming that electorates will behave rationally. Research suggests this assumption has power in terms of predicting the behavior of the public at large even when it does not predict the behavior of individual voters (e.g., Key 1966; Page and Shapiro 1992). The theory of this book deals solely with the public at large. (Naturally, it is also consistent with models of individual decision making that presume citizens behave rationally, such as Chong [1991] and Wlezien [1995].) In addition, I take care to base theoretical assumptions about the electorate on empirical evidence from the public opinion literature.

28. For a more thorough discussion of the benefits of testing rational choice theories, see Cameron and Morton (2002) and Morton (1999).

29. *Federalist*, No. 49, 315.

the twentieth century it is the president, not Congress, who has had the advantage in capturing the public's attention. According to this literature, the presidency metamorphosed from an office in which policy operations centered on relations with other elites into one in which public appeals, opinion polls, and other plebiscitary activities became a routine and significant component of the operations.[30] The structural factors thought to have contributed to the transformation include technological advances in mass communications, particularly radio and television; developments in transportation; the advent of the scientific polling of public opinion; the declining strength of political parties; and the growth of presidential primaries.[31]

The theoretical arguments of this book are not limited to a particular set of such activities; the arguments encompass all periods in which presidents have been capable of mobilizing and monitoring mass opinion. For this reason, I shy away from characterizing the study as an examination of the "modern presidency," the term that Neustadt (1990 [1960]) and others use to describe administrations since Franklin D. Roosevelt. At the same time, in order to examine a set of comparable political circumstances, I limit the testing of the theory to the period in which the president could reach a multitude of citizens through television. Specifically, I analyze Dwight Eisenhower's second term through Bill Clinton's second term. By 1957 over 78 percent of United States households owned a television while at the beginning of Eisenhower's first term only 44 percent of households owned one.[32] This focus has the additional advantage of comporting with work that suggests presidents' legislative capacities have been greater in the post–World War II era than in any other period of American history (e.g., Wayne 1978).[33]

---

30. See, for example, Gamm and Smith (1998), Geer (1996), Kernell (1997), Lowi (1985), Milkis (1998), Skowronek (1993), and Tulis (1987).

31. This list of structural factors that caused the growth of a "plebiscitary presidency" is by no means exhaustive. Also, some authors emphasize the influence of individual presidents in reconstructing the norms of executive behavior. See, for example, Tulis (1987) on the importance of Theodore Roosevelt and Woodrow Wilson and Lowi (1985) on the significance of Franklin D. Roosevelt.

32. *Historical Statistics of the United States, Colonial Times to 1970* (Washington, DC: Bureau of the Census), 1975.

33. Scholarly debate exists about the exact period in which plebiscitary activity became a significant feature of the presidency. For instance, Gamm and Smith (1998) argue that the transformation occurred during Theodore Roosevelt's presidency, Tulis (1987) maintains that Woodrow Wilson's presidency was critical, and Lowi (1985) asserts that Franklin D. Roosvelt's presidency was central. The empirical focus on the television era is not meant to delve into this debate but rather to center the analysis on an extensive yet comparable set of political circumstances.

For some of the tests, the availability of comparable public opinion data limits the analysis to 1972 forward. This limitation has a benefit, however, because several scholars identify Nixon's presidency as the beginning of the era in which presidents' public relations became a dominant feature of executive-legislative negotiations (e.g., Kernell 1997; Skowronek 1993). Specifically, Kernell and Stephen Skowronek argue that this development effectively ended the pluralist mode of governmental operations in which presidents' involvement in the policy process was epitomized by bargaining among lawmakers, interest groups, and other policy specialists. The tests that include data since 1972 establish findings for this period in isolation.

Having reviewed the main arguments, structure, and historical context of the book, we are now ready to develop them in more detail, beginning with the analysis of public appeals in part 1.

PART ONE

Public Appeals

Franklin D. Roosevelt fundamentally altered the politics surrounding State of the Union addresses when he became the first president to deliver the speech live over primetime radio on January 3 of 1936. Prior to this time, the practice had been to give the address during working hours without any sort of broadcast. FDR used the occasion to promote the continuation of his New Deal policies, claiming that dismantling them would favor an "economic autocracy" over the people at large. Daring his critics to pass legislation opposing the policies, he declared, "The way is open in the Congress for an expression of opinion by yeas and nays."[1]

Newspapers were quick to remark on the new form of presentation, and much of the commentary was derogatory. For example, the day following the speech, the *Salt Lake City Tribune* characterized it as follows: "Rather than a report on an urge to the Congress, it was an appeal to the people in which politics was the dominant note. It confirmed the worst fears of the Republican members who thought the night session was an unpleasant departure from the normal processes of American government."[2] The *Chicago Tribune* was more pointedly critical, stating that "The event was a degradation of the Presidency and of Congress."[3] Even more disparaging was the *San Francisco Chronicle,* which proclaimed that President Roosevelt had "misused his constitutional function and the machinery of Congress" by transforming the State of the Union into a mass appeal.[4]

Overall, these comments suggest that many political observers viewed Roosevelt's innovative transmission of the State of the Union as

1. "Annual Message to Congress," January 3, 1936, *Public Papers of the Presidents of the United States* (Washington, DC: Government Printing Office, 1936).

2. Cited in "Press Agrees the Roosevelt Message Was Political, Varies Widely in Opinion," *New York Times,* January 5, 1933, 33.

3. Ibid.

4. Ibid.

an unwelcome digression from typical policymaking; the notion that the president would use his constitutional prerogative of reporting to Congress as an excuse to advocate his agenda to the mass populace was not widely accepted. Despite this initial reticence to Roosevelt's actions, however, presidents since him have regularly employed State of the Union addresses to promote initiatives to the citizenry. More generally, and as many scholars have documented, public appeals have become a normal component of presidents' attempts to influence policymaking.[5] The chief executive is no longer likely to be criticized simply for seeking to mobilize public opinion in support of his agenda.

Yet while there is now relative consensus that public appeals are a prominent component of presidential activity, the policy ramifications are not much better understood than they were in the time of FDR. What sorts of influence, if any, do appeals engender? Do the politics of foreign policy appeals differ from those of domestic policy ones? To what extent do presidents use appeals to change mass opinion versus promote initiatives that are already popular? The chapters that constitute part 1 answer these and related questions.

Chapter 2 presents a theoretical framework of presidential appeals to the public. The framework, which I term the Public Appeals Theory, focuses on the relations among presidents, congressional members, and voters, combining elements of standard veto models with an explicit role for the mass electorate. The chapter begins by describing the intuition behind a simple spatial model. I proceed to discuss how the intuition of this model is influenced by assumptions regarding the cost of appealing to the public and the president's ability to alter citizens' policy preferences. Finally, following the literatures on public opinion and presidential power, I discuss how various assumptions are likely to differ between the contexts of foreign and domestic affairs. For example, research on public opinion suggests that citizens are less informed about foreign policy and that a president can thus more easily alter preferences over these issues. Consistent with this distinction, the hypotheses derived from the theory differ between the two domains. I therefore conduct the empirical analysis of domestic and foreign policy appeals separately.

Chapter 3 examines domestic policy appeals. The chapter begins by presenting summary statistics for all nationally televised discretionary speeches from the presidential administrations of Eisenhower through Clinton. These summary data establish for a broad range of policy areas basic patterns regarding the appeals, such as the popularity of the publi-

    5. E.g., Gamm and Smith (1998), Geer (1996), Kernell (1997), Lowi (1985), Milkis (1998), Skowronek (1993), and Tulis (1987).

cized initiatives. The chapter proceeds to develop analysis that compares policymaking when presidents do and do not go public, and that accounts for the possibility presidents go public strategically. In particular, I analyze annual budgetary negotiations for a recurring set of policy issues during the Eisenhower through Clinton presidencies. The policy issues range from the environment to economic development to drug control. For each issue and year, I have collected data on whether the president made a public appeal as well as on a variety of control variables, including whether the issue was a presidential priority, media coverage of the issue, and, where available, citizens' policy preferences. Using these data I estimate how political factors affect the likelihood of domestic policy appeals and the legislative influence obtained from them.

Chapter 4 assesses foreign policy appeals with empirics paralleling those in chapter 3. Accordingly, chapter 4 commences with descriptive statistics on the nationally televised speeches of Presidents Eisenhower through Clinton regarding foreign and defense issues such as arms control, economic aid, and trade agreements. I then examine the causes and legislative effects of foreign policy appeals using a data set of annual budgetary negotiations between the executive and legislative branches.

By the conclusion of part 1, we will have substantial evidence on the extent to which the theory developed in chapter 2 explains the politics of public appeals. Correspondingly, we will have a considerable understanding of the policy ramifications of this presidential activity.

CHAPTER TWO

A Theory of Public Appeals

THREE SEEMINGLY DISPARATE APPEALS

President Reagan appealed to the public about an initiative to terminate the Departments of Education and Energy on September 24, 1981. "There's only one way to shrink the size and cost of big government," he declared in a nationally televised address, continuing, "and that is by eliminating agencies that are not needed and are getting in the way of a solution."[1] Prior to the president's address, political commentators predicted Reagan would succeed in abolishing the departments. Only ten days before, *Newsweek* proclaimed that the Department of Education "seems doomed."[2] Earlier that year in the same periodical, commentator Bill Roedor opined, "It is now virtually certain that Ronald Reagan will eliminate two Cabinet departments [Energy and Education]."[3] After the speech, however, Reagan did not achieve these policy goals. According to *Congressional Quarterly,* members from both major parties gave the proposals a "chilly" reception.[4] Neither the House nor Senate even brought the matters to a vote.

This policy failure occurred only two months after legislative negotiations that helped to cement Reagan's title as "the Great Communicator." On July 27, less than two days before the House was scheduled to vote on a 25 percent income tax reduction proposed by the president, he appealed to the public about the initiative on primetime television. Before

1. "Address to the Nation on the Program for Economic Recovery," 24 September 1981, *Public Papers of the Presidents of the United States* (Washington, DC: Government Printing Office, 1981).

2. "Death Warrant for a Department," *Newsweek*, September 14, 1981, 95.

3. Bill Roeder, "A Cabinet Exit for Schools and Fuels," *Newsweek*, March 23, 1981, 17.

4. The *Congressional Quarterly Almanac* (1982, 501) stated that members' reaction to abolishing the Department of Education was "so cool that the administration decided not to push legislation" on the issue. The same almanac noted that Congress gave "a chilly reception" to the president's proposal to terminate the Department of Energy (p. 303).

the speech, Reagan was expected to face defeat. As his Chief of Staff James Baker surmised, "We thought we were beat on the tax bill."[5] Speaker of the House Tip O'Neill likewise assessed, "we [the Democrats] had this won."[6] After the speech, however, many Democrats switched positions. In the end, the president's initiative prevailed by a vote of 238 to 195.

The House similarly reversed course following an appeal made by President Clinton regarding the deployment of troops. On November 27 of 1995, Clinton used a primetime address to try to rally the public around his proposal to send 20,000 American troops to Bosnia for a NATO peacekeeping mission. Ten days earlier the House had voted 243–171 to block funding for the mission unless Clinton explicitly obtained congressional consent, and according to supporters of the majority position the purpose of the vote had been to prevent the troop deployment. For example, Rep. Porter Goss (R-FL) surmised, "The message is clear, and the message is, 'Don't send our young men and women to Bosnia.'"[7] Rep. Dana Rohrabacher (R-CA) similarly opined, "Whose nutty idea is this to send . . . Americans into the meat grinder called the Balkans?"[8] Despite this initial lack of congressional backing, the president achieved legislative victory following his speech. Sixteen days after it, the House changed course and voted 218–210 against cutting funds for the mission.

To what extent did Clinton's appeal concerning deployment of troops and Reagan's appeal concerning his tax reduction affect congressional support for these policies? If the addresses did contribute to the legislative victories, then why did Reagan's appeal regarding the Departments of Education and Energy receive such an unenthusiastic response from Congress? More generally, under what conditions do presidents generate legislative influence from championing proposals to the mass public? And how does this activity increase the extent to which mass opinion guides policymaking? To answer these questions, this chapter provides a theoretical framework referred to as the Public Appeals Theory.

As with any theory, mine contains a set of assumptions from which pre-

5. Lou Cannon, "The Master Politician Has His Day; Reagan Shows Skills as Master of Politics," *Washington Post,* August 2, 1981, A1.

6. "Tax Victory Gives Reagan a Clean Sweep on Economic Proposals," *National Journal,* August 1, 1981, 1363.

7. "House Rejects Idea of Sending U.S. Troops to Bosnia," *St. Louis Post-Dispatch,* November 18, 1995, 3A.

8. Ibid.

dictions are derived. The purpose of these assumptions and ensuing predictions is not to explain all variation in presidential behavior but rather to elucidate general patterns that we should observe across administrations. I state the theoretical assumptions in two successive sets: a basic set that focuses on critical relationships among current opinion, presidential preferences, and legislative preferences; and a broader set that incorporates phenomena such as the cost of public appeals and the president's ability to alter current opinion. The Public Appeals Theory accordingly becomes more complex as the chapter develops. In particular, it is presented in four sections that describe, in sequence, the basic set of assumptions, the results that derive from these basic assumptions, the integration of costly appeals to the theory, and an extension in which presidents can alter citizens' preferences over policy choices. This sequential presentation highlights how various structural conditions alter the politics of public appeals. After describing the theory, I delineate five testable hypotheses. The final section returns to the three examples of appeals that began the chapter, developing the cases more fully to illustrate the predictions of the Public Appeals Theory.

BASIC ASSUMPTIONS

The basic assumptions concern the relevant players, their preferences, actions, and behavior. These assumptions could be specified at a variety of levels of mathematical precision; I have chosen to present them largely through figures and narrative. Because the use of formal notation is minimized, footnotes are employed on occasion to offer a more precise description of the theory.[9]

The Players and What They Want

The Public Appeals Theory has three types of players: a president, congressional members, and voters. As often presumed in formal models (e.g., Downs 1957), all of the players have preferences over a given policy issue that can be represented on a one-dimensional line. The president's preferences are assumed to derive from motivations such as reelection, favorable historical evaluations, and ideological goals. The president has a most desired outcome, and he prefers outcomes closer to it over ones further from it. For example, if the issue is the income tax rate and the

9. Readers interested in a formal exposition of the basic assumptions are directed to Canes-Wrone (2001b).

president's most preferred policy is to reduce the rate by 50 percent, he prefers a decrease of 30 percent to one of 20 percent.[10]

The electorate and legislators also are assumed to have these types of well-ordered preferences. As in other models that concern the mass public (e.g., Ferejohn 1986; Groseclose and McCarty 2001), the electorate is characterized by a representative voter. One may interpret this entity to be the median voter, or the person for whom no majority prefers another option over her most preferred one. I also assume that congressional members' behavior can be captured by a unitary actor, who represents the Congress or legislature. This assumption is often employed in theories of executive-legislative bargaining (e.g., Groseclose and McCarty 2001; Matthews 1989; McCarty 1997). In the empirical analysis of subsequent chapters, I account for other complexities of the legislative process and public opinion. Here, the simplifications facilitate a straightforward explication of the theory.[11]

For the given policy issue, the electorate desires a particular outcome, and consistent with work on congressional members' incentives, the legislature's policy preferences depend in part on those of the electorate (e.g., Arnold 1990; Canes-Wrone, Brady, and Cogan 2002; Fiorina 1974; Mayhew 1974). In particular, the preferred outcome of the Congress is an induced function of the electorate's preferences as well as what I call "pull incentives," which pull the legislature from supporting the electorate's preferred choice. Research suggests that congressional members may vote against district opinion because of pressure from interest groups (Caldeira and Wright 1998; Hall and Wayman 1990), parties (Aldrich 1995; Rohde 1991; Sinclair 1983; Snyder and Groseclose 2000), and committees (Maltzman 1999; Shepsle and Weingast 1987), as well as because of specific policy or career goals (Fenno 1973). The existence of the pull incentives highlights the fact that under various conditions members have incentives not to be responsive to popular sentiment.

In the Public Appeals Theory, how much weight the Congress assigns to the electorate's preferences versus the pull incentives depends on the salience of the issue: the greater the salience, the greater the weight given to the electorate's preferences. This assumption follows the observations of classic works in legislative studies. For example, John Kingdon (1977) and E. E. Schattschneider (1960) argue that Congress is more responsive

10. Technically, he weakly prefers outcomes closer to it over ones further from it. Thus if he desires a tax cut of 50 percent, he prefers one of 30 percent no less than he prefers one of 20 percent.

11. For instance, incorporating the assumption that the president and Congress face different electorates would complicate the exposition without substantively altering the results.

to the public on highly visible issues. Vincent Hutchings (1998) and Ken Kollman (1998) have provided quantitative evidence of the effect. This tenet of the congressional literature comports with research that suggests a politician is more susceptible to criticism on issues to which the public has been attentive. On such issues, citizens have a "context" for comprehending an attack (Popkin 1994). Even if they do not recount the specifics of a policy debate, they may recall how they felt about the politician's actions (Lodge, McGraw, and Stroh 1989).

Appeals

The theory assumes that a president enhances the public salience of an issue by advocating it to the electorate, an assumption that comports with a variety of work on public opinion (e.g., Cohen 1995; Cornwell 1965; Hill 1998; Lawrence 2003; Schattschneider 1960).[12] In keeping with the previously discussed evidence that salience induces legislative responsiveness (e.g., Hutchings 1998; Kingdon 1977; Kollman 1998; Schattschneider 1960), an appeal in the theory causes the legislature to prefer the outcome the electorate desires.[13] This assumption could be relaxed so that an appeal merely shifted the legislature's preferences in the direction of the electorate's, but doing so would complicate the exposition without substantively altering the testable hypotheses.[14]

For ease of explication, I initially assume that appeals are costless to the president but that if he is indifferent between making one and not making one he will not go public. I also initially assume that appeals do not alter citizens' policy preferences. The literature suggests presidents face great difficulty changing citizens' policy preferences, particularly on domestic issues (e.g., Edwards 2003; Page and Shapiro 1984, 1992; Page, Shapiro, and Dempsey 1987). Indeed, George Edwards (2003) argues forcefully that presidents' attempts to do so generally fail. Later in the chapter, after

12. This argument is also consistent with work on priming in campaigns (e.g., Page 1978; Riker 1996).

13. The formalization of this assumption is akin to that in models of induced ideal points (e.g., Bawn 1995).

14. The theory does not focus on the role of the media in transmitting the president's information but, instead, builds on the well-established finding that presidential appeals do indeed increase the salience of the issues advocated. Others have shown how media coverage contributes to the president's ability to focus public attention on given issues (e.g., Behr and Iyengar 1985). Also, a substantial literature exists on the strategies presidents employ to receive coverage from the media (e.g., Ansolabehere, Behr, and Iyengar 1993; Grossman and Kumar 1981). Analyzing such behavior is not the purpose of this study. However, in the empirical work of future chapters, I control for the quantity of media coverage.

Figure 2.1 Effect of a Public Appeal on Congressional Preferences

Configuration 1: Movement toward the president's preferences

$$c^0 \qquad c^e = e \qquad\qquad p$$

Configuration 2: Movement away from the president's preferences

$$c^e = e \qquad c^0 \qquad\qquad p$$

describing the logic that derives from the basic set of assumptions, I discuss how it changes if appeals are costly or if the president can indeed alter citizens' preferences about policy choices. These extensions alter the substantive implications of the theory but not, as we shall see, by as much as one might expect.

Figure 2.1 depicts the impact of a public appeal under the basic set of assumptions. The figure represents the unidimensional policy space, with p representing the preferred outcome of the president, c^0 the preferred outcome of Congress without an appeal, c^e the preferred outcome of Congress with an appeal, and e the preferred outcome of the electorate. As the figure shows, an appeal can induce the legislature to prefer an outcome closer to or further away from the one desired by the president. If the president makes an appeal in the first configuration, the increased salience of the issue shifts the position of Congress toward the president's position because the electorate's preferred outcome is located in this direction. In the second configuration, in which the electorate's and president's positions are on opposite sides of the policy Congress initially desires, an appeal would shift Congress's preferred outcome away from that of the president.

Actions

The Public Appeals Theory involves three actions. First, the president can appeal to the public about an issue. Second, Congress can pass a bill or choose to maintain a given status quo q. Third, if Congress has enacted a bill, the president can veto it, with a veto resulting in the given status quo.[15]

---

15. In the formal exposition of Canes-Wrone (2001b), these actions are modeled in a repeated context; that is, the president has multiple opportunities to go public and Congress has multiple occasions to pass legislation that the president may veto or accept. Here, the substantive predictions do not require the sequence of action to be repeated.

Of course, in reality executive-legislative bargaining involves complexities not encompassed by these three actions. For instance, Congress can override a presidential veto, the passage of a bill requires approval from two chambers, and the chambers utilize different voting procedures. One way to rectify the assumptions with these facets of legislative politics is to interpret the legislative actor as the member who is pivotal in determining the congressional position.[16]

The theory also does not incorporate the possibility of congressional members appealing to the public. Altering the framework to encompass this feature would not change the testable predictions regarding the relationship among current opinion, the president's preferences, and the legislative influence a chief executive generates from appealing to the public. Moreover, the framework presented is consistent with the widespread view that presidents have an advantage over other politicians in commanding public attention (e.g., Edwards 1982; Kernell 1997; Key 1961; Miroff 1982). V. O. Key (1961, 416), for instance, observes that "no other official can match the president in his capacity to utilize the media of communication . . ." Bruce Miroff (1982, 219) similarly assesses that the president's "access to the political consciousness of ordinary American citizens is unmatched for directness and immediacy."[17]

Behavior

The theory presumes the players try to achieve legislative outcomes as close to their preferred ones as possible. Moreover, each player is assumed to know the others' preferences and behave as if everyone is trying to achieve their preferred outcome. For the president, this involves attaining a policy as near to his preferred outcome p as possible. Likewise, congressional behavior is aimed at achieving an outcome maximally close to c^e if the president issues an appeal and c^0 if he does not. Within this theoretical setup, the electorate does not take any explicit actions.[18]

16. See Brady and Volden (1998) and Krehbiel (1998) for models that predict which congressional member will be pivotal.

17. There are other features of presidential-congressional policymaking from which this model also abstracts. For instance, under some circumstances, presidents can enact an executive order that can only be overturned by two-thirds majorities in each congressional chamber, the federal courts, or a subsequent president. The Public Appeals Theory is explicitly concerned with legislation. Allowing the president to act unilaterally by passing an executive order would not change the key substantive predictions of the theory, although doing so would naturally make the president's influence less dependent on public appeals.

18. In the extension in which the president can alter public opinion, the electorate updates its beliefs. Technically, game theorists distinguish between the updating of beliefs and observable actions.

BASIC RESULTS

An important component of the results is that the president does not always want to make a public appeal. Indeed, under certain circumstances, the strategy would backfire and actually decrease his ability to achieve a policy close to his preferred one. In other circumstances, the action would neither aid nor hurt him; the outcome following an appeal would be identical to what it would have been if he had not gone public. Whether the president in fact has the incentive to appeal to the public depends on the location of the electorate's preferences in relation to those of the president and Congress, as well as in relation to the status quo.

The president will only want to make an appeal if the electorate's preferred outcome is closer to his own than is the status quo or the outcome initially desired by Congress. When the electorate's desired outcome e is further from the president's policy position p than the outcome Congress originally wants c^0, an appeal would move the legislature's preferences away from those of the president given that the action induces Congress to want e. The president thus has no incentive to make an appeal. He also lacks this incentive if he prefers the status quo q to the electorate's desired outcome e. In this case, he can simply use his veto to achieve the status quo q, which he prefers to the outcome Congress would want following an appeal.

Figures 2.2 and 2.3 depict how the configuration of preferences affects a president's incentives to appeal to the public. Figure 2.2 highlights how going public can aid a president when the veto does not grant him any influence, while figure 2.3 shows that taking an issue to the public can be advantageous even when the president is able to achieve some influence from the veto. In each figure, I have assumed that the players' preferences are symmetric around their policy positions; in other words, given two options that are equidistant from an actor's desired outcome, one to the left and another to the right of it, the actor prefers the two options equally. Figure 2.2 depicts these "symmetric preferences" around p, the presi-

Figure 2.2 Basic Results When President Lacks Veto Power

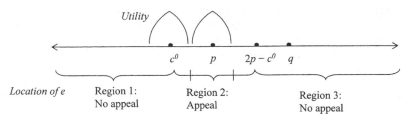

Figure 2.3 Basic Results When President Has Veto Power

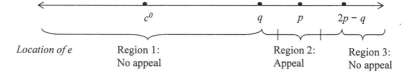

dent's policy position, and c^0, the outcome initially desired by Congress. The vertical axis represents the utility a player receives from an outcome; a player's preferences accordingly "peak" at his ideal outcome. The figure also divides the policy space into three regions based on possible locations of e, the electorate's desired outcome. The regions demarcate how the relative location of e affects whether the president will want to issue an appeal.

In all regions of figure 2.2, if the president does not issue an appeal, the outcome is c^0, the initial policy position of Congress.[19] This occurs because the president prefers c^0 to the status quo q and thus has no incentive to veto a proposal of c^0. The president's decision about going public is therefore based on whether he prefers the outcome this action would induce, or whether he prefers c^0.

When the electorate's preferred outcome e is located in the leftmost region, labeled Region 1, the president prefers c^0 to the outcome an appeal would generate. Specifically, going public would cause Congress to want to achieve e, and Congress would accordingly propose the policy as near e as possible among the set of options the president would not veto. In no part of Region 1 is this optimal congressional proposal any closer to p than is c^0. The president therefore has no incentive to make an appeal.

In comparison, in the middle region of the figure, Region 2, the president does move policy toward his preferred choice p by taking the issue to the airwaves. Region 2 is bounded at the left by c^0 and at the right by the outcome that is the same distance from p as c^0 (the position $2p - c^0$). The electorate's position e is thus closer to p than is c^0, the policy originally desired by Congress. Because an appeal induces Congress to want to enact e, and the president prefers this outcome to c^0, he issues an appeal and signs legislation equal to e.

The remaining region in the figure, Region 3, is akin to Region 1 in that the president has no incentive to issue an appeal. He prefers the outcome

---

19. The solution to the veto component of the Public Appeals Theory is identical to the well-known veto game of Romer and Rosenthal (1978). For details that concern this game but are not central to the argument here, I direct readers to the original Romer and Rosenthal article.

Congress initially desires to the one Congress would advance given increased salience to the issue, and therefore does not take the issue to the public.

Figure 2.2 highlights two critical implications of the basic framework of the Public Appeals Theory. The first implication is that public appeals can afford the president legislative influence; by increasing the salience of an issue, a president can encourage Congress to enact legislation closer to his policy position than would otherwise be enacted. The second implication is that this executive influence depends on the proximity of the president's and electorate's preferences. When the electorate's preferences are near those of the president, he is likely to gain legislative influence from commanding public attention to the issue; alternatively, when the electorate and president have quite dissimilar preferences, the president is likely to do better simply by staying silent than by appealing to the public. Consequently, all else being equal, a president's likelihood of issuing an appeal is higher the closer the president's preferences are to those of the electorate.

These implications hold even when a president can benefit from exercising his veto power, as illustrated by figure 2.3. Like the previous figure, figure 2.3 is divided into three regions of locations of the electorate's preferred outcome e, and these regions designate whether the president has an incentive to appeal to the public. Unlike the previous figure, however, in figure 2.3 the president prefers the status quo q to the initial position of Congress, c^0, and Congress prefers q to the president's position p. Thus if the president does not issue an appeal, the policy remains at the status quo q because the president would veto any policy that Congress would want enacted. The president's decision over whether to go public accordingly depends on whether he prefers q to the outcome that would occur following an appeal.

In Regions 1 and 3, the configuration of preferences is such that the president lacks any incentive to make an appeal. The action would encourage Congress to champion a policy the president considers inferior to the status quo q. As a result, the president and Congress would still not be able to agree on any movement from q.

In contrast, when the electorate's preferred outcome e is located in Region 2, a president achieves influence from appealing to the public. Doing so encourages Congress to support an option closer to the president's preferred outcome p than is the status quo q or the outcome the legislature initially desired c^0. Thus for this range of the electorate's preferred outcome the president makes an appeal, Congress proceeds to enact e, and the president signs the legislation.

Like figure 2.2, figure 2.3 shows that a president generates influence from appealing to the public but that this influence depends on the proximity of the president's preferences to those of the electorate. When these preferences are close, the president is likely to move policy in his direction by going public. Alternatively, when the electorate's desired outcome is located far from that of the president, he is likely to achieve little policy movement in his favor and even potentially harm his interests by appealing to the citizenry. Obviously, these implications assume all else is equal; the locations of the status quo and the outcome initially desired by Congress also affect a president's incentives. However, holding these positions constant, a president is more likely to acquire influence from appealing to the public the closer his desired outcomes are to those of the electorate. Consequently, he will be most likely to issue an appeal when he and the citizenry have similar policy positions.

The basic framework suggests that a president's public appeals should increase the influence of current opinion on legislative outcomes. Presidents have an incentive to draw public attention to issues on which they and the mass public share a desire to move policy away from the status quo as well as the option Congress would otherwise enact. Accordingly, presidential appeals should involve initiatives that are popular with the public; presidents have no incentive, and in many circumstances a *disincentive*, to publicize unpopular initiatives. A chief executive's speeches may consequently give the impression that he is something of a plebiscite, consistently following public opinion. Notably, this should be the case even if his more general policy agenda does not cater to current opinion.

EXTENSIONS

Costly Appeals

Research establishes that citizens have a limited attention span for politics (e.g., Brody 1991). Correspondingly, television networks restrict the availability of primetime exposure for presidential appeals (e.g., Kernell 1997). Presidents are therefore constrained in the number of times they can command the attention of the public. By appealing on a given issue, a president decreases his ability to do so on other matters. The Public Appeals Theory can incorporate this opportunity cost by assuming that an appeal imposes an exogenous cost on the president.[20]

20. More technically, the president's utility function is based on two additive terms: one that reflects the president's desire to achieve an outcome as close to p as possible and another that reflects the exogenous cost from appealing to the public, with this second term equaling the specified cost if he makes an appeal and zero otherwise.

Naturally, one might expect the cost of appealing to the public to vary by policy issue. Some matters require a good deal of explanation, and speechmaking about them could require presidents to forgo speechmaking about a multitude of other issues. On the other hand, the cost of appealing to the public could be extremely low for an issue associated with a major event such as an environmental disaster. Indeed, a president could be compelled to address the public about certain topics, such as the deployment of troops, placing the cost of an appeal at zero as in the basic set of assumptions.[21]

When the cost is greater than zero, there will be circumstances under which the president does not want to make an appeal even though the action would not harm his prospects for legislative success and could even increase them. In particular, if the cost of going public is greater than the policy benefit the activity affords, the president will not want to make an appeal. For instance, assume Congress initially prefers an outcome close to the one desired by the president. Because the president can achieve an outcome similar to the one he wants without taking to the airwaves, the cost of taking to them may well be greater than the policy benefits the activity would generate. However, as his policy position becomes more distant from the outcome likely to occur without an appeal, the policy benefits of going public will more likely outweigh the cost of the action.

Altering Citizens' Policy Preferences

Some research on public opinion suggests presidents can use public appeals to alter citizens' policy preferences. This research also indicates, however, that the impact will not be large in magnitude, and indeed under many conditions nonexistent.[22] For instance, Benjamin Page and Robert Shapiro (1992) find that only a popular president who makes repeated appeals regarding an issue can move mass opinion toward his position and then by a maximum of five to ten percentage points. Moreover, as the authors point out, even this effect cannot be established at a conventional level of statistical significance. John Zaller (1992, 97) presents a similar

---

21. Baum and Kernell (1999) suggest that the cost of commanding public attention via a televised appeal has changed over time. In particular, they argue that the dissemination of cable television has vastly increased this cost.

22. A related yet distinct topic is whether presidents shape public opinion through means other than direct public appeals. Certainly presidents try to do so, for instance, by trying to affect the content of media coverage. However, as Jacobs and Shapiro (2000) and Edwards (1983; 2003) discuss, a president's ability to craft public opinion is much more limited than commonly presumed.

account of presidents' ability to alter citizens' policy preferences. He observes that a popular president who does not face opposition from other members of the Washington community on a given issue can move public opinion five to ten percentage points in favor of his position. Yet Zaller does not attempt to stipulate the degree to which this capacity is systematic.

Only in the domain of foreign affairs has research established a routine impact of presidential appeals on citizens' policy preferences. In particular, James Meernik and Michael Ault (2001) find foreign policy appeals regularly move current opinion about six percentage points toward the chief executive's position.[23] The fact that the evidence for a routine impact is stronger in foreign affairs comports with research that argues citizens tend to have less information about these issues (e.g., Edwards 1983, Jacobs and Shapiro 2002b). As Edwards (1983, 43) observes, "people tend to defer more to the president on [foreign policy] issues than on domestic ones that they can directly relate to their own experience."[24]

Putting aside temporarily any empirical patterns distinguishing foreign and domestic affairs, the Public Appeals Theory can readily incorporate the possibility of presidents changing citizens' preferences about policy alternatives. In particular, the theory can include assumptions from a class of theories known as "cheap talk" games, in which a more informed actor alters a less informed one's preferences by sending her a signal (e.g., Austen-Smith and Banks 2000; Crawford and Sobel 1982; Gilligan and Krehbiel 1987; Matthews 1989).[25] Within the context of legislative politics, these games have been applied to situations in which there exists a difference between policy choices and policy outcomes. Each actor has a preferred outcome and wants to enact the policy option most likely to produce that outcome. There is uncertainty, however, about how the chosen option will affect the outcome. The actors have beliefs about this relationship, and one actor has more information than the others do about it.

A simple hypothetical example connects this setup to the basic set of assumptions. Assume the policy issue is arms reduction. The outcomes

23. The effect is statistically significant at conventional levels.

24. Edwards (2003) is less sanguine about presidents' ability to alter citizens' preferences on foreign policy issues. In particular, Edwards argues presidents' attempts to alter citizens' preferences generally fall on "deaf ears." Several of his examples suggest, however, that some presidential persuasion may occur, at least in the realm of foreign policy. These cases include Reagan's speech about the Invasion of Grenada (p. 59) and public opinion regarding the Strategic Defense Initiative (p. 58).

25. The term "cheap talk" refers to the fact that the signal the informed actor sends does not affect any cost he incurs from sending it.

are levels of arms reduction, and the policy choices are various arms control treaties. Further presume that the president, Congress, and electorate each have preferences over the level of arms reduction as well as a set of beliefs about how the choice of treaty will influence this level. The president has better information than the other actors have about the likely consequences of the treaties, and everyone is aware of this asymmetry in information. The president can accordingly utilize this informational advantage to try to convince the Congress and electorate that his preferred policy is the one that will advance their interests.

To apply the framework of cheap-talk games more generally to the Public Appeals Theory, I make the following set of assumptions. The president, legislature, and electorate each have preferences over a set of policy outcomes. The president has information the electorate and legislature lack about how the policy choice will affect the outcome. In the first stage of action, the president decides whether to make an appeal. Subsequently, he sends a signal about the expected policy effects.[26] The Congress and electorate then update their beliefs about the optimal policy choice, and Congress proceeds to enact legislation, which the president vetoes or accepts.

The solution to these assumptions follows the influential cheap-talk model of Vincent Crawford and Joel Sobel (1981) almost directly, and so I do not repeat it here except to highlight two substantive implications.[27] First, within this framework, the president can change the electorate's preferences about policy choices. Consequently, in comparison to the framework of the basic set of assumptions, the president's likelihood of appealing to the public is less influenced by the electorate's initial preferences; in the earlier framework, the electorate's preferences about policy choices were equivalent to those about outcomes, and were accordingly fixed. Here, the president can hope to move the preferences about policy choices toward his own. This ability derives from the fact that voters know the president has better information than they do about the relationship between the policy choices and outcomes. Thus when he tries to convince the electorate to support his preferred course of action, he can claim that his policy information warrants this action.

The extended framework does not suggest, however, that the president can simply convince the citizenry to support his preferred policy choice.

26. Regardless of whether the president incurs a cost from appealing to the public, the signal he sends does not affect the cost, placing the framework within the class of cheap-talk games.

27. A formal proof of this model is available upon request, although it differs only trivially from the original Crawford and Sobel (1982) one.

This is the second key implication. In particular, the president's ability to alter the electorate's preferences depends on the degree to which the actors desire similar policy outcomes. The further the president's desired outcome is from that of the electorate, the lower his capacity to alter public opinion about the policy choice. Intuitively, as the preferences over outcomes diverge, citizens become less trusting that the president has their interests at heart. Even when the preferences over outcomes are close enough that he can alter mass opinion about the optimal policy choice, he typically cannot convince the electorate to support his position. Instead, he merely has the capacity to move the electorate's position toward his own. Thus even when the president can achieve some movement in public opinion, the movement may not be sufficient to aid him in the legislative process; it is possible, for example, that after going public he may still prefer the status quo to the policy choice the electorate desires.

These implications are illustrated by continuing with the hypothetical example on arms control. In that example, the president can appeal to voters in an effort to convince them that his preferred treaty would produce the level of arms reduction they desire. The electorate, which by assumption knows the president's policy information is better than theirs, may be influenced by his efforts.[28] The president may therefore want to go public even if he deems that the treaty initially preferred by the electorate is inferior to the status quo. In contrast, under the basic set of assumptions, the president never has an incentive to go public if he prefers the status quo to the option initially desired by the electorate; in that case, given that he cannot alter voters' policy preferences, he is better off simply exercising his veto power.

Whether the president will want to appeal to the public depends in part on the extent to which voters perceive their interests to be aligned with his. Specifically, if the electorate's and president's preferences over the level of arms reduction are similar, then even if their initial beliefs about the appropriate treaty are widely disparate, the president may have considerable sway over voters' preferred course of action. However, if their preferences over the level of arms reduction are quite different, the electorate will be distrustful of the president's claims.

In sum, while the politics of public appeals differ when presidents can alter citizens' policy preferences, the difference is less dramatic than one might anticipate. The ability does make presidents' influence from going

28. For purposes of this theoretical extension, the president's information is indeed better than that of the public. Later in the book (in particular, chap. 5), I discuss contexts in which the president may move opinion even when the public has a more accurate impression of the state of the world than does the president.

public less dependent on the initial state of public opinion and, consequently, the decision to make an appeal less dependent as well. However, according to the theory, it is not the case that the chief executive can simply convince the electorate to support any given proposal. When the president's and electorate's preferences over outcomes are sufficiently divergent, he may not be able to move mass opinion at all. Moreover, even when he can move it to some extent, he may not be able to do so enough to increase his prospects for legislative success.

TESTABLE HYPOTHESES

The theoretical analysis offers a number of testable hypotheses concerning the relationship among current opinion, presidents' legislative influence, and the decision to make a mass appeal. The theory can also generate other hypotheses, for instance on veto politics, which are less central to the topic of how presidents' involvement of the mass public affects policymaking. To maintain focus on this topic, I do not specify such predictions. The stipulated hypotheses are only those tested in subsequent chapters.

In delineating these predictions, I distinguish at times between foreign and domestic policy. This distinction comports with the previously discussed evidence that presidents can more easily change the electorate's preferences on issues of foreign affairs, as well as with the oft-employed differentiation in the presidency literature between foreign and domestic policymaking. The section accordingly begins with a justification of the distinction, proceeds to stipulate the predictions, and then compares them to the existing literature.

Foreign versus Domestic Policy

The literature suggests that the executive politics surrounding foreign and domestic policy differ substantially. In particular, scholars have long contended that presidents have greater influence over foreign and defense policy (e.g., Dahl 1950; Fenno 1973; Huntington 1961; Wildavsky 1966).[29] While this thesis has been a subject of controversy (Oldfield and Wildavsky 1991; Shull 1991), recent work suggests presidents do in fact have certain advantages in foreign policy they lack in other domains (Peterson 1994; Sullivan 1991).[30] These advantages include greater

---

29. Henceforth, to minimize verbiage, I use the term foreign policy to refer to foreign as well as defense policy.

30. Shull's (1991) edited volume provides a series of studies on this topic.

agenda-setting power, a greater ability to lead public opinion, and less opposition from interest groups.

The advantage of most relevance to the Public Appeals Theory is the president's greater capacity to lead mass opinion. As discussed previously, the literature indicates that individuals tend to be less knowledgeable about foreign policy issues and hence more likely to look to the chief executive for guidance (e.g., Edwards 1983; Sobel 1993).[31] While on domestic issues presidents may occasionally move citizens' policy positions, they cannot expect to do so regularly (Page and Shapiro 1992). Alternatively, on foreign policy issues presidents routinely rally the public toward their positions (Meernik and Ault 2001).[32]

The empirical predictions of the Public Appeals Theory reflect this variation. The predictions for domestic affairs derive from the basic assumptions, where presidents cannot expect to alter citizens' preferences about policy choices. The predictions for foreign affairs, in comparison, derive from the theoretical extension in which presidents may be able to alter these policy preferences.[33] In making these generalizations, I am not arguing that a president can never move mass opinion about a domestic issue toward his position. Instead, I am highlighting that the asymmetry between the two policy domains is significant enough to warrant substantially different predictions regarding the politics of public appeals. Obviously, the empirical analysis will assess the extent to which this expectation is appropriate.

Legislative Influence, Position Popularity and Domestic Policy

The Public Appeals Theory suggests that a president's influence from appealing to the public is not independent of the initial popularity of the proposal he advocates.[34] Particularly when a president cannot expect to alter citizens' policy preferences, he will want to focus his appeals on

31. The analysis of Mueller (1973) suggests that citizens are particularly likely to support a president's decisions about U.S. military engagement.

32. Edwards and Wood (1999) suggests that presidents can more easily attract media attention on domestic than foreign policy issues. This work does not, however, distinguish between written and spoken presidential statements and thus does not necessarily imply that domestic policy appeals are more likely to garner public attention than foreign policy ones.

33. Henceforth, when I discuss the possibility of a president altering citizens' preferences about policy choices, I will use at will the phrasing "policy preferences" rather than "preferences about policy choices" in order to minimize verbiage.

34. Bond and Fleisher (1990, 3–4) make an important distinction between presidential influence and presidential success. The former refers to circumstances in which the president causes Congress to do something it otherwise would not have, and the latter to

initiatives that are already popular. If he does not, going public will fail to increase his legislative influence and may even decrease it. Accordingly, given presidents' difficulty in altering citizens' preferences about domestic policy issues, we should expect domestic policy appeals to concern popular proposals.

Predictions 2.1 and 2.2 summarize the relationship among the initially popularity of a president's position on a domestic policy issue, the influence generated by his appealing to the public about the issue, and the likelihood he promotes the issue to the public.

Prediction 2.1: Popularity of Domestic Positions. The more popular the president's position on a domestic policy issue is, the more likely he will be to appeal to the public about that issue.

Prediction 2.2: Influence over Domestic Affairs. Because a president's domestic policy appeals will typically concern issues on which he wants Congress to become more responsive to the electorate's existing policy preferences, the appeals will generally increase his legislative influence.

The predictions suggest presidents' involvement of the mass public encourages the enactment of domestic policies that follow current opinion. A president will tend to publicize domestic initiatives that he and the public would like to see enacted. After he does so, Congress will become more likely to support the initiatives. Domestic policy appeals thus increase the influence of presidents as well as the mass citizenry.

This set of predictions stands in contrast to the literature. Existing work suggests either that a president has no need to base the decision to go public on citizens' policy preferences or that public appeals do not regularly advance his prospects for legislative success.[35] For instance, while Gary Miller (1993) and E. E. Schattschneider (1960) each argue that presidents may generate legislative influence from publicizing initiatives, these arguments encompass initiatives that are not originally popular.[36]

---

circumstances in which legislative outcomes are consistent with the president's preferences for reasons that encompass but are not limited to presidents' efforts. In other words, while influence implies success, the converse does not hold. Here, because the predictions concern influence (and thus by implication success), I use the terms interchangeably.

35. The work most supportive of these hypotheses is focused not on the presidency but on interest groups. For example, Kollman's (1998) theory of "outside lobbying" suggests interest groups will only obtain influence from going public when they publicize issues that are already popular. Likewise, Smith (2000) argues that big business as a group only wields political power when it is fighting for policies that have popular support.

36. In related work, Barrett (2000) finds that a president's prospects for achieving legislative victory on an initiative are higher the more he refers to the proposal in his written

Miller (1993) develops a formal model in which a president generates influence from going public because the action shifts power within the legislature from committees to the floor, with which the president's interests are assumed to be aligned.[37] Public opinion is not an explicit component of the theory, and accordingly, Miller's analysis allows that a president's decision to go public may not depend on the popularity of his position.[38] The analysis of Schattschneider (1960) similarly suggests the Popularity of Domestic Positions prediction may be incorrect. He argues that the nationalization of an issue transfers power from interest groups toward the larger populace and the presidency.[39] Schattschneider does not, however, conjecture about the implications of variation in popular support for presidents' positions.

Other studies that diverge from the Popularity of Domestic Positions prediction explicitly link the policy effects of mass appeals to structural factors other than public support for the president's position. For example, Samuel Kernell (1997, 189) argues that the primary determinant of a successful appeal is a president's personal approval ratings. Kernell bases this argument on the presumption that a citizen's espousal of an executive initiative depends on her overall evaluation of the chief executive's performance.[40] Cary Covington (1987) focuses not on the president's personal popularity, but on the maneuvering room that "staying private" affords. In particular, he contends that presidents should not state policy

---

and spoken statements. Barrett does not consider the role of mass opinion in affecting presidential or congressional behavior, however, perhaps because he does not distinguish mass appeals from written messages to Congress.

37. This logic is consistent with Maltzman (1999), who argues that the floor has more influence on salient issues.

38. Ingberman and Yao's (1991a; 1991b) models of a credible commitment veto are also consistent with the conclusion that a president's influence from public appeals does not depend on the popularity of his policy position although importantly, these models concern only situations in which the president is trying to block legislation. In the Ingberman and Yao models, the president incurs a cost from reneging on a public veto threat. A president can therefore use the public threat to increase his veto power over an issue, and this ability is not constrained by the popularity of his policy position.

39. In particular, the presidency constitutes "the principal instrument" (Schattschneider 1960, 14) for the nationalization of an issue and "is likely to become more powerful" (p. 94) when conflict involves a national dimension.

40. Kernell's (1997) theory is described in his chapter "Opinion Leadership and Foreign Affairs," indicating at first glance that it is not applicable to domestic policy. However, in describing the theory, he cites domestic policy examples (e.g., Reagan's appeal concerning his proposed tax increase in 1982, p. 190) and compares the perspective to research that encompasses domestic policy appeals (e.g., Polsby 1978). I therefore discuss the perspective with reference to both domestic and foreign policy appeals.

positions when congressional members are cross-pressured by interest groups.

In these conceptions of the politics of mass appeals, the policy positions of the citizenry do not play a central role. The president's influence from publicizing a proposal is independent of the initial popularity of the proposal.[41] Correspondingly, citizens' positions do not affect the likelihood the chief executive takes to the national airwaves. Thus in contrast with the Public Appeals Theory, presidents' appeals do not necessarily increase the degree to which policymaking responds to current opinion.

Other research reaches a similar conclusion via a different line of argument. In particular, a number of studies indicate that presidents do not in general gain influence from appeals. For example, writing a few years later than Schattschneider (1960), Elmer Cornwell (1965, 303) argued that:

> In theory a public which [the President] has convinced will communicate its desires to Capitol Hill, and action will result. But Congress by its nature is far less responsive to national currents of opinion than to local pressures. Furthermore, well over half the membership come from safe seats and are immune to anything but a virtual tidal wave of popular demand . . . Finally, many of the most powerful individuals on the Hill, the committee chairmen, are from the safest districts and hence the most insulated from any White House-generated pressure.

Reaching a similar conclusion about the likely impact of appeals, Nelson Polsby (1978, 51–52) offers two reasons why presidents, at least at the time of his writing, could not count on generating policy influence through this strategy:[42]

> First, the appeal to public opinion itself is likely to fail because of the ephemerality of mass public attitudes on most issues . . . Second, even if by unusual combination of circumstances public opinion does for once yield to a president's entreaties, the effects may or may not reach Congress or influence congressional disposition of an issue. Congressmen after all have their constituencies and their own means of reaching them, and they may find themselves ill disposed toward a president who prefers to deal indirectly with

---

41. Several studies that are not focused primarily on studying the policy effects of presidents' public appeals also mention the possibility of appeals generating influence. These studies do not, however, specify how rare or common the influence might be, nor do they relate the likelihood of influence to the popularity of the president's policy position (e.g., Campbell and Jamieson 1990; Edwards 1983; Lowi 1985; Skowronek 1993).

42. Polsby (1978, 52) does acknowledge that "it may well be true in some future time that presidents will be able to get their way on matters of public policy by direct appeals to public opinion."

them through what they may interpret as coercion rather than face to face and in a spirit of mutual accommodation.

Supporting the arguments of Polsby and Cornwell, Jeffrey Tulis (1987) and Joseph Bessette (1994) observe that the only evidence of public appeals generating presidential influence comes from a few cases that do not reflect typical executive-legislative negotiations. Thus Tulis, Bessette, Polsby, and Cornwell indicate that even if the Popularity of Domestic Positions prediction holds, the Influence over Domestic Affairs hypothesis likely does not.

Legislative Influence, Position Popularity and Foreign Policy

The Public Appeals Theory indicates that a president's likelihood of appealing to the public will be less influenced by citizens' policy preferences when he can alter them, as he routinely can on issues of foreign affairs. In particular, this capacity makes a president's influence from going public less dependent on initial opinion, causing his decision to utilize this tactic to be less dependent on initial opinion as well. We should thereby expect the relationship among the initial popularity of a president's position, the likelihood he appeals to the public, and the legislative influence generated by this activity to differ between foreign and domestic policy. Predictions 2.3 and 2.4 specify hypotheses about these relationships.

Prediction 2.3: Popularity of Foreign Positions. The initial popularity of the president's position on a foreign policy issue will be less likely than the initial popularity of his position on a domestic issue to affect the probability he appeals to the public.

Prediction 2.4: Influence over Foreign Affairs. Foreign policy appeals will generate legislative influence even though they may not concern issues on which the president wants Congress to become more responsive to the electorate's initial policy preferences.

Because a chief executive's ability to alter citizens' policy preferences is greater for foreign affairs, the initial popularity of foreign policy proposals will pose less of a constraint on the legislative influence that an appeal can generate. In fact, presidents can have an incentive to go public about a foreign policy proposal that is marginally unpopular; an appeal may enhance the popularity of the proposal as well as its salience.

Notably, Predictions 2.3 and 2.4 do not imply that presidents can convince voters to support any given foreign policy initiative by advocating it to the public. In the extension of the Public Appeals Theory, in which the president may alter the electorate's preferences about policy choices, this ability depends on the proximity between his and the electorate's fundamental policy goals or interests; the further apart are these fundamental goals or interests, the less able the president is to convince citizens to support his position. Moreover, Predictions 2.3 and 2.4 do not suggest that presidents' influence from foreign policy appeals is necessarily larger than that achieved from domestic policy ones. According to the theory, this influence depends on the initial configuration of the president's, legislature's, and electorate's preferences over policy outcomes. For example, if the president's and electorate's but not the legislature's preferences are similar on domestic issues, while all of the players' preferences are similar on foreign issues, then the influence generated from domestic policy appeals may be more substantial than that from foreign policy ones.

The Popularity of Foreign Positions and Influence over Foreign Affairs predictions are not found in prior work. A few studies of public appeals distinguish between foreign and domestic policy, but these studies fail to confirm or contradict the predictions. For instance, Edwards (1983) and Kernell (1997) argue that presidents are better able to rally public support for foreign policy initiatives and hence more likely to achieve legislative success from appealing to the public about them. David A. Lewis (1997, 387) does not directly dispute this claim but cautions that in foreign policy presidents "have little need to resort to public appeals as a means of pressuring members of Congress."

Other research on public appeals does not distinguish between foreign and domestic policy and thus is not germane to the Popularity of Foreign Positions prediction. Some of this work, however, is relevant to the Influence over Foreign Affairs prediction. In particular, the latter hypothesis comports with the previously discussed studies that argue presidents routinely gain influence from public appeals (e.g., Miller 1993; Schattschneider 1960) and contradicts the studies that argue presidents typically do not gain influence from this activity (e.g., Bessette 1994; Cornwell 1965; Polsby 1978; Tulis 1987).

Sincerity of Policy Debate

In the Public Appeals Theory, when the president incurs at least a trivial cost from making a public appeal, he will not make one if he can achieve his preferred outcome without doing so. In other words, he will not simply publicize an inevitable legislative achievement. Indeed, among issues on which he would like Congress to follow mass opinion, his incentives to go public are greater the less is his influence absent the plebiscitary activity, *ceteris paribus*. This occurs because the net benefits from taking to the airwaves increase as his policy influence absent doing so declines. Prediction 2.5 summarizes this anticipated executive behavior.

Prediction 2.5: Sincerity of Policy Debate. The president's likelihood of appealing to the public will be negatively correlated with his expected legislative success absent doing so.

Like the other predictions, the Sincerity of Policy Debate hypothesis contrasts with earlier work. Specifically, Joshua Clinton et al. (2004) argue that presidents' likelihood of appealing to the public may be positively correlated with their prospects for legislative success. According to Clinton and his co-authors, chief executives have the incentive to demonstrate that they can produce legislative victories. Therefore, presidents may advocate proposals that Congress would enact even without the plebiscitary activity; the appearance of policy victory could merely be a facade. This view is consistent with what Roderick Hart (1987) terms the "Liberal" perspective of presidents' public communications. According to this perspective, presidents' public rhetoric "is but a harmless affectation reflecting certain media realities" and does not affect policymaking.[43]

Considering these studies in conjunction with the other parts of the literature, two recurring schools of thought about public appeals emerge, and each of these alternative schools contrasts with the Public Appeals Theory. The first is that presidents' appeals do not generally influence legislative decisions. This perspective encompasses the studies that contrast with the Sincerity of Policy Debate prediction as well as the previously discussed work that argues appeals do not typically generate policy influence. The second school of thought is that appeals do routinely affect policymaking but not in a way that depends on citizens' policy preferences. This perspective includes the studies that imply appeals generally grant presidents influence, as well as those that indicate this influence is dependent on factors other than citizens' policy preferences.

Which of the perspectives is correct? The subsequent chapters develop testing that compares the various perspectives against each other.

EXAMPLES

Before proceeding to the testing, I revisit the examples that began the chapter. These included two domestic policy appeals of President Reagan and a foreign policy appeal of President Clinton. More specifically, the examples involved President Reagan's 1981 appeal about abolishing the Departments of Education and Energy, his 1981 appeal about

---

43. This perspective from Hart would also be consistent with the likelihood of an appeal being unrelated to the president's expected legislative success.

cutting income taxes by 25 percent, and President Clinton's 1995 appeal about deploying American troops to Bosnia. The purpose of revisiting these examples is to explicate predictions of the theory. Accordingly, I do not account for factors that are outside the theoretical framework and yet may influence presidential and congressional behavior; such analysis is reserved for subsequent chapters.

In all three of the examples, Congress either did not adopt the president's proposed course of action or initially seemed unlikely to do so. As described at the outset of the chapter, Reagan's proposal to terminate the Departments of Energy and Education was never adopted, his tax cut was expected to fail, and the House voted against Clinton's Bosnia initiative before his speech. Thus, consistent with the Sincerity of Policy Debate prediction, the presidents' public appeals concerned negotiations in which legislative success was not a forgone conclusion; in no case was a president simply credit claiming or grandstanding. Where the cases differ from each other is in their relationships concerning current opinion, the president's preferences, and legislative behavior. The following descriptions highlight these differences, as well as how they relate to the testable hypotheses.

Two Domestic Policy Appeals of Reagan

The description of Reagan's appeals earlier this chapter underscored that each was associated with a legislative outcome that surprised observers. Political insiders had originally assessed the Democrats would defeat Reagan's proposal for a 25 percent income tax reduction, and yet the reduction was enacted. Likewise, pundits mistakenly conjectured that Reagan would succeed in terminating the Departments of Education and Energy. The Public Appeals Theory, in comparison, suggests that the legislative outcomes should not have been surprising.

In the case of the tax cut, Reagan's proposal was quite popular prior to his appeal. According to an NBC survey conducted two weeks before the address, 58 percent of the populace supported the tax reduction when asked about it in isolation. Moreover, 53 percent of respondents favored Reagan's proposal over a Democratic alternative of a 15 percent cut.[44]

44. Poll conducted by NBC News and Associated Press on July 13–14, 1981. Respondents of the first question were asked, "Reagan has also proposed cutting federal income tax rates by 25 percent over the next three years. Do you favor or oppose such tax cuts, or don't you know enough about them to have an opinion?" The respondents of the second question were asked, "Democrats in Congress have proposed a 15 percent cut in income tax rates over the next two years in place of Reagan's proposal for a 25 percent cut over three years. Which proposal would you most like to see adopted—a 15 percent tax rate cut over two years or a 25 percent tax rate cut over three years?"

Figure 2.4 Reagan's 1981 Tax Cuts

No tax reduction	15%	25%

$$\longleftrightarrow \qquad\bullet\qquad\qquad\bullet\qquad\qquad\bullet\qquad\qquad\longrightarrow$$

$$q \qquad\qquad C^0 \qquad\qquad P = E$$

Tax Reduction

Congress, however, seemed set to support the Democratic alternative. Speaker of the House Thomas P. (Tip) O'Neill, Jr., estimated that before Reagan's appeal, the alternative was likely to win by five or six votes.[45]

Figure 2.4 depicts a configuration of preferences consistent with the set of political circumstances before the appeal. The one-dimensional issue space represents the issue of tax reduction; the further to the right a player's preferred outcome, the greater the reduction desired. The status quo q represents no cuts in taxes, and there is space on either side of q to account for the possibility of preferring tax increases as well as tax cuts. Capital letters are used for the actors' preferences to reflect the fact that the available data concern preferences over policy choices and not outcomes. (This difference is substantively immaterial to the figures on the domestic policy cases.) The president's preferred choice P reflects his desire for a 25 percent cut, and following the public opinion data, I map the electorate's position E as identical to that of the president.[46] Finally, the congressional position prior to the appeal, C^0, is located between the president's position P and the status quo as the legislature was posed to enact the Democratic alternative of a 15 percent cut.

The Influence over Domestic Affairs prediction implies that Reagan's appeal in this circumstance should have advanced his prospects for legislative success. Because the mass public was more favorable to his proposal than Congress was, the appeal should have pressured members to switch their positions. In particular, given the configuration of preferences in figure 2.4, the theory predicts that the appeal should have induced Congress to support the president's policy.

Indeed, the evidence suggests this sequence of events occurred. After the appeal, a number of Democrats from moderate to conservative districts changed their positions to vote with the president. An aide to one of these members, Representative Beverly Byron (D-MD), defended the

45. Lou Cannon and Thomas B. Edsall, "Reagan Makes Appeal to Voters for Tax Bill," *Washington Post,* July 28, 1981, A1.

46. Obviously, it is possible that the electorate's ideal policy choice was not identical to that of the president; the available survey data does not allow one to make a more nuanced estimation of public sentiment.

switch by noting the office was "inundated with calls" in favor of Reagan's proposal the morning after the appeal. Offices throughout the Hill offered similar accounts.[47] Ultimately, the House enacted Reagan's proposal by a margin of 43 votes.[48]

The example of Reagan's appeal to abolish the Departments of Education and Energy presents a contrasting sequence of events. Before the appeal, the initiatives were very unpopular. Polling data suggest that 68 percent of the populace favored keeping the Education Department compared with 27 percent who wanted to eliminate it. Similarly, survey results indicate that 50 percent of the national adult population wanted to preserve the Department of Energy while only 40 percent were interested in abolishing it.[49] Congress, particularly the Democratic-controlled House, was also not predisposed toward supporting the terminations. Democratic members by and large backed the departments, which had been created during the Carter administration. Even some influential Republican members were opposed to Reagan's recommendation.[50] For instance, Senator William V. Roth, Jr. (R-DE), chairman of the committee with jurisdiction over the reorganization of agencies, wanted the Department of Education to remain a cabinet-level agency.[51]

Figure 2.5 characterizes these preferences of the president, Congress, and citizens using the notation of the Public Appeals Theory. Because the players' preferences about terminating the Department of Energy did not markedly diverge from those concerning the Education Department, I bundle the initiatives as if they were one proposal. The one-dimensional issue space represents the agency rank, which for purposes of these cases

47. Tom Raum, "Hill Flooded with Phone Calls, Telegrams," *Associated Press,* July 28, 1981.

48. Bessette (1994, 193) observes that Reagan's appeal, "though clearly helpful to his cause, had to be supplemented by private deals to secure the necessary congressional votes." I make no claims otherwise. As remarked at the outset of the section, these cases do not control for other influences on legislative behavior but merely explicate the theory. In the subsequent two chapters, I proceed to control for such factors.

49. Harris Survey taken September 19–24, 1981, of the national adult population. Respondents were asked, "President Reagan wants to close down the Department of Energy. Do you favor or oppose closing down the Department of Energy?" and then "President Reagan wants to close down the Department of Education. Do you favor or oppose closing down the Department of Education?" For subsequently cited surveys throughout the book, the sample is the national adult population unless otherwise noted.

50. See, for instance: Peter Behr, "Liberal Democrats Hit Reagan Pledge to Speed DOE's End," *Washington Post,* September 26, 1981, F9; Charles R. Babcok, "Reagan Delays Verdict on Education Department: Key Congressmen to Review Plan Calling for Foundation," *Washington Post,* November 18, 1981, A17.

51. Edward B. Fiske, "Some Republicans Oppose Efforts to Abolish U.S. Education Department," *New York Times,* December 26, 1981, A1.

Figure 2.5 Reagan's Initiative to Abolish the Departments of Energy and Education

Cabinet Level	Termination

$$q = C^0 = E \qquad\qquad\qquad\qquad P$$

Agency Rank

ranges from cabinet level to termination. In between these two extremes are options such as demoting the agencies to a subcabinet level. As in figure 2.4, P represents the president's preferred option, E the electorate's, C^0 the legislature's preferred policy absent a presidential appeal, and q the status quo policy, which was that the departments remain in the cabinet. The placement of P at the right end reflects Reagan's stated desire to terminate the departments, and the location of the congressional and electorate's preferences at the left end represents these actors' opposition to reducing the rank.

The Public Appeals Theory suggests that Reagan's televised address should not have advanced his initiatives. When a president cannot expect to change citizens' policy preferences, as is typically the case with domestic policy issues, the theory suggests the action will cause members to become more likely to cater to citizens' initial policy preferences. Accordingly, in this case, given that the congressional position was already in line with public opinion, Reagan's appeal should not have increased his prospects for success. Citizens' beliefs about the desirability of the agency closings should have remained relatively steady, and congressional opposition to the closings should not have diminished.

The aftermath of the appeal supports these expectations. Even in the days following Reagan's speech, his proposals received little public support. According to an ABC survey conducted in the days after the appeal, only 32 percent of the populace favored the abolishment of the Department of Education, and only 42 percent the elimination of the Department of Energy.[52] Moreover, consistent with the Public Appeals Theory, Congress never brought the proposals to the floor. By the subsequent congressional session, Reagan was presuming the continuation of the departments in his budget.

52. The survey was conducted September 25–26, 1981. Respondents were asked, "I'm going to mention some of the proposals President Reagan made in his speech (on the economy Thursday [9/24/81] night). After each would you please tell me whether you tend to agree or disagree with the proposal." For the Department of Education, the question wording was, ". . . His proposal to eliminate the Department of Education." For the Department of Energy, the wording was, ". . . His proposal to eliminate the Department of Energy."

Relatively obviously, in one notable way the example of the Departments of Energy and Education does not comport with the Public Appeals Theory. In particular, the Influence over Domestic Affairs prediction maintains that presidents will only publicize popular domestic initiatives. The example is still helpful for explicating the Public Appeals Theory, however, because it illustrates precisely why presidents have the incentive to avoid appealing to the public about unpopular domestic initiatives: namely, if a chief executive does publicize one, he is unlikely to see it enacted by Congress. Thus although the example does not comport with the predicted patterns of speechmaking, it supports expectations regarding the policy impact of public appeals.

Overall, the Reagan examples highlight how presidential, congressional, and citizens' preferences affect the legislative consequences of a domestic policy appeal. When, as in the case of the tax cut, public opinion is closer to a president's position than is the outcome desired by Congress, an appeal is likely to advance his prospects for legislative success. A president cannot, however, expect to gain influence from publicizing any given domestic policy proposal. As the example of the Departments of Energy and Education highlights, when citizens disfavor a domestic initiative, appealing to the mass public will not increase, and if anything will decrease the likelihood Congress enacts it. Thus in contrast to the other schools of thought from the literature, the examples suggest that a president's mass appeals influence policymaking in a way that depends on citizens' policy preferences.

A Foreign Policy Appeal of Clinton

The third example that began this chapter, President Clinton's November 27, 1995, appeal about sending 20,000 troops to Bosnia for a NATO peacekeeping mission, serves to underscore ways in which the theoretical predictions differ for foreign policy. In this case, neither the public nor Congress was terribly supportive of the president's initiative prior to his address. A Gallup poll taken a few weeks before it estimated that 49 percent of the public disapproved of dispatching a peacekeeping force to Bosnia while only 47 percent supported doing so.[53] Around the

53. The Gallup Organization conducted the survey on November 6–8, 1995. Respondents were asked: "There is a chance a peace agreement could be reached by all the groups currently fighting in Bosnia. If so, the Clinton Administration is considering contributing U.S. (United States) troops to an international peacekeeping force. Would you favor or oppose that?"

Figure 2.6 Clinton's Bosnia Mission

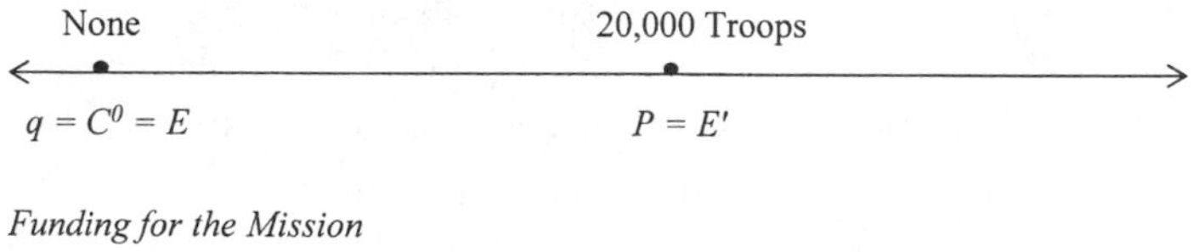

None   20,000 Troops

$q = C^0 = E$ $P = E'$

Funding for the Mission

same time, an ABC News-Washington Post poll found that 50 percent of respondents thought that Congress should have the final say over whether to send the troops as compared with 46 percent who thought that Clinton should have the final say.[54] Consistent with this public sentiment, the House had already voted to block funding for the Bosnia mission. The aim of the vote, as discussed at the outset of the chapter, was to prevent the deployment of troops for the peacekeeping mission.

Figure 2.6 maps the preferences of the public, Congress, and Clinton prior to the appeal. The familiar one dimensional issue space represents funding for the Bosnia mission. The policy choices that the electorate and Congress initially preferred, E and C^0 respectively, are located at the status quo q of no U.S. military involvement (and hence no funding). The placement of Clinton's preferred option P reflects the president's interest in deploying 20,000 troops.

The Influence over Foreign Affairs prediction is based on the premise that presidents can use the bully pulpit to alter citizens' preferences about a foreign policy issue. More precisely, the theory suggests that if citizens perceive their fundamental policy goals to be sufficiently similar to those of the president, an appeal may shift their preferences over policy choices toward his own. Clinton's appeal appears to have had such an effect.[55] An ABC poll conducted the night of the speech found that 50 percent of the public thought Congress should not try to thwart Clinton's proposal by blocking funding for the mission.[56] Likewise, a Gallup poll found the proportion of citizens who disapproved of the president's policy dropped

54. Poll conducted by ABC News November 10–13, 1995. Respondents were asked: "If they don't agree, who should have the final say on whether or not to send U.S. (United States) troops to Bosnia—Congress or the Clinton Administration?"

55. In an ideal world, we would have data on citizens' perception of the relationship between their and the president's fundamental policy goals over Bosnia as well as data on preferences about policy choices. Here, we have only the latter type of data.

56. The question asked by ABC was, "Do you think Congress should or should not try to prevent (President Bill) Clinton from sending U.S. (United States) troops to Bosnia by blocking the money for the mobilization?"

nine percentage points, to 40 percent, after the speech.[57] Thus Clinton's public appeal shifted public opinion to his advantage.

It was following the shift that the aforementioned House reversal occurred. On December 13, the House voted, along with the Senate, to support the Bosnia mission. The change in public opinion is depicted in figure 2.6 with the notation E', which represents the electorate's induced preference after the appeal. The policy position is placed at P, the president's position, in accord with the available survey data.[58]

It is worth noting that in addition to Clinton's appeal, another significant event occurred between the House votes. On December 8, the president dispatched a force of 700 troops by authority of an executive order (Executive Order 1282). One could obviously argue that this deployment of the troops affected congressional behavior as much or more than Clinton's appeal. There are reasons, however, to believe that the appeal was important. First, budgetary politics are one of the key ways in which unilateral action by the president can be thwarted (Howell 2003, 120–26); Clinton would have faced significant political and legal barriers to sustaining a force of 20,000 troops in Bosnia if Congress had continued to deny the mission any funding. Second, there is evidence that Republican Party leaders refused to fight with Clinton as soon as the speech was given rather than waiting until the advance deployment of troops. Speaker of the House Newt Gingrich failed to criticize Clinton's plan following the speech. Likewise, Bob Dole, then the Senate Majority leader, declined an invitation to respond on national television to Clinton's appeal.[59]

CONCLUSION

This chapter has developed a theoretical framework, the Public Appeals Theory, which suggests a president's appeals increase citizens' policy influence as well as his own. The theory finds that a president's success from appealing to the public depends on strategically choosing the initiatives he advocates. If he were to select an issue to promote to the citi-

57. The question wording was, "Now that a peace agreement has been reached by all the groups currently fighting in Bosnia, the Clinton Administration plans to contribute U.S. (United States) troops to an international peacekeeping force. Do you favor or oppose that?" The Gallup Organization conducted the poll the night of the appeal.

58. Again, it is possible that the electorate's ideal policy choice was not identical to that of the president but the available survey data does not allow one to make a more nuanced estimation of public opinion.

59. Mary McGrory, "The Price of Prevailing," *Washington Post*, November 30, 1995, A2.

zenry randomly, doing so could actually hurt his prospects for legislative success. When the president cannot expect to alter citizens' policy preferences, such as is typically the case with domestic policy, he has the incentive to publicize initiatives that are already popular. Even when he can likely move mass opinion toward his position, as is commonly the case with foreign policy issues, he will want to avoid publicizing unpopular initiatives if citizens perceive that his policy goals differ substantially from theirs.

As this chapter has detailed, these predictions contrast with other perspectives from the literature. One group of studies suggests that appeals only rarely influence policymaking in Washington. Another group indicates that appeals routinely influence policymaking but not in a way that increases the impact of current opinion on lawmaking. Therefore, it remains far from clear that the Public Appeals Theory will be borne out empirically. In the next two chapters, I assess the extent to which the theory indeed explains the politics of presidents' public appeals.

CHAPTER THREE

Domestic Policy Appeals

The predictions derived from the Public Appeals Theory suggest that a president's domestic policy appeals will increase his legislative influence as well as that of the mass public. According to the Influence over Domestic Affairs prediction, a president can achieve legislative success by publicizing issues on which he wants congressional members to be become more responsive to citizens' policy preferences. Consequently, and as specified by the Popularity of Domestic Positions hypothesis, a chief executive's likelihood of publicizing a domestic policy proposal is higher the greater is popular support for the proposal. This incentive to publicize popular initiatives does not, however, imply that a president goes public about issues on which he would achieve policy victory absent the plebiscitary activity. Indeed, the third prediction regarding domestic policy appeals, the Sincerity of Policy Debate prediction, suggests they are not actions of credit-claiming but instead involve genuine policy negotiations.

This perspective of domestic policy appeals, while arguably intuitive, contrasts with other perspectives from the literature. As discussed in chapter 2, some research indicates that appeals do not routinely increase the policy influence of presidents or the mass public. This school of thought encompasses work that argues appeals almost never influence policymaking because public opinion is ephemeral (Polsby 1978), because most congressional members hold "safe seats" and thus need not respond to public opinion (Cornwell 1965), or because appeals are about credit-claiming (Hart 1987; Clinton et al. 2004). Other research fits into yet another perspective, which is that appeals do regularly influence the policy process but not in a way that depends on citizens' policy positions. This strand of the literature includes the studies that contend appeals should, in general, grant presidents legislative influence (e.g., Miller 1993; Schattschneider 1960), as well as those that suggest this influence is contingent on factors other than citizens' policy preferences, such as the president's personal approval ratings (Kernell 1997).

Which perspective best fits the patterns of domestic policy appeals? Prior empirical work does not provide an answer. A number of excellent case studies have been conducted of famous presidential appeals about domestic initiatives, ranging from Theodore Roosevelt's efforts for the Hepburn Act of 1906 (Tulis 1987) to Bill Clinton's publicizing of his plan for nationalized health care (e.g., Hacker 1999; Jacobs and Shapiro 2000; Skocpol 1996).[1] These studies offer detailed evidence on significant successes (such as in the Roosevelt case) and failures (as in the Clinton case). Yet this work does not establish whether the successes are isolated, or as the Public Appeals Theory would suggest, related to the president's publicizing of popular domestic initiatives.

A study of Calvin Mouw and Michael MacKuen (1992) is more indicative of such an effect. Examining the major and minor addresses of Presidents Eisenhower and Reagan, Mouw and MacKuen find that congressional agenda-setters moderate their proposals in response to presidents' public statements. The analysis does not, however, investigate whether the moderation corresponds to presidential influence or whether it occurs in administrations other than those of Eisenhower and Reagan. Nor does the analysis address the relationship between the popularity of the president's proposal and the likelihood that he publicizes it. The Public Appeals Theory is thus neither confirmed nor challenged by Mouw and MacKuen.

This chapter examines the theory as it concerns domestic policy. I first present some descriptive statistics on the relationship among the popularity of a president's proposal, his likelihood of appealing to the public about it, and the likelihood of legislative success; I then proceed to conduct more rigorous tests of the hypotheses. The descriptive statistics revolve around the nationally televised, noncompulsory presidential speeches during the Eisenhower through Clinton presidencies. The purpose of this "first-glance analysis" is to describe public opinion about the domestic initiatives that presidents publicize. For instance, how popular are the policies that presidents promote in national addresses? Do certain presidents tend to push relatively popular initiatives while other presidents promote unpopular ones?

The first-glance analysis also examines how a president's legislative success is correlated with the popularity of his publicized initiatives. This correlation provides a rudimentary assessment of whether the Public Appeals Theory explains variation in the legislative outcomes associated

---

1. Case studies of famous foreign policy appeals also have been conducted. See, for instance, Tulis (1987) on Woodrow Wilson's efforts to secure support for the League of Nations and Kernell (1976) on the Truman Doctrine speech.

with domestic policy appeals. The correlation is not an appropriate test, however, because a positive correlation could simply reflect that presidents go public about forgone policy victories or that popular proposals are more likely to be enacted regardless of whether a president publicizes them. To account for these issues, what is needed is an analysis that deals with the potential endogeneity between presidents' public appeals and expected legislative success and that compares legislative outcomes with and without public appeals.

The second part of the chapter develops testing that incorporates these features. The testing revolves around a set of annually recurring budgetary issues during the presidencies of Eisenhower through Clinton. The examination of a set of comparable policies is important because it facilitates coding the variables of analysis similarly across observations. Thus, for example, I am able to utilize survey data with identical question wording. Correspondingly, a consistent set of control variables can be drawn upon.

What will all of this empirical analysis ultimately accomplish? If the theoretical predictions are inconsistent with the descriptive statistics and/or not supported by the econometric tests, the analysis will indicate that the Public Appeals Theory does not explain domestic policy appeals even if, in chapter 4, it ends up explaining foreign policy appeals. If, on the other hand, the first-glance analysis and subsequent tests substantiate the predictions, this chapter will have provided considerable support for the theory.

A FIRST GLANCE

The first-glance data set derives from all nationally televised, nonobligatory, primetime presidential addresses between 1957 and 2000.[2] These speeches include, for example, Bill Clinton's 1993 address on healthcare reform, Jimmy Carter's "crisis of confidence speech" in 1979, and Lyndon Johnson's speech on voting rights in 1965. I begin with Eisenhower's second term because, by 1957, 78 percent of homes owned a television set while in 1953, only 44 percent of homes owned one.[3] Thus throughout the span of the data, each president could reach a national audience via television.

2. The first-glance analysis excludes State of the Union addresses in order to evaluate whether basic patterns predicted by the Public Appeals Theory hold for discretionary speeches. In the subsequent section that presents the testing, I do not exclude State of the Union addresses.

3. *Historical Statistics of the United States, Colonial Times to 1970* (Washington, DC: Bureau of the Census, 1975).

The data consist of domestic policy appeals from these speeches for which I could obtain at least one survey estimating public approval versus disapproval of the initiative during the year leading up to the address.[4] To formulate this list of appeals, I read each address with the purpose of determining all legislative proposals that the president mentioned in his speech. Only proposals on specific policy initiatives or legislation were included.[5] Thus, I did not code a president's claim that he was "for the environment" or "concerned about health care" as a policy appeal.[6]

I obtained the public opinion data using Roper's R-POLL database.[7] For observations for which multiple polls exist, I used the one most proximate to the date of the address.[8] I did not use any polls taken after the speech because the theoretical predictions concern the popularity of initiatives prior to a president's decision to appeal to the public. Obviously, I could not find surveys with identical question wording for all of the various initiatives. In the subsequent testing of the budgetary data, only surveys with identical question wording are used. Here, in the interest of examining as broad a range of policies as possible, I do not impose this constraint, acknowledging that the different question wordings will create noise. A constraint I do impose, however, is that the answers must be structured such that they can be categorized into groups of those who favor the president's proposal, those who oppose it, and those who "don't know" whether they have a stated preference. Thus, for example, polls that ask respondents whether they prefer more, less, or "about the same" amount of spending on a given policy issue are not used in this portion of

4. Herbst (1998) documents how policymakers may measure public opinion through sources other than public opinion polls. This fact notwithstanding, polls are still a dominant means by which politicians (particularly federal ones) estimate public opinion, as Herbst (1993) herself describes elsewhere. For purposes of this analysis, polls are useful because they provide a reasonably consistent means of estimating public opinion across issue and time.

5. As discussed subsequently, I have examined the legislative histories of the initiatives promoted in the appeals using the *Congressional Quarterly Almanacs*. These histories suggest that the appeals corresponded to the presidents' actual legislative proposals.

6. To ensure that no legislative proposal was missed, I assigned a research assistant to conduct this data collection as well. The inter-coder reliability was 98 percent.

7. The availability of survey data determines the unit of observation. If the president repeatedly appealed to the public about a proposal and there are different public opinion polls for each appeal, I coded each one separately. If, however, the president repeatedly appealed to the public about a proposal and there exists only one survey, I included only one entry. The latter situation affected less than a handful of observations. Moreover, I have conducted the analysis by coding repeated appeals with one entry per speech even if only one survey exists for all of them and received substantively similar results.

8. If multiple polls were taken on that date, I averaged across them.

Table 3.1 Popularity of Initiatives in Domestic Policy Appeals, 1957–2000

Popularity Variable	Number of Observations	Mean (%)	Median (%)	Standard Deviation (%)	Minimum (%)	Maximum (%)
Approval	99	55	56	17	11	87
Approval – Disapproval	99	22	28	33	−71	81

the analysis. I restrict the data in this way to ensure that the ratings on policy approval are at least minimally consistent across the various surveys.

These efforts produced a data set of ninety-nine domestic policy appeals, which encompass many of the significant policy negotiations of the past decades. For example, John F. Kennedy's appeal to end segregation in public facilities, Richard Nixon's advocacy of welfare reform, and Bill Clinton's efforts to pass the Brady Bill are all included. Consistent with these examples, the data are not clustered into one or two administrations; each president is associated with at least four appeals. There is a slight trend toward more observations for the later presidents: the average annual number of domestic policy appeals is 1.4 for presidents through Richard Nixon's tenure and 2.8 for Gerald Ford through Bill Clinton.[9]

Popularity of Initiatives

Table 3.1 presents the summary statistics on the extent to which presidents' domestic policy appeals concern initiatives that are popular. Following Richard Brody's (1991) approach, popularity is measured in two ways, the first of which captures public support and the second of which captures the difference between public support and opposition. Accordingly, *Approval* represents the percentage of respondents who favor the policy, while *Approval − Disapproval* equals that percentage minus the percentage who disfavor it. The latter statistic, in addition to incorporating the degree of opposition to the president's proposal, indirectly helps to stipulate the percentage of "don't know" responses; that percentage equals $100 - 2* Approval + [Approval - Disapproval]$.

As the table shows, the descriptive statistics are consistent with the Influence over Domestic Affairs prediction, which maintains that a president will go public about popular domestic initiatives. The mean and median policy approval ratings, 55 percent and 56 percent, respectively,

9. This trend is largely a function of the increased quantity of available public opinion data for the later years.

Table 3.2 Popularity of Initiatives in Domestic Policy Appeals, by President

President	Number of Observations	Average Number of Observations per Year	Mean of Approval (%)	Mean of Approval – Disapproval (%)
Eisenhower	5	1.25	57	33
Kennedy	5	1.67	51	18
Johnson	4	0.80	54	17
Nixon	12	2.00	61	32
Ford	7	3.50	51	16
Carter	16	4.00	61	36
Reagan	23	2.88	50	10
Bush	9	2.25	50	11
Clinton	18	2.25	59	24

indicate that over half of the population is supportive of the typical domestic initiative publicized by the president. Likewise, the mean and median of the policy approval minus disapproval ratings, 22 percent and 28 percent, imply that more individuals favor than disfavor the typical domestic proposal he publicizes.[10] Table 3.1 thus indicates presidents tend to go public about domestic initiatives that are already relatively popular.

The data do not indicate that mass opinion always favors the proposals, however. Consistent with Lawrence Jacobs's and Robert Shapiro's (2000; 2002a) argument that presidents attempt to manipulate the citizenry, the descriptive statistics show that presidents at times make appeals about domestic policy initiatives that are not initially supported by a majority of the populace. The variable *Approval* has a range of 11 percent to 87 percent with a standard deviation of 17 percent, and *Approval – Disapproval* ranges from −71 percent to 81 percent with a standard deviation of 33 percent.

A possible cause of the variation could be that some presidents publicize popular domestic initiatives while other presidents attempt to change citizens' preferences. This state of affairs would comport with work that emphasizes the uniqueness of individual presidents' leadership styles (e.g., Greenstein 2000). Such variation would suggest that the Public Appeals Theory does not apply systematically across administrations. Table 3.2 examines whether this is the case, summarizing the means of

10. For seventy-six of the ninety-nine domestic policy appeals, the approval rating was higher than the disapproval rating.

Approval and *Approval — Disapproval* by president. Notably, the data indicate that all presidents tend to focus their domestic policy appeals on popular initiatives. For each president from Eisenhower through Clinton, the mean approval rating of the publicized proposals is at least 50 percent and the mean difference between the approval and disapproval ratings is at least 10 percent. In other words, public support is consistently greater than public opposition, and this support comes from at least a bare majority of the populace.

The descriptive statistics do not necessarily contradict Greenstein's general argument that leadership styles differ; the mean approval rating of the proposals varies from 50 percent to 61 percent. However, it is not the case that the Public Appeals Theory corresponds to the behavior of only a subset of presidents. Rather, as expected, each president generally appeals to the mass public about domestic initiatives that are aligned with national public opinion.

Legislative Outcomes

The theoretical analysis of chapter 2 suggests that if a president appeals to the public regarding an unpopular domestic policy initiative, this action will make congressional members less likely to enact the policy. The theory would therefore be inconsistent with the data if presidents routinely achieved legislative victories on unpopular domestic initiatives after publicizing them. Likewise, the theory would receive refutation if the correlation between legislative success and the popularity of publicized domestic policy initiatives were negative. To assess whether the first-glance data evince these patterns, I estimate the popularity of the policy initiatives according to the legislative outcomes.

I determined these outcomes using the legislative histories provided by the *Congressional Quarterly Almanac*. At first, I attempted to classify each proposal by whether Congress enacted it with "significant amendment," enacted it without significant amendment, or failed to enact the initiative. Owing to the difficulty in comparing the significance of amendments across the large range of policy areas, I ended up collapsing the first two categories and producing a binary coding. For nonbudgetary proposals, the initiative was coded as a legislative success if it became law in some form during the congress in which the president publicized the issue and a legislative failure otherwise.[11] For budgetary proposals,

---

11. In chapter 2, I observed that the terms "presidential influence" and "presidential success" have different connotations in the literature, with the former referring to circumstances in which the president's actions altered congressional behavior and the latter

Table 3.3 Popularity of Initiatives in Domestic Policy Appeals, by Legislative Outcome

Outcome	Mean of Approval (%)	Mean of Approval − Disapproval (%)
Legislative Success ($n = 64$)	59	28
Legislative Failure ($n = 35$)	49	11

I coded an outcome as a success only if the percentage change in enacted appropriations from last year was within three percentage points of the change in appropriations requested by the president. In the following section, where all of the data concern appeals over budgetary policy, I adopt a more nuanced accounting of legislative success.[12]

Table 3.3 presents the descriptive statistics on the legislative outcomes. Consistent with expectations, table 3.3 suggests that successful domestic policy appeals concern proposals supported by a majority of the population. The mean approval rating for the legislative victories is 59 percent. Were it alternatively the case that this approval rating was less than 50 percent, the table would indicate that initial policy popularity may not be critical to the legislative impact of a domestic policy appeal.

Also consistent with expectations, legislative success is positively correlated with the popularity of the publicized initiatives. Specifically, the mean approval rating for the legislative failures is 49 percent, a statistically significant difference from the mean approval rating of the victories ($p < 0.01$, one-tailed).[13] Likewise, the mean approval minus disapproval rating is 28 percent for the legislative victories and 11 percent for the failures, another statistically significant difference ($p < 0.01$, one-tailed). Were the average popularity of the enacted initiatives less than that of the failed

---

instances of influence as well as circumstances in which Congress would have adopted the president's position even if he had not. The analysis of this section does not try to distinguish success from influence. However, since the concept of success encompasses that of influence, the predictions on influence can be analyzed with data on legislative success.

12. The cutoff point of three percentage points is necessarily arbitrary. I base it partially on the fact that in the budgetary data used later in this chapter, the median absolute difference between the percentage change in appropriations requested by the president and that enacted is three percentage points. Changing the cutoff point to four or five percentage points does not in any way alter the results. Also, eliminating the budgetary observations from the first-glance analysis does not alter the substantive findings.

13. Overall, the appeals are associated with victory in 65 percent of the cases. This ratio of successful appeals is nearly identical to that found in Peterson's (1990) study of 229 presidential domestic policy initiatives. Peterson finds that of the 42 initiatives a president mentioned in a television or radio broadcast, Congress enacted 64 percent of them in some form.

ones, the data would suggest that presidents need not be concerned about the popularity of a domestic proposal when deciding whether to publicize it.

On the whole, the first-glance analysis has established that the Public Appeals Theory is consistent with summary statistics on presidents' domestic policy appeals. Presidents generally appeal to the public about popular domestic initiatives, and this relationship holds not only for the presidents as a group but also for each administration individually. Also as expected, the popularity of the publicized initiatives is positively correlated with whether a legislative victory occurs. The descriptive statistics therefore comport with the anticipated presidential and congressional behavior.

Despite this consistency with the theory, the empirical analysis has not yet confirmed the key theoretical predictions. An appropriate test of the Influence over Domestic Affairs hypothesis necessitates a comparison between the legislative outcomes that occur with and without appeals, as well as a means of accounting for the potential endogeneity between appeals and expected legislative success. Testing the Popularity of Domestic Positions and Sincerity of Policy Debate predictions, meanwhile, requires an assessment of the circumstances under which presidents do not issue appeals. Finally, a proper test of any of the hypotheses must control for other factors such as the ideological composition of Congress and the president's popularity. In the next section, I develop testing that addresses these issues.

TESTING

Because the theoretical predictions concern variation over whether a president takes an initiative to the public, the data for the testing should contain presidential proposals and legislative outcomes from situations in which appeals occur and comparable situations in which no appeal occurs.[14] Budgetary data are well suited for this purpose. Each year, the president submits written proposals for the funding of federal agencies, and Congress enacts legislation concerning this funding. In fact, the president cannot legally avoid making these annual proposals as the Budget and Accounting Act of 1921 requires them.

---

14. This section of chapter 3 extends the analysis conducted in Canes-Wrone (2001a) through the second Clinton administration. Unlike in Canes-Wrone (2001a), here I do not include a dummy variable for a president's start of term because of multicollinearity issues with other control variables. However, including this variable does not alter the major substantive results.

Budgetary data also offer many other benefits for purposes of testing the Public Appeals Theory. First, the quantitative nature of the data facilitates measuring legislative success more precisely than simply victory versus failure. Second, the appropriations process encompasses many of the most important presidential initiatives of the past forty years. For instance, Johnson's war on poverty, Ford's efforts at deregulation, and Reagan's initiative to cut domestic social spending all involved budgetary negotiations that are part of the data of this chapter. Indeed, over the past half-century, the budget has often been the central battleground between a president and congressional members who are recalcitrant to enact his agenda.

Third, because the Budget and Accounting Act requires presidents to submit an annual budget, the data are not censored by a president's decision to state a policy position. On most issues a president can avoid taking a position, and he has an incentive to "stay silent" when publicity is not an asset (Covington 1987). Thus, data based on noncompulsory presidential positions could be biased in favor of finding significant influence from going public. Budgetary data avoid this problem.

Fourth, because the data concern a set of comparable issues, the control variables are commensurate across observations. For example, I am able to utilize public opinion surveys with identical question wording. Fifth and finally, prior research establishes that budgetary data reflect active bargaining between the president and Congress (e.g., Brady and Volden 1998; Kiewiet and Krehbiel 2002; Kiewiet and McCubbins 1988, 1991; Krehbiel 1998; Su, Kamlet, and Mowery 1993). The observations therefore concern the type of policy negotiations addressed by the Public Appeals Theory.

The specific budgetary data employed revolve around the funding for forty-three domestic agencies during fiscal years 1958 through 2001. (Appropriations for a given fiscal year are generally enacted in the previous calendar year. Accordingly, the data concern the second Eisenhower term through both Clinton administrations.) An observation consists of a pairing of an agency i and fiscal year t. Each of the agencies was funded by discretionary spending, which means that Congress had to appropriate funds annually or else the relevant programs would have been terminated.[15] Thus all of the observations involve a similarly extreme "status quo policy" that would have resulted had no new legislation been passed in a given year. These budgetary data are based on those in D. Roderick Kiewiet's and Mathew McCubbins's (1991) analysis of party influence.[16]

---

15. Mandatory spending, in contrast, does not require annual appropriations.

16. I obtained the data from Joe White, who had extended them through fiscal year 1989 for his analysis of incrementalism in the budgetary process (White 1995). I have

For reasons that I will discuss in turn, the budgetary data analyzed in chapters 4 and 8 are not from the Kiewiet and McCubbins observations. However, for purposes of studying domestic policy appeals, the observations provide a good foundation on which to construct a data set.

The forty-three agencies span a range of policy issues, including the environment, crime protection, public works, tax collection, and economic regulation. For example, the data encompass the Environmental Protection Agency, the Federal Bureau of Investigation, the Immigration and Naturalization Service, the Internal Revenue Service, and the Securities and Exchange Commission.[17] Because some of the agencies did not exist for the entirety of the time period, the data set is not a balanced panel with an observation for each agency and year. Still, the number of budgetary negotiations examined is substantial. In total, I have 1,225 observations of a presidential proposal and the subsequently enacted appropriations for a given agency and fiscal year.

Measurement of Key Variables

The data include a set of key variables that directly pertain to the predictions of the Public Appeals Theory as well as a set of controls. The latter encompass factors from alternative predictions in addition to standard controls from the literature. Following the predictions of the Public

---

extended the data through fiscal year 2001 and also have eliminated any agency whose funding was at least 20 percent mandatory in any year. The data collection by Kiewiet and McCubbins was supported by the National Science Foundation grant SES-8421161.

17. The set of agencies includes the following: Administration of the Public Debt, Army Corps of Engineers, Bureau of Labor Statistics, Bureau of Land Management, Bureau of Mines, Bureau of Narcotics, Bureau of Reclamation, Census Bureau, Civil Aeronautics Board, Coastal and Geodetic Survey, Commodity Futures Trading Commission, Consumer Product Safety Commission, Customs Service, Drug Enforcement Administration, Economic Development Administration, Environmental Protection Agency, Federal Bureau of Investigation, Federal Communications Commission, Federal Prison System, Federal Trade Commission, Fish and Wildlife Service, Food and Drug Administration, Forest Service, Geological Survey, Immigration and Naturalization Service, Internal Revenue Service, Interstate Commerce Commission, National Aeronautics and Space Administration, National Highway Traffic Safety Administration, National Institute of Standards, National Oceanic and Atmospheric Administration, National Park Service, Natural Resources and Conservation Service, National Science Foundation, Occupational Safety and Health Administration, Patent and Trademark Office, Rural Electrification Administration, Secret Service, Securities and Exchange Commission, Small Business Administration Loan and Investment Fund, Soil Conservation Service, United States Mint, and the Weather Bureau.

Appeals Theory, the key variables concern public appeals, the popularity of the president's proposal, and legislative success.

I collected the data for *Public Appeal* by reading all of the nationally televised primetime addresses that presidents gave between 1957 and 2000, the years during which the fiscal year 1958 through 2001 budgets were passed. The speeches include nonobligatory ones as well as State of the Union addresses. For each observation of an agency and fiscal year, I coded a public appeal as occurring if the president spoke about his budgetary proposal or policy issues that could only refer to it. This coding does not encompass broad declarations such as "I am the education president."[18] Using this approach, seventy-eight of the observations are associated with a presidential appeal.

The second key variable is *Policy Approval,* which I measure with responses from the following survey question: "We are faced with many problems in this country, none of which can be solved easily or expensively. I'm going to name some of these problems, and for each one I'd like you to tell me whether you think we're spending too much money, too little money, or about the right amount on [the particular policy issue]."[19] For almost every year since 1971, the General Social Survey and/or a Roper survey have asked this question with reference to six policy issues that match the agencies in the data. Specifically, the question has referred to crime, drug control, the environment, poverty assistance, parks and space exploration, which I map, respectively, to the Federal Bureau of Investigation, the Drug Enforcement Agency, the Environmental Protection Agency, the Economic Development Administration, the National Park Service, and the National Aeronautic and Space Administration.[20]

Policy Approval equals the percentage of responses that express at least weak agreement with the direction of spending the president proposes. Thus if the president requests a 5 percent increase in appropriations for NASA, policy approval equals the percentage of respondents that thought there was either "too little" or "about the right amount of" spending on

18. Analysis of these open-ended statements is consistent with Cohen's (1997) claim that they are merely symbolic. In particular, unlike the specific appeals I analyze, these broad statements often are not linked to presidents' actual proposals.

19. Jacoby (1994) and Wleizen (1995) also have utilized these survey data, and the studies suggest the responses indeed reflect citizens' viewpoints about the policy issues. Jacoby shows citizens evaluate the various budgetary programs differently, while Wleizen establishes that responses vary predictably with outside events.

20. The specific question wordings for each issue are as follows: (1) crime: ". . . halting the rising crime rate?"; (2) drug control: ". . . dealing with drug addiction?"; (3) environment: ". . . improving and protecting the environment?"; (4) poverty assistance: ". . . assistance to the poor?"; (5) parks: ". . . parks and recreation?"; (6) space exploration: ". . . the space exploration program?"

space exploration. I have also conducted the analysis with the variable equaling the percentage of responses that strongly agree with the direction of the proposal minus the percentage that strongly disagree (thus disregarding the "about the right amount" responses), and the results are substantively similar to those presented.[21] If both the General Social Survey and a Roper survey were conducted for a given policy issue and year, *Policy Approval* is based on the average of the responses; if only one survey was conducted, the variable is based on these responses alone. Because the public opinion data are available for only a subset of the budgetary observations, I conduct the analysis twice: once on those observations for which the policy approval data are available and once on the full set of budgetary observations.

The final key variable reflects the president's success in achieving his budgetary proposal. *Presidential Budgetary Success* equals the absolute difference between the percentage change in appropriations requested by the president and the percentage change enacted. Formally, for a given agency i and year t, the variable equals:

$$- | \; \%\Delta \text{Presidential Proposal}_{it} - \%\Delta \text{Enacted Appropriations}_{it} | \; .$$

The measure assumes that the lower the absolute difference between the enacted spending and the president's requested appropriations, the greater is the legislative success achieved by the president. The specification comports with existing spatial models of the budgetary process (e.g., Ferejohn and Krehbiel 1987; Kiewiet and McCubbins 1988), which presume that a president has a most preferred outcome and likes other outcomes less the further they are from his preferred one, just as in the Public Appeals Theory. *Presidential Budgetary Success* is based on percentage changes rather than mere levels of spending to reduce autocorrelation that would otherwise plague the testing. Furthermore, the use of percentage changes is consistent with the literature on the incrementalism of the budgetary process (e.g., Schick 1995, 53–54; White 1995; Wildavsky 1992).

In utilizing the president's proposals as a proxy for his policy preferences, I acknowledge that the proposals may be affected by strategic behavior. In particular, a president who wants to increase (cut) spending may recommend a higher (lower) level of spending than he truly desires. To deal with this possibility, I adopt an econometric specification in which this behavior would not affect the signs or significance of the key estimated effects. The next section describes the details of this empirical model.

---

21. Specifically, all three of the main hypotheses are supported at conventional levels of statistical significance ($p < 0.05$, two-tailed).

Empirical Model

The standard empirical model for analyzing a president's ability to affect the legislative process consists of a one-equation specification in which presidential success is regressed on a variety of factors. For example, in Jon Bond's and Richard Fleisher's (1990) influential study of the role of presidential success, the main specification is a one-equation probit model in which the dependent variable reflects whether presidential victory occurred on a roll-call vote. For the purpose of testing the Public Appeals Theory, a one-equation model would be problematic because the theory suggests a president's decision to appeal to the public will not only influence the likelihood of success but also be affected by this likelihood. We therefore need a specification that accounts for the potential endogeneity between presidents' budgetary success and public appeals.

The econometric specification termed a simultaneous equations model is tailor-made for this type of problem. These models, while not new to the study of the presidency (e.g., Brace and Hinckley 1992; Ostrom and Simon 1985; Rivers and Rose 1985), are not employed frequently. Unlike the prototypical regression model, simultaneous equations specifications involve multiple dependent variables. The standard approach for estimating these models is to include in each equation at least one independent variable, called an "instrument," which is correlated with the dependent variable of that equation but outside of this relationship is not correlated with the other dependent variable(s).[22] The instruments serve to ensure that each dependent variable is explained by a separate equation.

The empirical model that I employ to test the theoretical predictions incorporates this method. Formally, I estimate the following system of equations for each budgetary agency i in year t:

(3.1)   Public Appeal$_{it}$ = f (Presidential Budgetary Success**$_{it}$,
Policy Approval$_{it}$, Control Variables$_{it}$,
Instrument 1_{it}, ε_{1it})

22. See Greene (1993, 578–634) for an overview or Kennedy (1989, 115–16) for a basic introduction. Generally the most difficult component of analyzing a model that requires instrumental variables is finding an appropriate set of instruments. If an instrument is in fact correlated with the error term of the equation from which it has been excluded, the estimates will be inconsistent. Likewise, instruments that are only weakly correlated with the independent variable with which they are associated will produce high standard errors that could obfuscate a significant relationship. (In extreme cases, where the correlation is nonexistent and the equations are not otherwise differentiated, the system may be unidentified.)

(3.2) Presidential Budgetary Success$_{it}$ = f(Public Appeal**$_{it}$,
   Policy Approval$_{it}$, Control Variables$_{it}$, Instrument 2$_{it}$, ε_{2it}),

where the set of control variables and the two instruments are defined in the following section; and where ε_1 and ε_2 are identically and independently distributed normal error terms. In equation (3.2), the president's budgetary success is regressed on whether the president appeals to the public, the popularity of the president's proposal, a set of control variables, and an instrument that identifies the equation uniquely within the system. The right-side factor *Presidential Appeal*** is a predicted value based on equation (3.1), which analyzes the probability of an appeal as a function of proposal popularity, the set of control variables, an instrumental variable that is unique to the equation, and the president's predicted budgetary success as estimated by equation (3.2). Takeshi Amemiya (1978) provides a method for estimating systems of simultaneous equations that have one dichotomous and one continuous dependent variable like the specification here, in which the measure of public appeals is dichotomous and the measure of budgetary success continuous. I adopt his approach.[23]

Equations (3.1) and (3.2) capture each of the three theoretical hypotheses that concern domestic policy—the Popularity of Domestic Positions prediction, the Influence over Domestic Affairs prediction, and the Sincerity of Policy Debate prediction. Equation (3.1) tests the first of these hypotheses by estimating how the likelihood of a domestic policy appeal is affected by the popularity of the president's proposal. The equation also tests the Sincerity of Policy Debate hypothesis by examining the effect of presidents' expected budgetary success on the likelihood of an appeal. The Influence over Domestic Affairs prediction is analyzed in

---

23. Amemiya (1978) recommends estimating simultaneous equations models that have one continuous and one dichotomous dependent variable via maximum likelihood, and he provides the likelihood function. For equations (3.1) and (3.2) the likelihood function is:

$$\log L = \sum_{it} \log f_1 (x'_{it}\, \beta) + \sum_{it} \text{Public Appeal}_{it} \log F (x'_{it}\, \gamma + \rho \text{Presidential Budgetary}$$
$$\text{Success}_{it}) + \sum_{it} (1 - \text{Public Appeal}_{it}) \log [1 - F (x'_{it}\, \gamma + \rho \text{Presidential}$$
$$\text{Budgetary Success}_{it})],$$

where F is the standard normal distribution function; f_1 is the density function of $N(0, \sigma_1^2)$, with σ_1^2 equaling the sum of squared residuals for equation (3.2); x is the set of exogenous variables; and β, γ, and ρ are parameters to be estimated. Amemiya describes how the estimated parameters translate into the coefficients, and interested readers are directed to his article for further details.

equation (3.2), which estimates the impact of a domestic policy appeal on presidential budgetary success.

As mentioned previously, strategic proposing by the president would not influence the signs or significance of the coefficients that test the predictions.[24] Such behavior would influence the magnitudes of the effects, but notably, would not bias in favor (or against) confirmation of the predictions given that they do not concern the magnitudes. Moreover, assuming that a president offers proposals further from Congress's desired outcomes than his true preferences are, the estimated size of the coefficient on public appeals will be *underestimated*. The impact of proposal popularity will not be influenced, while the effect of presidential budgetary success on the probability of an appeal will be overstated, regardless of whether the effect is positive or negative. As a result, I focus on the sign and significance of the effect of expected budgetary success.[25]

24. If the president's proposal were further from the outcome Congress desired than was the president's true preference, *Presidential Budgetary Success* would be higher by a given multiplicative factor k. Notably, any random measurement error would not bias the testing given that presidential budgetary success is an endogenous variable (Greene 1993, 280–81). The consequence of strategic proposing consequently depends on the impact of k. Following the derivations of Heckman (1978), the effect of a public appeal equals the effect of Instrument 1 in the reduced form of equation (3.1) divided by the effect of Instrument 1 in the reduced form of equation (3.2). Increasing presidential budgetary success by k would inflate the coefficient on the instrument in the reduced form of equation (3.2) but not influence the analogous coefficient in the reduced form of equation (3.1). The estimated impact of a public appeal would therefore be understated by $1/k$, and the sign and significance of the estimate would not be affected.

25. I considered alternative models in which the president's proposal is predicted from a first-stage equation, but they present problems that could bias in favor of accepting the Public Appeals Theory. In particular, such a specification requires regressing enacted appropriations on the predicted presidential proposal, an interaction of the predicted proposal with the likelihood of an appeal, and interactions of the predicted proposal with each of the control variables (as well as all of the corresponding main effects). Perhaps not surprisingly, the specification involves an enormous amount of multicollinearity; nine correlations between the various factors are equal to or greater than 0.9. As a result, not only the standard errors but also the signs of the coefficients could be biased, potentially in favor of the theory (Greene 1993, 267). The standard "fix" to this problem, which is simply dropping the collinear factors, is not an attractive option given the large number of collinear variables and their importance in controlling for determinants of presidential success other than public appeals. (One cannot simply add to the system of equations (3.1) and (3.2) a third identified equation in which the president's proposal is the dependent variable; any factor that predicts the president's proposal should also affect the absolute difference between the percentage change in the president's proposal and enacted appropriations.) I have also conducted specification testing to assess whether the analysis requires an endogenous regime-switching model that estimates the president's influence from public appeals separately according to whether the president preferred

Measurement of Instruments and Control Variables

Instruments

Budget Share (Instrument 1). For each observation of an agency i in fiscal year t, *Budget Share* equals enacted appropriations for the agency in fiscal year $t-2$ as a percentage of total discretionary spending in that year. The variable serves as the primary instrument for equation (3.1) because the factor should affect the likelihood of an appeal but not, independent of this impact, presidential budgetary success. The predicted relationship is based on the fact that federal spending is ultimately subject to constraints. Politicians do not want to increase deficit spending or taxes to such an extent that the national economy is put into turmoil, and, correspondingly, throughout the twentieth century solid majorities have opposed high deficits and taxes (Modigliani and Modigliani 1987). Thus the greater the fiscal size of a budget item, the less funding there is for other items. In other words, the larger the program, the higher its impact on the president's overall agenda. Larger programs are consequently more likely to be the subjects of appeals.

The relative fiscal size of a program should not otherwise be correlated with presidential budgetary success, however. Just as larger programs should be more important to a president's agenda, they should also be more important to congressional members' agendas. Consequently, if the relative level of funding did not affect the likelihood of an appeal, then I would not expect *Budget Share* to affect *Presidential Budgetary Success*.

Unified Government (Instrument 2). The variable equals one if the president's party has a majority in each chamber of Congress and zero otherwise. The expectation is that presidential budgetary success will be higher under unified government. This presumption is supported by work that argues legislative outcomes are typically affected by whether government is unified or divided (e.g., Cameron 2000; Howell et al. 2000), as well as work that suggests this distinction is commonly not critical outside the context of budgetary politics (e.g., Brady and Volden 1998; Krehbiel 1998).[26] *Unified Government* serves as the instrument for equation (3.2)

---

more or less spending than Congress. The specification testing suggests that the influence is statistically equivalent between these two regimes ($p > 0.7$, two-tailed). This result is consistent with several recent studies of budgetary politics (Kiewiet and Krehbiel 2002; Krehbiel 1998).

26. Brady and Volden (1998) and Krehbiel (1998) find that the threat of a veto or filibuster often makes the distinction between unified and divided government nonpivotal in legislative-executive negotiations. However, these scholars also find that the distinction is

because the factor should not have an effect on the likelihood of an appeal other than by affecting presidential budgetary success. In other words, the specification presumes that if a president's legislative influence were uncorrelated with whether government was unified, then his decision over whether to appeal to the public would not be affected by this factor.

Control Variables

The control variables account for alternative hypotheses regarding the causes and effects of public appeals, as well as standard factors that the literature suggests may affect a president's legislative influence. In general, the inclusion of such controls should bias against finding support for the Public Appeals Theory.

Prior Media Salience. Two variables account for the public salience of the issue prior to the president's appeal, the first reflecting media coverage and the second public opinion. The Public Appeals Theory does not imply that prior issue salience should be correlated with presidents' legislative success, but I include the variables to account for the suggestion of E. E. Schattschneider (1960) and others that salience generally advantages the president. The first of these controls, *Prior Media Salience*, follows Brody's (1991) use of front-page *New York Times* articles to measure media attention to an issue. Specifically, the variable equals the number of *New York Times* articles on the agency from the two months prior to the president's appeal if he made one or, if he did not, during the two months prior to the submission of his budgetary proposal. The period of two months is used to cover the lengthiest interval during which the core planning for a major presidential address would generally occur.[27]

Public Concern. The second control for prior issue salience has the benefit of directly reflecting public opinion. The factor is based on the recurring Gallup survey that asks respondents "What do you think is the most important problem facing this country today?" (Only surveys that do not limit the available responses are used.) Because the interval between "Most Important Problem" polls varies across time, I utilize all surveys from the year prior to the president's appeal if one was given or, absent an appeal, from the year prior to the submission of the budgetary proposal.

---

likely to be pivotal when the status quo policy is extreme, such as in the case of discretionary appropriations, where the formal status quo is zero funding.

27. This length comports with the descriptions of presidential speechwriting given in Dallek (1998), Hartmann (1980), and Schlesinger (1965).

The variable equals the percentage of surveys during this period in which at least 1 percent of the responses concern an issue specific to the agency.

Personal Popularity. This variable is an important control in equation (3.1) as well as equation (3.2). In equation (3.1), the factor accounts for the possibility that personal popularity influences a president's likelihood of appealing to the public. The effect should be positive if Samuel Kernell (1997) is correct that personal popularity determines the success of an appeal, as under this reasoning a president should be more likely to go public when he is popular. In equation (3.2), *Personal Popularity* accounts for whatever legislative success approval ratings engender. Numerous studies indicate that personal approval may increase a president's bargaining power with Congress.[28]

The variable is based on the standard Gallup approval ratings, which derive from responses to the question "Do you approve or disapprove of the way [the current president] is handling his job as president?" Because research suggests that a legislative effect of personal approval is more likely to be found when the factor is measured in ranges (e.g., Bond and Fleisher 1990), I code presidential popularity as an indicator that depends on whether the president's approval is at least 50 percent.[29] Specifically, the indicator equals one if the average approval rating during the time between the submission of his budgetary proposal and the enactment of appropriations is above this threshold and zero otherwise.

Priority. Research suggests that a president will exert more pressure on congressional members when an issue is a personal priority (e.g., Fett 1994; Peterson 1990). To account for this variation across legislative negotiations, I include a variable that reflects presidents' personal budget priorities. The factor is based on content analysis of presidents' annual Statements of Budget Priorities and Budget Messages. Specifically, *Priority* is an indicator that equals one if, for a given agency i in fiscal year t, the president specifies funding for the agency or programs within it to be a priority.

Targeted Address. As Kernell (1997) documents, presidents routinely give minor addresses to specialized audiences. *Targeted Address* controls for the possibility that presidents obtain influence from these addresses.

---

28. See Brody (1991) and Canes-Wrone and de Marchi (2002) for reviews of this literature.

29. I also have conducted the analysis with a variable reflecting marginal changes in the approval ratings and received substantively similar results.

I coded the variable through content analysis of all minor presidential addresses in the *Public Papers of the Presidents*.[30] For a given agency and fiscal year, the variable equals one if the president gave a specialized address about the agency or programs within it, and equals zero otherwise.[31]

% Change in Gross Domestic Product (%Δ GDP). I include a macroeconomic control to account for the direct effect of the economy on appropriations. The variable equals the percentage change in gross domestic product (GDP) during the year prior to the president's proposal. The analysis cannot account for GDP as well as unemployment and inflation because of multicollinearity. Substituting any of these macroeconomic controls does not substantially affect the results however.

Individual Presidents. Studies of the presidency routinely account for differences specific to the individual holding office, and the final set of control variables serve this purpose. For each chief executive from Eisenhower through Clinton, I include an indicator that equals one for the years in which he held the office of the presidency and zero otherwise. Thus if a given president is particularly effective at bargaining with Congress, or is particularly likely to appeal to the public, this behavior should be reflected in the findings.

Results

The results strongly support the theoretical predictions on domestic policy appeals. I begin by discussing the findings for equation (3.1), which tests the Popularity of Domestic Positions and the Sincerity of Policy Debate predictions. Table 3.4 presents these estimates. The first column of estimates concerns observations on which there exist data on the popularity of the president's proposal, while the second concerns the full sample of budgetary observations.

Focusing initially on the first column, it provides clear support for the Popularity of Domestic Positions prediction. Specifically, the effect of *Policy Approval* is positive and solidly significant at conventional levels ($p < 0.05$, two-tailed), suggesting that presidents are more likely to publicize their domestic proposals the more popular these proposals are.

---

30. *Public Papers of the Presidents of the United States* (Washington, DC: Government Printing Office, 1957–2000).

31. In constructing this variable, I did not include speeches that presidents delivered to agency officials. Research on targeted addresses describes them as speeches given to the public, not to other members of the executive branch (e.g., Hager and Sullivan 1994).

Table 3.4 Determinants of Domestic Policy Appeals

Independent Variables	Policy Approval Observations	All Budgetary Observations
Policy Approval	4.599	
	(2.205)	—
Presidential Budgetary Success**	−20.160	−13.121
	(8.760)	(9.117)
Budget Share	0.675	0.239
	(0.351)	(0.096)
Prior Media Salience	0.371	0.230
	(0.353)	(0.112)
Public Concern	−0.264	1.056
	(0.634)	(0.198)
Personal Popularity	0.067	0.018
	(0.477)	(0.182)
Priority	0.324	0.452
	(0.414)	(0.161)
Targeted Address	0.131	0.482
	(0.554)	(0.280)
% Δ GDP	−0.021	−0.929
	(0.091)	(3.625)
Constant	−4.890	−2.576
	(1.846)	(0.323)
President Indicators	Dropped due to Multicollinearity	Jointly Significant $\chi^2_{(8)} = 21.621$ ($p = 0.003$) Details in Text
Number of Observations	100	1225
Joint Fit of Estimates in Simultaneous System	$\chi^2_{(20)} = 202.391$ ($p < 0.000$)	$\chi^2_{(34)} = 704.024$ ($p < 0.000$)
Exogeneity of Budgetary Success	$\chi^2_{(10)} = 70.087$ ($p < 0.000$)	$\chi^2_{(18)} = 187.202$ ($p < 0.000$)

Note: The table reports structural probit estimates from the simultaneous system of equations (3.1) and (3.2); standard errors are in parentheses. In each sample, the dependent variable is Pr (Public Appeal) = 1. Presidential Budgetary Success** is a function of equation (3.2), the results of which are described in table 3.5.

Notably, table 3.4 indicates that this relationship holds even controlling for a range of other political factors.

Interpreting the substantive impact of the effect is not a matter of simply discussing the coefficient given that the estimates derive from a probit analysis; in such analyses, the magnitude of an effect depends on the particular values of the right-hand variables. Thus as is standard, I interpret the impact assuming the other right-hand side variables are at their means. Under this assumption, when the initial popularity of a president's domestic policy proposal is 50 percent, a ten percentage point increase will augment the likelihood that he appeals to the public by 17 percent. Similarly, a ten percentage point increase from initial policy approval of 60 percent will make a president 13 percent more likely to go public, and such an increase from initial policy approval of 40 percent will increase the probability of an appeal by 18 percent.

These magnitudes indicate that a president's decision over whether to go public about a domestic initiative is substantially influenced by the degree to which the initiative comports with citizens' existing policy preferences. The result is also consistent with the argument that presidents avoid publicizing domestic initiatives that are unpopular. To see whether such avoidance occurred routinely, I examined whether any of the appeals concerned policies on which the president's position was opposed by at least 50 percent of respondents. In 19 of the 100 policy approval observations, the president offered a proposal that faced such popular opposition, and notably, only two of these proposals were the subject of an appeal. Thus overall, the presidents tended to avoid publicizing unpopular domestic policy initiatives.

These results on policy approval indicate that presidents strategically choose the domestic proposals to advocate to the public. The more popular the proposal, the more likely a president is to publicize it. Likewise, presidents generally avoid publicizing initiatives that face strong public opposition. Thus any influence chief executives generate from domestic policy appeals derives in part from strategic behavior in deciding which initiatives to take to the public.

The second row of results provides further evidence of strategic executive behavior. For each sample of the data, the coefficient on presidential budgetary success supports the Sincerity of Policy Debate prediction, which stipulates that a president is more likely to go public about an initiative the less likely Congress is, absent any plebiscitary activity, to enact the initiative. The effect is highly significant ($p < 0.05$, two-tailed) in the policy approval sample and at least marginally significant in the full set of budgetary observations ($p = 0.08$, one-tailed). These findings contradict the school of thought that suggests presidents use public appeals for credit-claiming and grandstanding. Instead, presidents tend to go public about genuine policy debates.[32]

32. At the means of the independent variables, an increase of five percentage points in the president's expected budgetary success decreases his likelihood of appealing to the public by 16 percent in the policy approval sample and by 24 percent in the full sample of budgetary observations. As previously discussed, the magnitude (but not the sign or

Notably, this result suggests that a simple negative correlation between the likelihood of an appeal and presidential success would not necessarily imply that appeals reduce presidents' bargaining power; instead, such a correlation could merely reflect that presidents go public over the initiatives that Congress is least likely to enact. In other words, a simple correlation would reflect not only the effect of appeals on success but also that of expected success on the likelihood of an appeal. The difficulty in disentangling these effects highlights the need for the simultaneous equations specification.

The results regarding the exogeneity of presidential budgetary success further highlight the appropriateness of the empirical model. As table 3.4 describes, in each sample of the data the log-likelihood test indicates that the probability of presidential budgetary success is endogenous to the likelihood of an appeal. In other words, as expected, budgetary success both affects and is affected by the likelihood of an appeal.

The estimates for the instrumental variable *Budget Share* provide additional support for the empirical specification. The variable is positive and statistically significant in each sample of the data, indicating that presidents are more likely to appeal to the public about larger budgetary programs. The primary importance of this effect is the identification of the statistical model but, in addition, the finding supports the claim that presidents utilize appeals to achieve policy ends. In particular, the estimates imply that all else being equal, a president will be more likely to go public about a proposal the more it affects his overall policy agenda.

In comparison with the results regarding budget share and expected success, which are relatively similar across the two samples of the data, the results for several of the control variables differ markedly across the samples. In particular, all of the controls have insignificant effects in the policy approval sample, while *Prior Media Salience, Public Concern, Priority,* and *Targeted Address* each has at least a marginally significant impact in the sample of all budgetary observations ($p < 0.1$, two-tailed). The findings in the latter sample indicate that presidents are more likely to go public about a proposal the greater are media attention and public concern over the issue, when the proposal is a priority, and when the initiative is the subject of a targeted address. A potential explanation for the discrepancy between the samples is that the effects of these four controls are insignificant once the popularity of the president's proposal is accounted for. Another possibility is that the difference derives from the variation in the sets of observations. Analyzing the policy approval observations

significance) of this effect may be overestimated owing to the possibility of strategic proposing by the president. I therefore do not make much of these magnitudes.

without controlling for policy approval, I find evidence for the second of these explanations. Even without controlling for the popularity of the president's proposal, the effects of the four control variables are insignificant in the smaller sample.

The remaining controls are insignificant with the exception of the president indicators. Before describing the results on the indicators, it is worth highlighting the insignificance of personal popularity; if only popular presidents could use appeals to achieve legislative success, one would expect personal approval ratings to influence the likelihood of an appeal. The fact that they do not, and that policy approval has a large impact, supports the argument that it is the popularity of the proposal rather than that of the president which determines the success of an appeal.

The indicators for the individual presidents are included only in the sample of all budgetary observations because of the high collinearity between the Carter indicator and the instrument for presidential budgetary success, *Unified Government,* in the policy approval sample.[33] In the larger sample, these individual effects are jointly significant, suggesting that Presidents Eisenhower through Clinton were not equally likely to appeal to the public about the budgetary issues. A few specific differences are also worth noting. In particular, Kennedy, Johnson, Eisenhower, and Reagan were the presidents most likely to make a domestic policy appeal; Nixon, Bush, and Carter were the least likely to do so.[34] The fact that Nixon, Bush, and Carter were not prone to taking their domestic proposals to the airwaves is consistent with these presidents' lackluster reputations for public communication (e.g., Greenstein 2000). It is possible that they were less apt to utilize the bully pulpit precisely because they did not view the strategy as one that fit well with their personal skills.

While these results, and the aforementioned results on the control variables, suggest that a myriad of factors may influence the likelihood of an appeal, the results of table 3.4 are still highly supportive of the Public Appeals Theory. *Ceteris paribus,* presidents are found to be more likely to publicize a domestic proposal the more popular it is and almost never publicize unpopular proposals. In addition, as predicted, the appeals are not simply about presidential grandstanding but concern genuine policy negotiations. Presidents therefore utilize national speechmaking to

33. The factors are correlated at $\rho = 0.8$. When the indicators are included in the policy approval sample, they are not jointly significant and the effect of presidential budgetary success becomes insignificant, consistent with econometric theory on multicollinearity. Also consistent with econometric theory, the coefficient on *Policy Approval,* which is not affected by the collinearity, remains positive and significant.

34. Each pairwise comparison between these two groups is at least marginally significant ($p < 0.1$, two-tailed).

Table 3.5 Determinants of Domestic Policy Success

Independent Variables	Policy Approval Observations	All Budgetary Observations
Public Appeal**	0.119	0.164
	(0.054)	(0.077)
Policy Approval	0.636	
	(0.083)	—
Unified Government	0.117	0.081
	(0.050)	(0.046)
Prior Media Salience	−0.026	−0.007
	(0.033)	(0.014)
Public Concern	−0.110	0.011
	(0.047)	(0.024)
Priority	−0.027	−0.022
	(0.037)	(0.018)
Targeted Address	0.035	−0.057
	(0.052)	(0.035)
Personal Popularity	−0.062	0.005
	(0.039)	(0.016)
% Δ GDP	0.493	0.037
	(0.826)	(0.328)
Constant	−0.557	−0.151
	(0.074)	(0.053)
President Indicators	Dropped due to Multicollinearity	Jointly Significant $\chi^2_{(8)} = 40.928$ $(p < 0.000)$ Details in Text
Number of Observations	100	1225
Joint Fit of Estimates in Simultaneous System	$\chi^2_{(20)} = 202.391$ $(p < 0.000)$	$\chi^2_{(34)} = 704.024$ $(p < 0.000)$
Exogeneity of Public Appeal	$\chi^2_{(10)} = 90.127$ $(p < 0.000)$	$\chi^2_{(18)} = 466.451$ $(p < 0.000)$

Note: The table reports structural least squares estimates from the simultaneous system of equations (3.1) and (3.2); standard errors are in parentheses. In each sample, the dependent variable is Presidential Budgetary Success. Public Appeal** is a function of equation (3.1), the results of which are described in table 3.4.

attempt to generate influence over domestic policy. Of course, it still remains an open question whether influence is routinely engendered by the plebiscitary activity.

Table 3.5 addresses this remaining issue by presenting the findings on equation (3.2), which tests the Influence over Domestic Affairs prediction. The estimates provide strong support for the prediction. In both samples of the data, the effect of a domestic policy appeal is positive and solidly significant ($p < 0.05$, two-tailed). It is worth emphasizing that the earlier validation of the Sincerity of Policy Debate prediction establishes that this estimated impact of an appeal does not reflect credit-claiming but, instead, reveals policy influence.[35] Accordingly, the results contradict research that suggests public appeals only rarely affect policymaking; table 3.5 indicates they have a routine impact on legislative decisions.

Moreover, the magnitude of the impact is nontrivial. The two samples suggest a public appeal increases a president's budgetary success by twelve to sixteen percentage points, meaning that the percentage change in enacted appropriations is eleven to sixteen percentage points closer to the president's requested change. (The lower of these estimates is from the policy approval sample, the higher from the set of all budgetary observations.) As discussed previously, the econometric specification is such that this magnitude arguably *underestimates* the actual effect. To the extent that the president's preferred level of spending is closer to that of Congress than he proposes, the impact of an appeal will be understated.[36]

Of course, these results do not imply that a president could generate legislative success on any domestic initiative he promoted in a national address. The analysis has already established that presidents strategically choose the domestic initiatives to take to the public; specifically, presidents generally do not make appeals regarding proposals likely to mobilize popular opposition. Thus, together with table 3.4, the results indicate that a president can use public appeals to achieve domestic policy goals but that, as predicted, this influence is dependent on a president's decision to advocate popular initiatives.

The estimates on the instrument for presidential budgetary success, unified government, are also consistent with expectations. Like a good deal of prior research (e.g., Bond and Fleisher 1990; Kiewiet and McCubbins 1988), these estimates suggest that presidential influence depends on the degree of ideological congruence between executive and legislative preferences. In each sample, the effect of unified government is positive and reasonably significant ($p < 0.5$, one-tailed). More specifically, unified government is found to increase presidential budgetary success by

35. Consistent with this earlier finding, specification testing suggests a president's likelihood of making an appeal is endogenous to *Presidential Budgetary Success;* in other words, the president's decision to appeal to the public not only affects his influence with Congress but is also affected by his expected influence. Statistical details are given in table 3.5.

36. It is worth noting that this result does not depend on the use of the simultaneous equations specification. In a basic, ordinary least squares regression of equation (3.2), the impact of a public appeal is positive and significant ($p < 0.05$, two-tailed) in each sample of the data.

eight to twelve percentage points, depending on the sample of observations. These results, in combination with the findings on public appeals, imply that, for popular domestic policy initiatives, an appeal may counteract the legislative consequences of divergence in presidential and congressional preferences.

Among the control variables, the estimates regarding ex-ante salience are the most relevant to the Public Appeals Theory. Consistent with it, the effects of public concern and prior media salience suggest that a president's appeals would not generate influence if he randomly selected domestic initiatives to promote to the public. The coefficients on these factors are insignificant except for that on public concern in the policy approval sample, and this effect is negative. Thus, according to table 3.5, presidents are not more likely to achieve legislative victory on an issue merely because it is salient to the citizenry.

The other control variables typically have insignificant effects, with the key exceptions of policy approval and the president indicators. The estimates for policy approval suggest that a president's ability to enact a proposal is greater the more popular is the proposal, a result consistent with much of the literature on policy responsiveness (e.g., Erikson, MacKuen, and Stimson 2002a; Page and Shapiro 1983; Stimson, MacKuen, and Erikson 1995). The findings on the president indicators are also consistent with previous work in that their joint significance suggests executive influence differs across administrations even controlling for institutional factors (e.g., Greenstein 2000; Neustadt 1990 [1960]).[37] In terms of more specific individual differences, the most notable are that Nixon achieved greater budgetary success and Clinton less than did the other chief executives. The result on Nixon comports with Bond and Fleisher (1990, 206–7), who find that he enjoyed greater legislative success than purely structural factors would predict. The Clinton effect may be a function of his impeachment battles and, correspondingly, his relatively poor congressional relations.

The insignificant effects of the remaining control variables are consistent with Bond and Fleisher (1990). While the null result on presidential popularity is arguably still surprising, Cary Covington and Rhonda Kinney (1999) offer a possible explanation for the finding.[38] In particular,

---

37. As already discussed, the indicators are not included in the smaller sample owing to issues of multicollinearity between the Carter indicator and unified government. When they are included, they are not jointly significant and the effect of public appeals is nearly identical to that presented. The only major change is that the effect of unified government declines in significance.

38. I have investigated whether presidential popularity is endogenous to budgetary success and found no evidence of this endogeneity. Moreover, the effect of presidential

Covington and Kinney argue that a president's personal approval affects his ability to get policy initiatives onto the legislative agenda but does not otherwise influence members' behavior. Given that discretionary appropriations are on the legislative agenda each year, a president's personal popularity should not increase his influence over these policy issues if Covington and Kinney are correct.[39]

All in all, tables 3.4 and 3.5 provide a depiction of domestic policy appeals that supports the Public Appeals Theory. The findings indicate that presidents typically generate legislative influence when they appeal to the public about domestic initiatives. Moreover, this impact is substantively consequential. It is not the case, however, that presidents achieve legislative success by publicizing any randomly selected initiative. Instead, the results imply that the influence derived from domestic policy appeals depends on presidents' willingness to advocate proposals that are in line with citizens' policy preferences.

CAVEATS

Almost any study of political activity has its limitations, and the analysis of this chapter is no exception. In the interest of enabling readers to achieve a thorough and balanced understanding of the findings, I highlight a few of the caveats, as well as discuss why they may not be as critical as initial rumination might suggest.

Arguably the most obvious limitation regards the difficulty in accounting for elite behavior that occurs outside of the public eye. The specific concern is that influence attributed to presidents' public actions may be the consequence of unobserved private activity. This issue pervades all studies of political influence or success.[40] Unlike most of these studies,

---

popularity was not at all significant when I specified the variable as endogenous. In particular, I conducted a Hausman test in which the first-stage equation estimated presidential popularity as a function of the other control variables in equation (3.2), the variable *Public Appeal*, and the instrument *Scandal*, which equaled one for the years of the Watergate, Iran-Contra, Whitewater, and Monica Lewinsky scandals and otherwise equaled zero. Further details are available on request.

39. Research I have conducted with Scott de Marchi (Canes-Wrone and de Marchi 2002) provides another possible explanation for the null effect of presidents' personal popularity. We establish that a president's approval ratings affect legislative success only for issues that are salient and "complex," where a complex issue is one on which voters have little information and relatively unstable preferences. Given that many of the policies in the data here are relatively "simple" or "easy," e.g., crime and drug control, the overall null effect of presidential popularity should not be surprising.

40. Even work that is based on elite interviews or first-hand observations of events risks missing private bargaining that the political actors keep concealed.

however, I have made an explicit attempt to account for the likelihood of private bargaining by including a variable that measures presidential priorities. Moreover, analysis of this variable suggests that it differs from public appeals in ways consistent with the claim that it captures behavior of a less public nature. In particular, unlike *Public Appeal*, *Priority* is not affected by the popularity of the president's position.[41]

A second caveat, and one that will be relevant to other parts of the book as well, is that I have not examined all policy negotiations. Of course, any study of policymaking limits the set of negotiations examined in one way or another. The question is whether these limitations affect the universality of the results. Here, two potential biases are worth highlighting. First, the analysis regarding public opinion is limited by the availability of survey data, and it may be that presidential behavior differs when such data are not readily available. This possibility, while it obviously cannot be excluded, is at least diminished by the president's ability to acquire his own polls; the ability would seem to minimize the likelihood he would be stuck without any public opinion data if he so desired them.[42] The other potential bias, which is perhaps of greater concern, is the heavy reliance on budgetary data in the latter portion of the chapter. While these data cover a range of substantive domains, and have other advantages that were highlighted earlier, they differ from most legislation in that the budget is on the legislative agenda every year. Accordingly, the president may have more influence over budgetary issues than he does over issues on which Congress could simply fail to consider legislation that relates to his proposals. It was this limitation that inspired me to collect the data for the first-glance analysis that began the chapter. Notably, this analysis suggests that the results from the budgetary data do not disappear once one examines the other types of policies that presidents advocate in mass appeals.

CONCLUSION

The literature reviewed in chapter 2 suggested two perspectives about presidents' public appeals. One was that appeals influence the policy process but not in a way that depends on citizens' policy preferences (e.g., Kernell 1997; Miller 1993; Schattschneider 1960). The second was that appeals

---

41. This is the case regardless of whether policy approval is measured with marginal changes or a dummy variable for whether at least 50 percent of respondents agreed with the president's position.

42. Also, in tables 3.4 and 3.5, the results are relatively consistent between the sample that depends on the existence of public opinion data and the sample that does not.

do not in fact regularly alter the policy process. The latter perspective emerged in studies that argue there exists scant evidence appeals routinely affect policymaking (e.g., Bessette 1994; Tulis 1987), research that maintains members lack incentives to follow public opinion (e.g., Cornwell 1965; Polsby 1978), and in work that asserts appeals are primarily about presidential grandstanding (Clinton et al. 2003).

The Public Appeals Theory diverges from each of these perspectives. According to the theory, domestic policy appeals regularly affect policymaking, but the effect depends on citizens' policy positions. Only on popular domestic proposals can presidents increase their prospects for legislative success by going public; on unpopular initiatives, the strategy is not of assistance and may even harm legislative efforts. Going public thus grants power to the mass public as well as to presidents.

This chapter has provided two types of evidence that together support these predictions over the alternative perspectives. The chapter began with a "first-glance" analysis that examined basic relationships regarding the domestic policy appeals of Presidents Eisenhower through Clinton. According to these findings, presidents' domestic policy appeals tend to concern popular initiatives; this pattern holds not only for the presidents as a group but for each individual administration as well. Also according to the first-glance analysis, a positive correlation exists between the popularity of the initiatives promoted in the domestic policy appeals and the likelihood the initiatives are associated with legislative success. The first-glance analysis thus establishes that the basic relationships concerning domestic policy appeals, legislative success, and the popularity of the president's proposal are consistent with the Public Appeals Theory.

The chapter proceeded with testing that controlled for a variety of influences on presidential and congressional behavior and also accounted for the possibility of presidents going public about inevitable legislative victories. The results of this testing provide further support for the Public Appeals Theory. Specifically, presidents are shown to be more likely to publicize a domestic initiative the more popular it is and almost never appeal to the public about an initiative likely to mobilize popular opposition. Presidents do not, however, merely go public about foregone policy achievements. In fact, all else equal, presidents are more likely to publicize a domestic initiative the less legislative success they expect to achieve without the plebiscitary activity. Consistent with this strategic behavior, presidents are found to obtain legislative influence from domestic policy appeals. Moreover, the influence is comparable to that of other, more established determinants of policymaking.

Chapter 3 thus suggests that domestic policy appeals increase the extent to which presidents and the mass public affect legislative decisions and that the details of these effects are consistent with the Public Appeals Theory. Naturally however, it remains possible that the theory correctly characterizes the politics of domestic policy appeals but mischaracterizes the politics surrounding foreign policy ones. Do the politics of foreign and domestic policy appeals differ in the ways predicted in chapter 2? Are presidents able to generate influence from publicizing foreign policy initiatives? For answers to these questions, we turn to chapter 4.

CHAPTER FOUR

Foreign Policy Appeals

Michael Waldman, President Clinton's director of speechwriting from 1995 to 1999, discusses his experience at the White House in *POTUS Speaks: Finding the Words that Defined the Clinton Presidency* (Waldman 2000).[1] In the book, Waldman describes the behind-the-scenes process of creating presidential addresses *other* than foreign policy ones. Waldman, even though he was officially the director of speechwriting, had little control over the content of foreign policy appeals, which were the responsibility of the National Security Council. This division of speechwriting operations is similarly highlighted in Dick Morris's recollection of his White House experience. For example, he recounts that the foreign policy portions of the 1995 State of the Union address "arrived on stone tablets" from the National Security Council. "Spelling and punctuation could be corrected if a dictionary or style book proved them wrong," Morris (1997, 245) notes, "but that was about it."

Clinton's decision to maintain separate speechwriting organizations for foreign and domestic affairs comports with numerous distinctions the literature draws between the policy domains. As detailed in chapter 2, research suggests that on foreign policy issues presidents have a greater ability to change public opinion (e.g., Edwards 1983; Page and Shapiro 1992), greater unilateral capacities (e.g., Howell 2003), and greater overall influence (e.g., Dahl 1950; Fenno 1973; Huntington 1961; Peterson 1994). In keeping with this variation, the predictions of the Public Appeals Theory differ for foreign versus domestic policy appeals. For example, the Influence over Foreign Affairs prediction asserts that appeals will generate influence but that, unlike the case of domestic policy, this influence does not depend on presidents' choosing to publicize proposals that are already popular. Similarly, the Popularity of Foreign

---

1. For those readers unfamiliar with Washingtonian lingo, POTUS stands for President of the United States.

Positions prediction states a president's likelihood of appealing to the public will be less dependent on the popularity of his position if the issue concerns foreign rather than domestic affairs. Only the Sincerity of Policy Debate prediction, which is that the president's expected legislative success will be negatively correlated with the likelihood of an appeal, applies similarly to the two policy domains.

This chapter tests these predictions as well as examines other issues regarding the politics of foreign policy appeals. For example, how does the influence generated by these appeals, assuming there is any, compare to that for domestic policy initiatives? How popular is the typical foreign policy initiative a president publicizes? And do foreign policy appeals increase the probability that mass opinion will guide the policy process?

The empirical analysis is similar to that in chapter 3. I begin by presenting summary statistics in a "first-glance analysis" and proceed to conduct econometric testing. As before, the first-glance analysis examines nationally televised, noncompulsory presidential speeches of the second Eisenhower administration through the Clinton administrations. For the foreign and defense initiatives promoted in these speeches, I assess the average popularity of the policies, how this average popularity varied by president, and how it was correlated with presidential success in achieving the initiatives. I also compare these summary statistics to those for the domestic policy appeals, evaluating the degree to which the patterns of presidential speechmaking differ between domestic and foreign affairs.

The first-glance analysis determines whether the general trends of foreign policy appeals are consistent with the predictions of the Public Appeals Theory. For more rigorous analysis of the predictions, however, I need to compare presidents' legislative success when they go public with when they do not, account for the possibility that presidents publicize inevitable policy successes, and control for other influences on executive and legislative behavior. To conduct such testing I again turn to budgetary data, which have the nice properties of being readily quantifiable, broad in substantive scope, and significant in terms of American public policy. For example, the data of this chapter include Ford's initiatives to provide military aid to Cambodia and Vietnam, Reagan's efforts to increase defense spending, and Clinton's proposals to increase U.S. humanitarian assistance abroad.

By the end of chapter 4, we will have considerable evidence on whether the politics of foreign policy appeals differ from those surrounding domestic policy appeals. Furthermore, assuming these politics do differ, we will have evidence on the degree to which the theoretical predictions account for the variation.

A FIRST GLANCE

I collected the data for the first-glance analysis of foreign policy appeals in the same manner as the first-glance analysis of chapter 3; consequently, I do not repeat the full details of the compilation. Briefly, the data set revolves around the legislative proposals Presidents Eisenhower through Clinton promoted in nationally televised, nonobligatory, primetime speeches between 1957 and 2000. I examine all such foreign policy initiatives for which there exists at least one survey regarding public approval versus disapproval of the policy initiative during the year prior to the address. In other words, I use only surveys for which the data can be categorized into respondents that favor the president's proposal, those that do not favor it, and those who "don't know" their position.

As before, I include only specific legislative proposals. A claim to desire for "peace with country X," for example, is not coded as an appeal. Nor do I include appeals for government action by other countries. While analyzing the effects of U.S. presidents' speechmaking on the policy processes of other nations would be a valuable undertaking, it is beyond the scope of this analysis. Finally, I do not include descriptions of foreign policy events unless the president relates them to a legislative proposal. Therefore, speechmaking about the progress of a war or a foreign crisis, e.g., Carter's failed attempt to rescue the American hostages in Iran, does not count as an appeal unless the president calls for legislative action.

This coding produced a data set of thirty-five foreign policy appeals. The number is limited in part by the fact that I use only surveys for which the opinionated responses can be classified into the categories of approval versus disapproval. For example, the subsequent analysis of budgetary data concerns forty-three foreign policy appeals that relate to a different set of polls, which ask whether respondents prefer more, less, or about the same amount of spending for a given issue. Here, the use of surveys for which the opinionated responses can be categorized into policy approval versus disapproval allows for the examination of nonbudgetary issues and provides comparability with the first-glance analysis of chapter 3. Moreover, these thirty-five foreign policy appeals have substantial breadth; they include at least one observation for each president from Eisenhower through Clinton and encompass many of the significant foreign policy appeals during the latter part of the twentieth century. For example, the data encompass Kennedy's 1963 speech about his Nuclear Test Ban Treaty, Carter's 1978 appeal about the Panama Canal Treaties, and Reagan's efforts in 1983, 1984, and 1986 to generate popular support for aiding the Nicaraguan Contras.

Popularity of Initiatives

Table 4.1 summarizes the popularity of the initiatives prior to the president's speeches. Notably, the mean and median of *Approval*, 44 and 46 percent, imply that the typical foreign policy initiative a president publicizes lacks support from a majority of the population. In other words, presidents do not generally go public about foreign policy proposals that are already popular. This situation contrasts with that for domestic policy in chapter 3, where the mean and median policy approval ratings were 55 and 56 percent, respectively. A t-test suggests that the difference between the mean policy approval ratings is statistically significant ($t = 3.235$; $p < 0.01$, two-tailed), indicating that the relationship between citizens' preferences and presidential appeals differs substantially between the domains. This variation is consistent with the Popularity of Foreign Positions prediction, which maintains that the initial popularity of a president's position on a foreign policy issue will be less likely than that on a domestic issue to affect the likelihood he makes an appeal.

Other statistics in table 4.1 also suggest variation between the popularity of foreign and domestic policy appeals. The mean and median of the *Approval – Disapproval* ratings, 3 and 4 percent, respectively, are substantially lower than were the analogous ratings for the domestic policy appeals in the previous chapter, 22 and 26 percent. Moreover, the difference in means is statistically significant ($t = 2.819$; $p < 0.01$, two-tailed). The fact that the foreign policy ratings are positive suggests that presidents do not tend to publicize highly unpopular initiatives. In other words, although the difference between popular support and opposition is significantly lower for foreign policy appeals, it is still the case that presidents do not regularly go public about foreign policy proposals that face mass opposition.

The variation in the popularity of the initiatives is considerable but not as large as it was for the initiatives of the domestic policy appeals. *Approval* ranges from 16 to 74 percent with a standard deviation of 14 percent, while *Approval – Disapproval* ranges from −59 to 60 percent with a standard deviation of 29 percent. The lowest values of each meas-

Table 4.1 Popularity of Initiatives in Foreign Policy Appeals, 1957–2000

Popularity Variable	Number of Observations	Mean (%)	Median (%)	Minimum (%)	Maximum (%)	Standard Deviation (%)
Approval	35	44	46	16	74	14
Approval – Disapproval	35	3	4	−59	60	29

Table 4.2 Popularity of Initiatives in Foreign Policy Appeals, by President

President	Number of Observations	Average Number of Observations per Year	Mean of Approval (%)	Mean of Approval − Disapproval (%)
Eisenhower	2	0.50	51	18
Kennedy	2	0.66	57	37
Johnson	1	0.20	51	18
Nixon	1	0.17	48	6
Ford	6	3.00	41	−6
Carter	3	0.75	43	14
Reagan	14	1.75	42	−3
Bush	3	0.75	52	21
Clinton	3	0.38	42	−1

ure represent popular sentiment over Ford's proposal to increase military aid to South Vietnam, an initiative he publicized in April 1975. The maximums reflect the popularity of the Intermediate Range Nuclear Forces (INF) Treaty, which Reagan advocated in a primetime address in December 1987.

To what extent is this range in the popularity of the initiatives explained by variation in the willingness of individual presidents to try to change citizens' policy preferences? Table 4.2 addresses this question, showing for each administration the mean popularity of the foreign policy initiatives he publicized. The descriptive statistics suggest that the range in policy popularity is not a consequence of one group of presidents publicizing highly popular policies and another group promoting exceedingly unpopular policies. The mean approval rating of each president's publicized initiatives is within a standard deviation of the overall mean for all foreign policy appeals. Likewise, for each president, excepting Kennedy, the mean of the approval minus disapproval rating is within a standard deviation of the overall mean of the rating.

The statistics suggest somewhat of a time trend. The mean policy approval rating of Presidents Eisenhower, Kennedy, and Johnson is above 50 percent, while that for all of Presidents Nixon through Clinton, excepting Bush, is consistently below 50 percent. The intertemporal change is consistent with Lawrence Jacobs's and Robert Shapiro's (2000; 2002a) argument that presidents since Ford have become more likely to try to "craft" public opinion; indeed, the difference in the average popularity of the initiatives between the first four and latter five presidents is statistically significant at conventional levels ($p < 0.05$ in a two-tailed t-test). The intertemporal variation is also noteworthy because the analogous set of domestic policy appeals examined in chapter 3 did not demonstrate such a pattern. For instance, using Jacobs and Shapiro's cutoff point of the Ford presidency, the difference in average initiative popularity between the earlier and later presidents is not at all significant ($p = 0.65$, two-tailed). Thus the Jacobs and Shapiro prediction of a time trend holds only for the policy domain for which I maintain presidents can indeed "craft" mass opinion.

Overall, the descriptive statistics of tables 4.1 and 4.2 provide support for the Popularity of Foreign Positions prediction. In particular, the average popularity of the publicized foreign policy proposals is significantly lower than that for the domestic policy ones of chapter 3. Yet even in the domain of foreign policy, current opinion is not irrelevant. Presidents tend to avoid going public about proposals that face mass opposition, preferring instead to publicize issues for which initial opposition is not substantially higher than the initial level of support. Moreover, this result is not an artifact of the behavior of one or two presidents but holds across administrations.

Legislative Outcomes

The final summary statistics concern the legislative outcomes associated with the foreign policy appeals. In particular, I assess whether the basic patterns of legislative success comport with the Influence over Foreign Affairs prediction, which states that presidents may increase their prospects for legislative success by promoting initially unpopular foreign policy initiatives to the public. If it were the case, for example, that foreign policy appeals were always associated with legislative failures, then it would seem unlikely that the appeals were generating influence. Alternatively, if success were only achieved on popular initiatives, the descriptive statistics would indicate that presidents cannot achieve legislative success from publicizing initially unpopular foreign policy proposals.

I code legislative success exactly as in the first-glance analysis of chapter 3. Accordingly, a simple binary coding categorizes the observations of foreign policy appeals into those associated with legislative achievements versus those associated with legislative failures. Table 4.3 presents the mean popularity of the initiatives according to this classification.

Table 4.3 Popularity of Initiatives in Foreign Policy Appeals, by Legislative Outcome

Outcome	Mean of Approval (%)	Mean of Approval – Disapproval (%)
Legislative Success ($n = 24$)	48	8
Legislative Failure ($n = 11$)	36	−6

Arguably the most conspicuous result is that the mean approval rating for the legislative successes is only 48 percent. The statistics are thus consistent with the Influence over Foreign Affairs prediction. Presidents are routinely publicizing foreign policy initiatives that lack support from a majority of the population and achieving legislative victory after doing so.

This situation contrasts with what was found for domestic policy appeals. In fact, the mean approval rating for the category of foreign policy successes is almost identical to that for the category of domestic policy failures, which was 49 percent. The domestic policy successes, in comparison, were associated with proposals that initially enjoyed support by 59 percent of the population. The difference in the approval ratings between the foreign and domestic policy successes is statistically significant at conventional levels ($t = 2.819$; $p < 0.01$, two-tailed). Likewise, the average *Approval − Disapproval* rating for the foreign policy victories, 8 percent, is significantly lower than the analogous statistic for the domestic policy victories, which was 28 percent, and this difference is statistically significant ($t = 2.712$; $p < 0.01$, two-tailed).

These statistics indicate that the relationships concerning presidential appeals, policy approval, and legislative success differ across the two policy domains. The one common pattern is that the popularity of the publicized proposals is positively correlated with the likelihood that Congress enacts them. As table 4.3 shows, even for foreign policy appeals, the mean approval and approval minus disapproval ratings are higher for the policy achievements than for the failures. This trend is consistent with our expectations as well as the literature (e.g., Bartels 1991; Page and Shapiro 1983; Stimson, MacKuen, and Erikson 1995); indeed, it would have been surprising if popular support for an initiative were negatively correlated with the likelihood that congressional members endorse it.

In sum, the first-glance analysis of the relationship between foreign policy appeals and legislative success provides preliminary support for the Influence over Foreign Affairs prediction. The data suggest that the appeals routinely concern marginally unpopular initiatives on which the president ultimately achieves legislative success. Of course, a proper assessment of whether the appeals actually engender the success requires evaluating presidents' prospects for legislative victory absent the plebiscitary activity; here I have merely established basic patterns of presidential and congressional behavior. The subsequent section addresses this issue.

TESTING

As in chapter 3, the testing utilizes budgetary data. The results on foreign policy appeals can accordingly be readily compared with those on domestic policy ones. Furthermore, the advantages of budgetary data for the analysis of domestic policy—the annual recurrence of the president-congressional negotiations, the fact that presidents by law must offer proposals, the quantitative nature of the data, and the policy significance of the budgetary programs—hold for foreign policy too. The specific data analyzed in this chapter revolve around three policy issues: defense, economic assistance, and security assistance.

The data set is constructed at the level of policy issues rather than agencies for several reasons. First, presidents have considerable latitude to shift funding on foreign and defense issues (Ragsdale 1998, 301–2; Fisher 1975). For instance, by the Foreign Assistance Act of 1961, presidents can transfer up to 10 percent of the funds from various foreign assistance accounts to others (Ragsdale 1998, 301–2). Likewise, presidents enjoy "drawdown authority," which enables them to give Department of Defense equipment to other countries unilaterally and then replace the equipment with subsequent spending. A second reason for constructing the data set at the level of policy issues is that foreign policy appeals often involve budgetary requests specific to an issue but not an agency. For example, when President Reagan extolled his defense budget in a nationally televised address on April 28, 1981, the programs encompassed by this budgetary proposal were in the Departments of Defense, Energy and Transportation, among others.

The analysis of these budgetary data largely follows the structure of the testing in chapter 3 with two main differences. First, in this chapter I examine only budgetary observations for which public opinion data exist on the popularity of the president's proposal. (In chapter 3, I conducted the testing twice according to whether such data existed.) The testing therefore concerns the presidencies of Nixon through Clinton, beginning with appropriations for fiscal year 1973. I focus on these observations because the key theoretical differences between foreign and domestic policy appeals concern popular support for the president's proposals. Moreover, in the analysis of domestic policy appeals, the results on other relationships of interest were substantively similar across the two specifications.

The second key difference from the testing in the previous chapter relates to the fact that the Popularity of Foreign Positions prediction involves a direct comparison between domestic and foreign policy appeals. Analyzing this prediction requires pooling the domestic and foreign policy data sets. The analysis is therefore divided into two parts. I first assess the Influence over Foreign Affairs and Sincerity of Policy Debate predictions and then separately assess the Popularity of Foreign Positions prediction.

Influence over Foreign Affairs and Sincerity of Policy Debate Predictions

The econometric model used to test the Influence over Foreign Affairs and Sincerity of Policy Debate predictions is akin to that in chapter 3. Formally, it consists of the following system of simultaneous equations for each policy issue i in year t:

(4.1) $\Pr(\text{Public Appeal}_{it} = 1) = \Phi\,(\beta_0 + \beta_1 \text{ Presidential Budgetary Success}_{it}{}^{**} + \beta_2 \text{ Policy Approval}_{it} + \beta_3 \text{ Budget Share}_{it} + \beta_4 \text{ Prior Media Salience}_{it} + \beta_5 \text{ Public Concern}_{it} + \beta_6 \text{ Personal Popularity}_{it} + \beta_7 \text{ Priority}_{it} + \beta_8 \text{ Targeted Address}_{it} + \beta_9\ \%\,\Delta\,\text{GDP}_{it} + \beta_{10} \text{ War}_{it} + \beta_{11} \text{ Drawdown}_{it} + \tau \text{ President Indicators}_{it} + \varepsilon_{1it})$

(4.2) $\text{Presidential Budgetary Success}_{it} = \kappa_0 + \kappa_1 \text{ Public Appeal}_{it}{}^{**} + \kappa_2 \text{ Policy Approval}_{it} + \kappa_3 \text{ Unified Government}_{it} + \kappa_4 \text{ Prior Media Salience}_{it} + \kappa_5 \text{ Public Concern}_{it} + \kappa_6 \text{ Personal Popularity}_{it} + \kappa_7 \text{ Priority}_{it} + \kappa_8 \text{ Targeted Address}_{it} + \kappa_9\ \%\,\Delta\,\text{GDP}_{it} + \kappa_{10} \text{ War}_{it} + \kappa_{11} \text{ Drawdown}_{it} + \tau \text{ President Indicators}_{it} + \varepsilon_{2it},$

where *Public Appeal, Presidential Budgetary Success, Budget Share, Unified Government, Prior Media Salience, Public Concern, Personal Popularity, Priority, Targeted Address,* and *% Δ GDP* are defined in chapter 3; where *Policy Approval, War,* and *Drawdown* are described below; where *Presidential Budgetary Success*** equals the predicted values from equation (4.2); where *Public Appeal*** equals the predicted values from equation (4.1); and where ε_1 and ε_2 are identically and independently distributed normal error terms.[2]

The variables from chapter 3 are coded similarly here with the natural exception that policy popularity is measured with survey questions pertaining to the foreign policy issues. The factor is again based on the recurring General Social Survey and Roper surveys that ask: "We are faced with many problems in this country, none of which can be solved easily or inexpensively. I'm going to name some of these problems, and for each one I'd like you to tell me whether you think we're spending too much money, too little money, or about the right amount on [a particular policy issue]?" For the observations on defense, the question concludes with the wording "the military, armaments, and defense." For the observations on humanitarian and security assistance, the question finishes with the phrase "foreign aid."[3]

2. As in chapter 3, *Budget Share* and *Unified Government* serve as the instrumental variables. As I discuss later in the text, I also used *Drawdown* as an instrument in lieu of *Unified Government* and received substantially similar results.

3. The only other variable for which coding differs from the econometric analysis in chapter 3 is *Budget Share*, which is transformed because it and *Policy Approval* are

The new variables, *War* and *Drawdown,* are control factors that pertain to foreign and defense policy. The first of them is included to account for the possibility that presidents have greater influence over foreign and defense matters during active wars. I therefore expect presidential budgetary success to be positively affected by the variable, which equals one for the years of the Vietnam and Gulf Wars and zero otherwise.[4] *Drawdown* is also a binary indicator, equaling one if in the previous year the president exercised drawdown authority and zero otherwise.[5] The factor controls for the possibility that Congress responds differently to a president's budgetary requests on foreign and defense issues after he has unilaterally given Defense Department equipment to another nation. Hypothetically, this effect could be positive or negative. On the one hand, the exercise of drawdown authority requires future appropriations, suggesting that the president's budgetary success may be higher in the year following the use of this capacity. On the other hand, Congress may resent the president's unilateral action and respond by being less likely to accept his budgetary recommendations.

Table 4.4 presents the results for the analysis of the Influence over Foreign Affairs and Sincerity of Policy Debate predictions. The findings solidly corroborate the first of these predictions but only weakly support the latter. The first column of findings concerns equation (4.1), which tests the prediction on sincerity of debate. The second column pertains to equation (4.2), which examines the influence prediction. I begin by discussing the results for equation (4.1).

As the table shows, the coefficient on budgetary success is negative but not significant at any conventional level. The parameter estimates thus provide only weak support for the Sincerity of Policy Debate prediction. Notably, however, this result does not advance the alternative hypothesis that public appeals concern foregone successes; that is, there is no evidence that presidents are simply credit-claiming or grandstanding. The analysis simply does not establish with confidence that the likelihood of a

---

otherwise highly collinear. To deal with the problem, I transform *Budget Share* by taking the rank of the variable and log-transforming this rank, which decreases the correlation from 0.63 to 0.41. (In the domestic policy data in chapter 3, the correlation was only 0.25.) Without the transformation, the results are substantively similar except that the impact of policy approval on presidential budgetary success is insignificant. Full results are available on request.

4. Given the time period covered by the data, *War* equals one for 1972–73 (fiscal years 1973–74) and 1990–91 (fiscal years 1991–92), and zero otherwise.

5. The sources for this variable include table 7.13 in Ragsdale (1998) for all years until 1994 and the *Code of Federal Regulations* for each year since 1995.

Table 4.4 Determinants of Foreign Policy Appeals and Legislative Success

Independent Variables	Equation (4.1)	Equation (4.2)
Public Appeal**	—	0.022
		(0.012)
Policy Approval	−0.015	0.096
	(0.015)	(0.043)
Presidential Budgetary Success**	−108.194	—
	(487.369)	
Unified Government	—	0.011
		(0.049)
Budget Share	1.385	—
	(0.523)	
Prior Media Salience	0.494	0.001
	(0.205)	(0.003)
Public Concern	−1.769	−0.048
	(0.861)	(0.024)
Personal Popularity	1.171	−0.029
	(0.703)	(0.023)
Priority	0.124	−0.032
	(0.690)	(0.023)
Targeted Address	0.704	−0.012
	(0.587)	(0.023)
% Δ GDP	0.372	−0.010
	(0.237)	(0.007)
War	−1.613	0.035
	(1.103)	(0.036)
Drawdown	2.129	−0.093
	(1.920)	(0.032)
Constant	−5.716	−0.089
	(2.430)	(0.079)
President Indicators	$\chi^2_{(5)} = 7.152$	$\chi^2_{(5)} = 47.657$
	$(p = 0.210)$	$(p = 0.000)$
	Details in Text	Details In Text

Number of Observations		74
Joint Fit of Estimates		$\chi^2_{(34)} = 165.529$
		$(p < 0.000)$
Exogeneity Test	$\chi^2_{(17)} = 177.971$	$\chi^2_{(17)} = 45.619$
	$(p < 0.000)$	$(p < 0.000)$

Note: The dependent variable for equation (4.1) is *Pr* (Public Appeal) = 1; for equation (4.2), it is Presidential Budgetary Success. Standard errors are in parentheses. Budgetary Success** is a function of equation (4.2), and Public Appeal** is a function of equation (4.1).

foreign policy appeal is lower the more legislative success a president expects.

This result differs from that for domestic policy appeals, where the Sincerity of Policy Debate prediction received stronger confirmation. A possible explanation for the discrepancy relates to citizens' lower level of information about foreign affairs. In particular, it could be that presidents feel the need to inform citizens about certain foreign policy initiatives even when these initiatives are relatively likely to be enacted absent any public statements.

Among the other results on equation (4.1), the most notable one is that the impact of policy approval is not significant at any conventional level and even has a negative sign. According to the estimates, a marginal change in popular support for a foreign policy proposal does not influence the likelihood that the president takes the issue to the public. This result contrasts with that from the domestic policy data, where change in the variable *Policy Approval* had a substantial impact on the likelihood of an appeal. The analysis therefore provides preliminary support for the Popularity of Foreign Positions prediction, which suggests that the impact of policy approval on the likelihood of an appeal will be less in the realm of foreign affairs.

The lack of a significant effect of policy approval in table 4.4 suggests that the probability a president will publicize a foreign policy initiative could be utterly independent of the popularity of the initiative. A separate possibility, however, is that marginal changes in policy approval do not affect the likelihood of a foreign policy appeal even though large changes in policy approval do. This possibility is consistent with the first-glance analysis, which found that presidents tend to avoid publicizing foreign policy proposals that face mass opposition. To assess whether that pattern holds after controlling for a variety of other influences on presidential behavior, I reanalyzed the determinants of foreign policy appeals with a dichotomous measure of policy approval that equaled one if the original variable was greater than 50 percent and zero otherwise. The results of this analysis suggest that presidents are significantly more likely to go public about a foreign policy initiative if it has support from a majority of the populace. Specifically, at the means of the independent variables, a president is 31 percent more likely to make a foreign policy appeal about an initiative if it has majority support.[6] Thus nonmarginal change in policy approval does influence the likelihood of a foreign policy appeal, even though marginal change does not.

6. The coefficient on the dichotomous measure of policy approval equals 0.858, and the standard error is 0.456. The results on the other variables are available on request.

Returning to table 4.4, the remaining parameter estimates on equation (4.1) are largely consistent with expectations. For instance, budget share has a significant, positive effect. Just as predicted, presidents are found to be more likely to go public about a budgetary item the larger its percentage of total spending. This result is consistent with the claim that a president will be more likely to publicize an initiative the larger the impact of the initiative on other programs.[7]

The coefficients on the variables representing prior issue salience are each significant although the signs of the effects vary, with *Prior Media Coverage* having a positive impact and *Public Concern* a negative one. The positive influence of prior media salience comports with research that finds media attention to a foreign policy issue increases a president's attention to the issue in his public statements and writings (e.g., Edwards and Wood 1999). The result on public concern is, at first glance, surprising but explainable upon scrutiny of the Most Important Problem survey responses that constitute the variable. In particular, the responses concerning foreign aid generally articulate a negative disposition, i.e., that the biggest problem in the country is the expense of resources on international assistance. It would therefore seem that presidents are less likely to publicize proposals on foreign aid when significant segments of society name the existence of the program to be the most important problem in the United States.

The other control variables do not have a substantial effect on the likelihood of a foreign policy appeal. Even the president indicators are jointly insignificant, suggesting that individual presidents do not vary in their propensity to appeal to the public about foreign policy initiatives once structural factors are taken into account. The reason for including most of these factors in the simultaneous system was to control for the effect they may have on presidents' budgetary success, not the likelihood of an appeal. (However, once included in the equation on budgetary success, I took the standard, conservative approach of including them in each equation of the simultaneous system.) The insignificance of the estimates is therefore not entirely unexpected.

Turning to the results on the determinants of presidential budgetary success, the table provides further support for the theoretical expectations. Most important, the impact of a public appeal is in the expected direction and significant at conventional levels. According to the estimates, presidents achieve greater budgetary success on foreign and defense initiatives by advocating them to the public. The analysis thus supports the Influence over Foreign Affairs prediction, which holds that

---

7. The statistical significance of the factor supports using it as an instrument.

a president will obtain policy ends from foreign policy appeals even though they may not concern issues on which he wants Congress to become more responsive to citizens' existing policy preferences.

The magnitude of the effect, while not inconsequential, is considerably smaller than that for a domestic policy appeal. The results suggest that when a president goes on primetime television to promote a foreign budgetary proposal, his budgetary success increases by a little over two percentage points. That is, the percentage change in enacted appropriations is two percentage points closer to that requested by the president.[8] In comparison, a domestic policy appeal was estimated to affect the president's budgetary success by eleven to sixteen percentage points. A possible reason for the difference is that presidents obtain more of what they want in foreign affairs even absent plebiscitary activity (e.g., Dahl 1950; Fenno 1973; Huntington 1961; Peterson 1994); thus, the influence an appeal can generate is less than that for domestic affairs.

The other determinants of presidential success, which include the instrumental and control variables, generally have the predicted effects. Perhaps most important among these results is that the popularity of the president's proposal has a significantly positive impact. The analysis thus implies that marginal change in popular support for a foreign policy proposal increases congressional members' willingness to enact it. Because the literature suggests presidential speechmaking can change citizens' preferences about foreign policy issues (e.g., Edwards 1983; Meernik and Ault 2001), the significant effect of policy approval on presidential success is not inconsistent with the insignificant effect of the factor on the likelihood of an appeal. Indeed, a president's incentive to try to change citizens' preferences depends on the existence of a relationship between public opinion and legislative outcomes. Moreover, as discussed earlier, supplementary analysis shows that current opinion does affect the likelihood a president publicizes a foreign policy initiative in that he is more likely to do so when popular support for the initiative is above 50 percent.

In contrast to the results on policy approval, public concern is found to have a negative impact on presidents' budgetary success. The latter result comports with the previously discussed fact that the Most Important Problem survey responses regarding foreign aid register disapproval of the program. The negative effect may accordingly be a function of presidents achieving less of their foreign aid requests the more often the issue is cited as a problem. Consistent with this explanation, when I

---

8. As discussed in chapter 3, the magnitude of this effect will be underestimated to the extent that a president who prefers more (less) spending than Congress prefers will propose more (less) spending than he actually desires.

estimate the impact of the responses on budgetary success for each issue individually (by running for each issue a regression of *Presidential Budgetary Success* on *Public Concern*), only for humanitarian aid do the responses have a significant effect and it is a negative one.

The remaining variables with significant effects include the exercise of drawdown authority and the president indicators. The negative impact of the former indicates that when presidents unilaterally give other nations defense equipment, congressional members are less likely to enact the president's proposals for foreign and defense spending in the subsequent year. Members thus appear to resent presidents' circumventing of the legislative process.

The jointly significant effect of the president indicators suggests that even controlling for a myriad of factors, individual presidents differ in their ability to convince Congress to adopt foreign policy proposals. This result supports work that argues that a president's ability to negotiate with congressional members is in part a function of his personal qualities (e.g., Greenstein 2000; Neustadt 1990 [1960]). Among the individual differences, the most noteworthy is that Nixon was significantly less successful than the other presidents, who had largely indistinguishable effects from one another. Nixon's relatively poor performance may well be a function of the particular circumstances he faced with regard to the Vietnam War in the years of these data (which begin in calendar year 1972). In the final years of the war, increasing numbers of citizens no longer supported the military engagement (e.g., Lunch and Sperlich 1979). Given this widening opposition, congressional members had incentives not to grant the president deference over foreign and defense policy.

The lack of significance of the other variables is consistent with the results in chapter 3 with a couple of exceptions. Most notably, the effect of *Unified Government,* while positive, is not significant at conventional levels.[9] This finding is consistent with Aaron Wildavsky's (1966) original argument for why presidents should have greater influence in foreign affairs. Specifically, he argued that greater bipartisanship exists in this domain.[10] A potential statistical concern about this null effect is that it

9. One might presume this null effect results from the collinearity between *Unified Government* and the Carter administration indicator. Indeed, in chapter 3, I presented the analogous results without the president indicators because of this collinearity (which is 0.8). Here, even without the president indicators, *Unified Government* has an insignificant effect and all substantive results regarding the Public Appeals Theory remain. I therefore present the results with the indicators in order to provide insight into the individual differences among the presidents.

10. Oldfield and Wildavsky (1991) recant this argument, claiming it is "time bound" to the height of the Cold War.

may engender problems of identification given that *Unified Government* serves as the primary instrument for presidents' budgetary success. The fact that the econometric model contains one linear and one nonlinear equation contributes to identification by ensuring that *Public Appeal* is identified by an equation distinct from that explaining *Presidential Budgetary Success*. Still, I have conducted an alternative analysis to assess whether the substantive findings are a function of using *Unified Government* as the primary instrumental variable for equation (4.2). In the alternative analysis, I employ as this instrumental variable *Drawdown*, which according to tables 4.4 and 4.5 influences a president's budgetary success but not the likelihood of an appeal. These results are consistent with the ones presented. In particular, the findings corroborate the Public Appeals Theory excepting the Sincerity of Policy Debate prediction, which again receives only weak support.

Another finding that does not comport with expectations is the insignificant effect of war. According to table 4.4, presidents are not given greater deference over foreign and defense spending during a time of active military engagement. As with the Nixon effect, this result may be a function of the fact that the data concern the last two years of the Vietnam War, when the public was increasingly dissatisfied with the military engagement. In fact, these final years of Vietnam constitute half of the years in which a war occurs during the time period covered by the data.

Overall, table 4.4 provides support for the theoretical expectations and no evidence for the alternative perspectives of public appeals. In contrast to research that suggests public appeals only rarely aid presidents in the legislative process, the evidence indicates foreign policy appeals routinely advance chief executives' agendas. The results thus corroborate the Influence over Foreign Affairs prediction that presidents routinely achieve legislative influence from publicizing foreign policy initiatives. Only weak support is offered for the Sincerity of Policy Debate prediction that presidents are less likely to go public the greater the expected legislative success without doing so, but, notably, the findings do not suggest presidents are simply claiming credit or grandstanding. Accordingly, the finding that the appeals generate influence is not an artifact of presidents publicizing foregone successes. Finally, in combination with the results of chapter 3, the table provides preliminary support for the Popularity of Foreign Positions prediction that a president's likelihood of appealing to the public about an issue is less influenced by the popularity of his position if the issue concerns foreign rather than domestic affairs. The next section tests this prediction directly.

Popularity of Foreign Positions Prediction

To directly examine the Popularity of Foreign Positions prediction, I pool the budgetary data on foreign and domestic policy. The testing can therefore utilize interaction terms to assess whether the relationship between the likelihood of an appeal and the popularity of a presidential proposal differs between the two domains. Specifically, I analyze a probit equation in which the probability of an appeal is regressed on the following variables: policy approval, policy approval interacted with an indicator for whether the issue concerns foreign affairs, the main effect of the foreign policy indicator, and a set of control variables. The interaction term evaluates the degree to which the impact of proposal popularity differs for foreign policy. A negative coefficient on the factor would provide support for the Popularity of Foreign Positions prediction, while a positive coefficient would suggest that the popularity of a president's proposal has a greater effect on whether he goes public if the proposal concerns foreign affairs.

The set of the control variables includes the independent variables in equation (4.1). Like policy approval, each control factor is interacted with the indicator for foreign policy issues. Specification testing supports the inclusion of these interactions, which allow for the possibility that various factors may affect the likelihood of a foreign policy appeal differently than they affect the likelihood of a domestic policy one.[11] Intuitively, these factors allow that the politics of foreign and domestic policy appeals may vary fundamentally.

Table 4.5 presents the key results, which include the main effect of policy approval, the impact of this factor interacted with the foreign affairs indicator, and the main effect of the foreign affairs indicator. The other findings are consistent with those of earlier analyses and are available on request. The table provides strong confirmation of the Popularity of Foreign Positions prediction. The coefficient on the interaction between the foreign affairs indicator and policy approval is negative at conventional levels of statistical significance ($p < 0.05$, two-tailed). In other words, as expected, a president's likelihood of going public is found to be less influenced by the popularity of his position if the issue concerns foreign affairs. The result corroborates the evidence from the first-glance analyses of this chapter and chapter 3, which showed that the average initial popularity of the foreign policy initiatives a president takes to the public is substantially lower than that of the analogous domestic policy initiatives.

11. In a log likelihood ratio test, $\chi^2 = 22.53$ ($p = 0.05$).

Table 4.5 Test of the Popularity of Foreign Positions Prediction

Independent Variables	Probit Coefficient (Standard Error)
Policy Approval × Foreign Affairs	−0.023
	(0.011)
Policy Approval	0.018
	(0.007)
Foreign Affairs	−0.919
	(2.072)
Number of Observations	174
Joint Fit of Estimates	$\chi^2_{(30)} = 86.778$ ($p < 0.000$)

Note: The dependent variable is Pr (Public Appeal) = 1. Standard errors are in parentheses below probit coefficients. The set of control variables is defined in the text.

The findings in table 4.5 on the other major variable of interest, the main effect of policy approval, are also consistent with the Public Appeals Theory. In particular, the estimates suggest that when a proposal does not concern foreign affairs, a marginal increase in policy approval will significantly increase the likelihood that the president publicizes the proposal. These estimates therefore offer further confirmation of the Popularity of Domestic Positions prediction.

CONCLUSION

The results of chapter 4 provide a good deal of support for the Public Appeals Theory developed in chapter 2.[12] The tests as well as the basic patterns illuminated by the summary statistics indicate that foreign policy appeals largely function in the predicted ways. For example, consistent with the Influence over Foreign Affairs prediction, the findings establish that foreign policy appeals increase a president's influence with Congress. Likewise, consistent with the Popularity of Foreign Positions prediction, the popularity of an initiative is found to be less likely to affect a president's propensity to go public if the initiative concerns foreign policy.

The only theoretical prediction that does not receive strong corroboration is the Sincerity of Policy Debate prediction. The effect of expected legislative success on the likelihood of a public appeal is negative but not

---

12. Because the methodological approach of chapter 4 largely follows that of chapter 3, I do not repeat the caveats to this approach here. Interested readers are directed to the "Caveats" section of the earlier chapter.

at all significant at conventional levels. The analysis thus does not reject the possibility that the likelihood of a foreign policy appeal is unrelated to a president's expected legislative success. Notably, however, the results provide no support for the alternative prediction that presidents use plebiscitary appeals for credit-claiming or grandstanding. In other words, even though the foreign policy appeals do not concern the initiatives least likely to be enacted, neither do they concern foregone successes. Thus, as a whole, the evidence of the chapter provides support for the Public Appeals Theory.

The results, in providing support for the theory, suggest that foreign policy appeals are less likely than domestic policy ones to increase the impact of current opinion on policymaking. Notably, however, this variation does *not* imply that foreign policy appeals fail to increase the impact of current opinion. The summary statistics show that presidents generally avoid going public about foreign affairs initiatives that face mass opposition. Furthermore, even controlling for a variety of determinants of policy appeals, presidents are found to be significantly more likely to publicize foreign policy initiatives if the initiatives are favored by majority opinion. Thus, although the specific findings on foreign policy appeals differ from those on domestic policy ones, there are some notable consistencies with regards to mass opinion. In particular, in both domestic and foreign affairs, presidents strategically publicize relatively popular initiatives and, by doing so, increase the degree to which mass opinion guides policymaking.

This importance of mass opinion to the politics of public appeals, even in the realm of foreign policy, highlights the need for understanding the conditions under which presidents endorse initiatives simply because they are popular. In particular, there may be circumstances under which presidents not only advocate popular proposals to the public but also design the executive agenda in response to the initial popularity of the various policy options. While this type of agenda-setting has attractive features—for instance, it limits the ability of leaders and specialized groups to impose their personal agendas on the citizenry—such policy responsiveness may not always be in citizens' interests.

Indeed, as discussed in the chapter 1, scholars have typically lamented the fact that public appeals may give presidents an incentive to follow public opinion. For example, Sidney Milkis (1998, 401) notes, "With the liberation of the executive from many of the constraints of party leadership and the rise of the mass media, presidents have resorted to rhetoric . . . But, as the nation has witnessed all too clearly since the 1960s, this form of 'populist' presidential politics can all too readily degenerate into rank opportunism." Likewise, Jeffrey Tulis (1998, 111–13) questions whether one can permit rhetorical leadership without allowing for the possibility of demagoguery. These reflections suggest that a president's involvement of the mass public may encourage him to follow public opinion at the expense of societal welfare. For instance, a president may endorse popular policies even when he has information suggesting that they will produce bad outcomes for society.

Thus far, the analysis has shown that presidents' involvement of the mass public increases the policy influence of majority opinion but has not considered whether this influence entails the president endorsing popular policies he believes are not in citizens' long-term interests. In part 2, I turn to this issue and examine the impact of mass opinion on chief executives' policy choices. By doing so, I provide a more comprehensive understanding of the relationship among presidents, the mass public, and policymaking. Moreover, part 2 assesses whether, as others have feared, the influence presidents achieve from petitioning the citizenry is indeed problematic because it entails policies that presidents believe will ultimately harm society.

PART TWO

Policy Pandering and Leadership

In recent years, observers of American politics from inside and outside the academy have expressed the belief that presidents as well as other politicians harm society by involving the mass public in the policy process. For instance, Joseph Bessette (1994, 212) suggests presidents' arousing and monitoring of public opinion encourage the enactment of policies catering to an opinion that is "spontaneous, less well informed, and less reflective" than the policies that would be enacted as a result of deliberation among elites. In less erudite language, Arianna Huffington has expressed similar dismay over the attention that politicians give to mass opinion. She argues that they are now "pathological people pleasers, addicted to the short-term buzz of a bump in the polls and indifferent to the long-term effect . . . Today's new poll-happy pol has replaced the old-fashioned leader—one unafraid to make difficult, unpopular decisions" (Huffington 2000, 73).[1]

Part 1 established that these concerns have some plausibility. When presidents appeal to the public, they are not grandstanding but rallying the populace in an effort to pressure Congress to enact initiatives that are relatively popular. And subsequent to this speechmaking, Congress does become more likely to enact the popular initiatives that were advocated. Thus to the extent that mass influence over policymaking is indeed detrimental to societal welfare, presidents' public appeals advance this detrimental effect.

Of course, not all aspects of mass influence over policymaking are detrimental. As Paul Quirk and Joseph Hinchliffe (1998, 20–21) point out, mass influence "can help to overcome the organized interest groups and other narrow forces that have often dominated American politics."

---

1. As discussed in chapter 1, numerous other thinkers have made similar arguments. See, for instance, Lippman (1922), Kennan (1951), Morgenthau (1948), Tulis (1987), and Weissberg (2001).

This is also the view of E. E. Schattschneider (1960), who maintains that interest groups dominate politics except when the scope of conflict embraces the more general public. Numerous studies provide evidence for this perspective, documenting specific cases in which companies, industries, or other segments of society have obtained policy ends that were not necessarily in the interests of the populace.[2]

The set of normative concerns provoked by presidents' involvement of the mass public clearly needs to be defined separately from the broader question of whether this involvement increases the influence of current opinion over policymaking. One such concern, which some might argue is the primary normative issue, is identified by Alexander Hamilton in Federalist Paper No. 71.[3] In particular, he describes optimal executive behavior by admonishing that "when occasions present themselves, in which the interests of the people are at variance with their inclinations, it is the duty of the persons whom they have appointed to be the guardians of those interests."[4] Adopting Hamilton's language, the central question is whether presidents cater to citizens' inclinations when they believe doing so would harm citizens' interests. In other words, when a president cannot simultaneously go along with public opinion and pursue the policy he deems will advance societal welfare, what will he do? Will he follow current opinion? Do structural factors—for example, the electoral cycle or his personal popularity—influence the likelihood that he endorses a popular policy?

Part 2 examines these and related questions. In particular, it analyzes whether presidents follow public opinion when they believe citizens are misinformed about their interests, behavior I call *policy pandering*.[5] In

---

2. For instance, see Baron (2003), Derthick and Quirk (1985), Jacobs (1993), Peltzman (1976), Stigler (1971), and Wilson (1989).

3. There obviously exist other normative concerns about democratic responsiveness, including questions about the potential tyranny of the majority (see, for instance, Madison in Federalist Paper No. 10) and whether a coherent popular will even exists (Riker 1982).

4. *The Federalist Papers* 1987 [1788], No. 71, 410.

5. The use of the term pandering here differs from that in Jacobs and Shapiro (2000). In particular, Jacobs and Shapiro allow that the term may be applied to situations in which presidents believe citizens are well-informed about their interests as well as situations in which presidents believe citizens are misinformed. The definition of pandering employed here is also narrower than that in Maskin and Tirole (2004). For instance, Maskin and Tirole define "full pandering" as occurring when a government official always selects the policies voters want at the moment. This behavior accordingly includes circumstances in which the official believes voters correctly perceive their interests. Also, Maskin and Tirole define "forward-looking pandering" equivalently to what this book terms policy leadership.

examining this phenomenon, I simultaneously assess the extent to which presidents engage in the opposite behavior, which is termed *policy leadership*. In the latter case, the president pursues the policy he believes will promote societal welfare despite a lack of popular support for doing so.[6] I concentrate the analysis on circumstances in which the policy issue has at least some degree of salience to the public. This focus ensures that the examination corresponds to the normative concerns provoked by the findings of part 1. Furthermore, a president's incentive to follow public opinion should be greatest when voters are attentive to his policy decisions.

Part 2 has three major components, each of which comprises a chapter. Chapter 5 presents a theory, the Conditional Pandering Theory, which analyzes the incentives of presidents to follow public opinion when they believe doing so would not advance societal welfare. In chapter 6, the theory is examined through historical narrative. I develop three case studies that concern, respectively, Carter's proposal in early 1980 to reduce humanitarian assistance, Bush's policy reversal on the extension of unemployment benefits in 1991 and 1992, and Reagan's 1983 initiative to enact a "standby tax." In each of the historical studies, the Conditional Pandering Theory helps to explain an ostensible incongruity in the president's decision making. Chapter 7, which is co-authored with Ken Shotts, assesses the Conditional Pandering Theory with a larger data set of presidential decisions. More specifically, these data concern annually recurring presidential proposals on eleven policy issues across three decades. This analysis not only assesses the verisimilitude of the theory but also reveals general patterns in the relationship between public opinion and presidential policymaking.

A number of challenging questions are associated with the study of policy pandering. For instance, how does one distinguish pandering from more straightforward concurrence between a president's policy beliefs and current opinion? How does one distinguish informational from ideological differences? Even assuming these distinctions can be accomplished, how does one ascertain whether a president's policy decision is a function of structural incentives rather than his personality? Finally, is it reasonable to assume that presidents have better information than citizens do about their interests? The remainder of this introduction reflects on these questions, describing how the subsequent analysis addresses them.

---

6. This definition differs from what Geer (1996) terms "democratic leadership," which occurs when a politician moves public opinion toward his or her policy position.

PANDERING VERSUS CONCURRENCE

The most obvious challenge in studying the topic of pandering is that this behavior can be observationally equivalent to the president supporting a popular position simply because he and the public concur about the appropriate course of action. For instance, assume the vast majority of the public desires an income tax cut. A president could take this course of action because he believes that doing so would aid the economy, because he wants to appeal to a given constituency that supports the tax cut, or simply because the policy is widely supported. Perhaps because of this difficulty in determining a president's policy motivations, existing work on presidential responsiveness generally analyzes only the subject of *policy congruence*, i.e. the extent to which presidents' policy decisions are congruent with current opinion. Whether the congruence reflects policy pandering or instead *concurrence* between the president's policy desires and current opinion is not assessed.[7]

The following chapters discriminate between policy pandering and concurrence with a three-pronged approach that combines theoretical, narrative, and quantitative analyses. Because pandering and concurrence are distinct conceptually, the differentiation is most straightforward in the development of the Conditional Pandering Theory in chapter 5. The theory allows for the possibility that the president believes voters correctly perceive their interests in addition to the possibility that the president believes voters are misinformed about the optimal policy choice. Accordingly, the theory offers predictions on the likelihood of pandering as well as on concurrence and congruence.

In the case studies of chapter 6, which examine individual presidential decisions, I employ historical evidence to document whether a president's beliefs about the optimal course of action differed from public opinion. In all of the contexts analyzed, the evidence suggests that the president believed citizens were misinformed, or uninformed, about the likely consequences of policies. Thus none of the cases concern simple concurrence between the president's position and public opinion; the president either panders or takes an unpopular position.

The remaining empirical analysis—the statistical analysis of chapter 7—focuses not on the details of individual policy choices but, instead, on

---

7. For instance, when Erikson, MacKuen, and Stimson (2002a, 2002b) analyze whether presidents' roll-call positions are congruent with the public mood, the scholars do not attempt to assess the reasons for the congruence that occurs. Likewise, when Cohen (1997) and Jacobs and Shapiro (2000) present evidence that presidents are not substantively responsive to current opinion, the scholars do not attempt to ascertain the extent to which policy leadership is occurring.

broad patterns of decision making. For this examination, I utilize the predictions on policy congruence derived from the Conditional Pandering Theory, comparing them to existing predictions on congruence from the literature. In the theory, any predicted variation in congruence is entirely a consequence of variation in the likelihood of pandering; thus the predictions on congruence should be validated only if the predictions on pandering are correct. Moreover, according to the prior literature, the Conditional Pandering Theory predictions on congruence should not be validated by the data. The analysis therefore directly tests the theory and in doing so indirectly assesses its predictions on pandering.

In sum, the following chapters distinguish policy pandering from policy concurrence in three ways. First, the behaviors are differentiated theoretically. Second, for individual policy decisions, historical evidence is brought to bear on presidents' beliefs about the appropriate course of action and public opinion. Finally, a data set of presidential decisions is employed to evaluate whether the patterns of policy congruence correspond to the ones that should exist if presidents do indeed pander to public opinion.

INFORMATIONAL VERSUS IDEOLOGICAL DIFFERENCES

American presidents may disagree with citizens about the optimal course of action on a given policy issue either because of informational differences about which policy choice will likely produce the best outcome for society or, alternatively, because of ideological or "distributive" differences that are unrelated to informational asymmetries. Part 1 focused on this latter type of conflict, which may result from partisan alliances, interest groups, or personal ideological leanings, among other factors. Part 2 focuses on informational differences and, accordingly, the theoretical analysis abstracts from the other type of conflict. The purpose of the abstraction is to assess how informational differences unto themselves may provide perverse policy incentives; it is these incentives that are at the heart of the normative concern about policy pandering. The empirical analysis still accounts for ideological conflict, however, both in the case studies and the examination of the larger data set of presidential decisions. These empirics establish that the predictions of the theory hold even after accounting for ideological differences.

PERSONAL QUALITIES VERSUS INSTITUTIONAL INCENTIVES

The presidency literature has a long-standing tradition of examining executive behavior as a function of the personal qualities of the man who inhabits the office. Much of the analysis of Richard Neustadt (1990 [1960]), for example, is focused on individual presidents' strengths and weaknesses in bargaining with other policy elites. Another well-known example of this line of inquiry is the work of James David Barber (1977), who classifies chief executives into four personality types he claims shape executive behavior. More recently, Fred Greenstein (2000) has examined how various personal qualities, such as emotional intelligence and organizational capacity, affect a president's management style.

The subsequent theoretical analysis does not concentrate on presidents' personal qualities but instead on the institutional incentives for policy pandering. In other words, the theory assumes that a president will not endorse unpopular policies he believes are likely to advance societal welfare simply because he is an honorable person. Nor does it permit a chief executive to pander to public opinion solely as a function of his personality. The theory does incorporate, however, that presidents may differ in their abilities to ascertain how policies will affect citizens' well-being.

Furthermore, in testing the theory, the empirical analysis allows that presidents' personal qualities may affect their decisions. The historical narratives address this matter in a couple of ways. First, two of the cases analyze a policy issue on which a president initially bucks current opinion but then subsequently panders. The decision to pander to public opinion cannot, therefore, be ascribed solely to the president's personality; at least initially, the chief executive did not feel driven to take this course of action. Second, I have tried to select cases for which the president's behavior is not entirely consistent with historical assessments of his personality. Thus, for instance, the Carter narrative focuses on policy pandering even though Carter has a reputation for placing the public interest above political expediency (e.g., Hargrove 1988; Jones 1988).

The analysis of patterns of presidential decisions also accounts for differences in chief executives' personal qualities. The standard means by which statistical tests control for such differences is to include a dummy variable for each president. I adopted this approach in part 1 to allow that individual leaders may vary in their likelihood of appealing to the public and/or skill in legislative negotiations. In the econometrics of chapter 7, I again adopt this approach, this time to control for differences among individual presidents in their propensities to endorse popular policies.

PRESIDENTS, THE MASS PUBLIC, AND POLICY EXPERTISE

An underlying premise of the study of pandering is that presidents sometimes have what the literature refers to as "policy expertise" (e.g., Bawn 1995; Gilligan and Krehbiel 1987), or better information than citizens have about the expected consequences of policies. In the ensuing analysis, this information is not necessarily perfect. That is, a president can have policy expertise and still hold erroneous beliefs about the consequences of policies. He is simply more likely than the mass public to have accurate beliefs.

The premise of policy expertise is implicit in the work that argues presidents should not cater to current opinion (e.g., Bessette 1994; Lippmann 1922; Kennan 1951; Morgenthau 1948; Tulis 1987; Weissberg 2001). The premise also has an empirical basis. Chief executives have advisors and substantial bureaucratic resources dedicated to providing policy information. Moreover, on matters of national security, presidents typically have privileged information.

Even so, as Benjamin Page and Jason Barabas (2000) point out, leaders do not *always* have superior information. The following chapters do not dispute this claim. The underlying supposition is simply that there are normal circumstances under which presidents do indeed have superior knowledge. In chapter 8, the concluding chapter, I describe implications of the results for circumstances in which presidents do not have better information than citizens have.

CHAPTER FIVE

Incentives for Policy Pandering

What are a president's incentives to enact a popular policy when he has information that indicates the policy would produce a bad outcome for society? Work on presidential responsiveness to public opinion does not answer this question. Most of the existing work examines the level of and/or variation in responsiveness rather than whether presidents will pander in the sense of following current opinion when they believe it is misguided. For instance, Robert Erikson, Michael MacKuen, and James Stimson (2002a; 2002b) find high responsiveness yet do not analyze how the level is affected by a president's incentives to disregard current opinion when he deems citizens to be misinformed. The amount of responsiveness is also assessed by scholars such as Jeffrey Cohen (1997) and Lawrence Jacobs and Robert Shapiro (2000; 2002a), who argue the level is low. Likewise, Jeff Manza and Fay Lomax Cook (2002) propose that responsiveness should be greatest for unpopular presidents but do not examine the extent to which this greater responsiveness reflects pandering.

The strand of research that is perhaps most conceptually related to the topic of pandering derives from V. O. Key's (1961) discussion of latent opinion, or the opinion that citizens can be expected to have once they learn the consequences of policy choices. According to Key (1961), and more recently John Zaller (2003), politicians may rationally choose an unpopular policy if they believe that latent opinion supports it.[1] In other words, presidents may have incentives not to pander to current opinion when they believe it is misguided. Yet this line of work still leaves open many questions about politicians' incentives. For example, is it the case that presidents almost always care about latent opinion? Or, consistent

---

1. The work of Arnold (1990) and Fiorina (1981) is also consistent with this perspective.

with Manza and Cook (2002), are unpopular presidents particularly likely to cater to current opinion and disregard latent opinion?

The theoretical analysis of this chapter answers these and related questions. The analysis is based on the logic of a formal theory that I developed with Michael Herron and Ken Shotts (Canes-Wrone, Herron, and Shotts 2001), which I call the Conditional Pandering Theory.[2] The model itself is rather technically complex. Thus, unlike chapter 2, which extended a relatively simple model and therefore outlined a full set of assumptions, this chapter does not take the reader through such a detailed description. Indeed, I invoke no formal notation; I simply describe the intuition of the theory.

The Conditional Pandering Theory has two primary contributions. First, it generates predictions about the conditions under which a president who believes that citizens are misinformed will nonetheless cater to this mass opinion. Second, the theory produces hypotheses about overall congruence between the president's policy choices and public opinion. In other words, in addition to explaining variation in the likelihood of policy pandering, the Conditional Pandering Theory also explains variation in presidential responsiveness more generally.

The chapter proceeds as follows. I first present the theory in three sections: an outline of the conceptual background; a discussion, with hypothetical examples, of the policy incentives induced by this framework; and a statement of the general results. I then return to the literature on political responsiveness. Comparing the Conditional Pandering Theory to this work highlights the contributions of the theoretical analysis, both in terms of understanding policy pandering as well as overall congruence between presidents' policy choices and public opinion.

THE CONDITIONAL PANDERING THEORY

Conceptual Background

Policy Information

The primary goal of the theory is to assess whether presidents who have information that suggests a popular policy would not serve citizens' interests will pander to current opinion. The theory accordingly analyzes the policymaking of a president who has better information than the electorate does about the expected consequences of various policy options.

---

2. I focus on what we call the basic theory in Canes-Wrone, Herron, and Shotts (2001).

The president and voters are aware of this informational asymmetry, which, as mentioned in the introduction to part 2, the literature refers to as "policy expertise."[3]

The specific nature of the expertise takes the following form. There are two possible policy options that the president may choose and two sets of circumstances or "states of the world." Each of the policy options will succeed, in the sense of producing a good outcome, in exactly one of the sets of circumstances. The citizens have information indicating which set of conditions exists, but the president's information is better than theirs is.

For example, the president could face a decision over whether to send in troops to a foreign crisis that could affect U.S. security. In one state of the world, the crisis will not resolve without American intervention, and the optimal decision is to authorize the use of force. In the other state of the world, the crisis will be settled independently of American intervention, and the optimal policy is to keep the troops home. The public may believe that the crisis requires American assistance and therefore favor dispatching the military, but the president's intelligence could suggest that such assistance is not needed. The president therefore cannot simultaneously follow public opinion and endorse the policy he believes is in the national interest.

The president in the theory knows that the electorate will be attentive to the policy process. That is, the electorate learns the policy choice of the president and he is aware of their attentiveness when making his choice. This assumption comports with the normative concern that motivates the theoretical analysis: namely, that on salient issues a president may be motivated to placate the mass public even when he believes doing so will ultimately harm societal welfare.

While citizens are assumed to pay attention to the president's policy decision, he cannot credibly convey to them all of his policy information. Otherwise, he could simply report it and not face a decision between pandering and choosing a policy he believes will produce a good outcome. This assumption reflects contexts in which presidents have information that is too technical for the average citizen given her attention span for politics, is classified, or is not observable for some other reason. For example, during a time of high inflation, a president could have data that suggests the economy would recover more quickly without price controls, but he might not be able to persuade the citizenry of this fact.

3. As discussed in more detail in the introduction to part 2, the assumption of policy expertise is not meant to suggest that presidents always have more information than the public does. Instead, the assumption concentrates the analysis on the question at hand, which is whether presidents have the incentive to utilize expertise when they have it.

Alternatively, a president could have intelligence indicating that a foreign leader is involved in illegal activity such as drug trafficking but be unable to reveal the information without endangering undercover agents.

The purpose of assuming that a president cannot transmit all of his policy information to the electorate is obviously not to claim that a chief executive can never convince a reticent public to support his policies.[4] Instead, the purpose of the assumption is simply to focus the theory on analyzing the incentives for policy pandering, a behavior which by definition occurs only when the public and president do not agree about the optimal course of action. Once a president has shifted mass opinion to favor his position, the concern about policy pandering naturally becomes irrelevant.

Chapter 2 discussed how presidents have a greater ability to alter citizens' preferences about foreign affairs in comparison with domestic affairs. I was careful to note, however, that even on foreign policy issues presidents cannot universally command public support for their positions. In international as well as domestic affairs, a president may be forced to choose between following public opinion and supporting the course of action he believes would best serve society. Notwithstanding this applicability of the theory, in the empirical analysis I allow that a president's greater ability to alter citizens' preferences about foreign policy may cause pandering to be less likely in this domain.

Actors and Interests

The theory revolves around the actions of three types of players: a president, challenger, and electorate. This president wants to hold office as well as enact policies that are successful in the sense of producing good outcomes for voters. Scholars routinely claim that a president's behavior is also affected by his desire for a favorable historical legacy (e.g., Moe 1985; Skowronek 1993), and the policy motivation reflects this desire. Presidents are limited to serving two terms, and first-term presidents are assumed to discount the future. That is, given the choice between enacting a good policy now or in a subsequent term, they would prefer to do so right away.

The other actors include an electoral challenger and an electorate. The challenger's motivations are analogous to those of the incumbent president. He wants to hold office and enact policies that will give him a positive historical legacy.

---

4. However, it is worth underscoring that the literature suggests a president's ability to craft public opinion is more limited than commonly presumed (e.g., Edwards 1983 and 2003; Jacobs and Shapiro 2000).

Voters want to elect the candidate who will choose successful policies.[5] The theory assumes that the citizenry has common interests and accordingly analyzes it as a single representative voter; this assumption is adopted in other theories that analyze informational differences between the mass public and elected officials (e.g., Fearon 1999; Persson and Tabellini 1990). The purpose of abstracting from ideological or distributive differences is obviously not to suggest that they are unimportant. Indeed, the first half of the book focused on such differences, and they are accounted for in the empirical analysis of subsequent chapters. The purpose of abstracting from these types of conflicts here is to focus the Conditional Pandering Theory on the question at hand, which is whether informational differences in and of themselves give presidents perverse policy incentives.

Congress is not a player in the theory. The primary reason for this abstraction is to maintain focus on the matter of presidential pandering to public opinion. However, in the empirical examination, I control for factors related to executive-legislative bargaining.

Policy Competence

The Conditional Pandering Theory assumes that the president's ability to enact successful policies depends on his competence or quality. Thus while all presidents are presumed to have more policy information than the electorate has, different chief executives do not necessarily have the same level of expertise. These assumptions reflect that a president's policy information depends on institutional as well as personal factors. All inhabitants of the Oval Office have at their disposal a vast bureaucracy headed by personal advisors. Chief executives differ, however, in their ability to manage this apparatus, a skill Fred Greenstein (2000) refers to as "organizational capacity."

In the theory, the incumbent president and challenger may be either "high quality" or "low quality" in terms of policy competence.[6] High-quality

5. In assuming that voters have policy motivations, I am not claiming that the American electorate is well informed about all salient policy issues. Rather, I am maintaining that voting is influenced by candidates' positions. The degree to which this influence is direct or, instead, depends on heuristics (e.g., Lupia 1994; Popkin 1991; Sniderman, Brody, and Tetlock 1991; Zaller 1992) is a matter outside the theoretical analysis.

6. This role of competence is one of the key differences between the Conditional Pandering Theory and the theory developed in Maskin and Tirole (2004). In Maskin and Tirole, all elected officials have the same level of competence. (Officials differ primarily by whether their preferences are congruent with those of voters.)

executives learn the state of the world with perfect accuracy, whereas low-quality ones do not. The candidates do not necessarily have the same level of competence, and each candidate's level is his private information.[7]

Voters' Beliefs

Voters do not initially know whether the incumbent or challenger is more likely to choose better policies. They only have an initial perception about the competence of each candidate. The electorate may initially believe that the incumbent is more competent than the challenger, that the two candidates are similarly competent, or that the challenger is more competent. Regardless of the initial perception, the electorate updates its beliefs about the incumbent's competence by observing his policy choice and any policy outcome that occurs.

Policy Resolution

A policy "resolves" in the theory when the electorate learns whether the choice was indeed in their interests. In other words, a policy resolves when voters learn whether it will succeed or fail. This concept of policy resolution does not rest on any claims that policies necessarily have one, final outcome but, rather, reflects that voters may learn more about the likely consequences of policies after they are enacted. The concept is therefore related to Key's (1961) notion of latent opinion.

In the Conditional Pandering Theory, the president does not know when a policy will resolve at the time that he enacts it. He only knows the probability that it will resolve prior to the upcoming election. One may interpret this assumption as reflecting that a president commonly does not know whether voters will learn the consequences of a policy choice by the next election; citizens may or may not acquire information that causes them to update their beliefs about whether the choice was a good one. I assume in the theory that the policy decision itself does not affect the likelihood that voters learn before the next election whether the enacted option is indeed in their interests. In other words, each option is associated with the same likelihood of resolving before the election.[8]

---

7. The key assumption is simply that high-quality presidents have better information than low-quality ones, not that the information of high-quality presidents is perfect.

8. The formal model in Canes-Wrone, Herron, and Shotts (2001) examines the consequences of allowing the president's choice to affect the probability of policy resolution prior to the election. The most significant effect of this change is that the president can have the incentive, under certain circumstances, to enact a policy that is not only unpopular but also that he believes will produce a bad outcome.

Action

The Conditional Pandering Theory analyzes actions that take place during two presidential administrations separated by an election. In each administration, the president is responsible for choosing a policy. As described above, the optimal choice corresponds to the given set of circumstances about which the incumbent president has information the public lacks. The two administrations face potentially different sets of circumstances.

Prior to any activity by the president, challenger, or electorate, the incumbent president observes a policy signal, which gives him expertise about the way in which the policy choice is likely to affect the policy outcome. After learning this information, the president proceeds to endorse a policy option. Voters then either learn whether the option will produce a good outcome or, instead, discover that this information will not be revealed until after the election. At the time of the election, the citizenry decide whether to retain the president for a second term or to replace him with the challenger. This decision is based on their beliefs about which candidate is most likely to enact policy in their interests. In the second administration, like the first, the president in office observes information about the optimal course of action and proceeds to endorse a policy option.

Behavior

The theory assumes that each actor maximizes his or her interests. In addition, the players update their beliefs about the optimal policy choice and the president's level of competence whenever possible.[9]

Policy Incentives

The assumptions of the Conditional Pandering Theory produce a relatively intricate set of policy incentives. I describe them by highlighting the ways in which the structural conditions influence the likelihood that the president chooses to endorse the popular policy option. In the theory, the president and electorate either agree about the appropriate course of action or have different beliefs about which policy should be selected. When their beliefs conform, the president's incentives are straightforward.

---

9. In the formal model that motivates the logic, the equilibrium concept employed is what is called "perfect Bayesian." The concept requires that the players' strategies comport with their updating of beliefs according to Bayes's Rule and that this updating incorporates the fact that each player will maximize his or her self-interest.

His desire for reelection and a positive historical legacy induce him to choose the popular policy, which he expects will produce a good outcome. It is when the president thinks a popular policy will ultimately fail that his incentives can be more complex. In this circumstance, he faces motivations to pursue the option he believes will succeed, but he can also have motivations to pander to public opinion.

The incentives for pandering are related to the electoral motivations. When the president is not running for reelection (i.e., when he is in his second term), his desire for a positive historical legacy induces him to support the policy he believes to be in citizens' interests even if it is currently unpopular. Of course, in reality American presidents who are serving a second term may behave as if they are running for reelection. For example, a chief executive could want his vice-president or another fellow partisan to succeed him. As a result, in the empirical analysis I allow that second-term presidents may not behave like first-term ones. Specifically, I separately examine the behavior of first- and second-term presidents.

Although the incentives for pandering derive from the president's electoral motivations, voters in the theory paradoxically want to elect a candidate who is unlikely to pander to them. Their interests are best served by having a leader who will choose the optimal policy, regardless of whether it is popular. The president's incentive to pander to public opinion derives from the electorate's uncertainty about whether the president or challenger is most likely to choose good policies. Voters only have an initial estimate of each candidate's level of competence and update their estimate of the president's competence immediately after his policy decision. At that point, they increase their assessment of him if he chooses the policy they believe to be in their interests, regardless of the accuracy of that belief.

The president thus faces two types of tradeoffs when his information implies citizens are misinformed about the optimal course of action. The first tradeoff concerns the distinction between short- and long-run public opinion. Immediately after the president enacts a popular policy, voters think more highly of him. However, as soon as the outcome of the policy becomes known, their evaluations depend entirely on whether it succeeded or failed. The president's concern about short-run public opinion thus encourages him to enact the popular policy, while his concern about long-run public opinion encourages him to pursue the policy he believes will produce a good outcome. The second tradeoff involves the president's desire for a strong historical legacy. Under certain conditions, this desire may propel the president to choose an unpopular policy that he believes will produce a good outcome. Under other conditions, however, the president would prefer to choose the popular policy in order to get reelected for another term, during which he could establish a favorable legacy.

Precisely when will the president's optimal strategy be to exercise policy leadership as opposed to pandering? I describe these incentives as a function of his popularity relative to that of his challenger. This relative popularity can be divided into three main categories: highly popular, unpopular, and marginally popular. The first category refers to situations in which the incumbent's relative popularity is high enough that voters would reelect him even if he enacted a policy that lacked public support and they did not learn the consequences of the policy. The unpopular category encompasses the inverse set of circumstances. In this case, the president's relative popularity is low enough that he would not be reelected if he supported a popular policy that did not produce an outcome prior to the election. Marginally popular presidents are the ones whose relative popularity is between these two thresholds. In this category, if voters did not learn before the election whether the president's choice was a good one, they would reelect him if and only if he had chosen the option they initially supported.

I first describe the policy incentives for highly popular presidents. One might suppose that electorally motivated presidents always have the incentive to increase their popularity by pandering to public opinion. However, the Conditional Pandering Theory predicts that a highly popular president will not pander. Such an incumbent will lose an impending election only if voters realize beforehand that he has made a bad policy choice. Therefore, he has the incentive to support policies he believes will succeed. By doing so, he minimizes the probability that a policy failure occurs before voters cast their ballots.

For instance, assume a highly popular president faced public pressure to allow fewer legal immigrants into the country, and he had information suggesting such a reform would negatively affect the economy. If the president were to impose the restrictions on immigration, his popularity would increase immediately after enacting the policy. However, voters already have high evaluations of his competence relative to that of his likely challenger, and if the economy were negatively affected by the reform, voters would substantially decrease their assessments of his competence. His optimal strategy is thus to avoid the temptation to pander to public opinion.

Given highly popular presidents' incentives to avoid policy pandering, one might expect unpopular presidents to be strongly motivated to engage in this behavior. After all, an unpopular incumbent cannot retain his position unless he improves voters' perception of him, and pandering would increase this perception right after the policy decision is announced. An unpopular president's optimal strategy, however, is to exercise policy leadership. These presidents fall into two subgroups. In the first, the president is so unpopular that regardless of his policy decisions, he will be removed from office. Given this lack of electoral motivations, the incumbent's desire for a strong historical legacy induces him to pursue the program he believes will succeed. The second subgroup concerns presidents who, while unpopular, may still retain office if they can prove their policy competence to voters. For these presidents, the best way to demonstrate such competence is to endorse an option that succeeds before the election. An unpopular incumbent's electoral incentive is therefore to choose the option recommended by his policy information and hope voters learn his judgment was sound before casting their ballots.[10]

Consider the case of an unpopular president who is deciding whether to deploy U.S. troops to fight anti-U.S. rebels in another country. The president believes the rebels could pose a danger to U.S. interests and has information suggesting the operation could be accomplished without a loss of troops. The public, while it does not support the rebels, believes they do not pose any danger and would prefer not to send troops because of fears of casualties. If the president wages the mission and it is accomplished without casualties, voters' evaluations of the president's competence will rise dramatically. If, on the other hand, the president follows public opinion, his popularity will increase slightly until voters learn whether the decision was a good one, but the increase is not sufficient to win him reelection. Moreover, if the president panders to public opinion and voters learn before the election that the lack of military engagement has harmed American interests, then the pandering actually decreases his prospects for reelection.

The Conditional Pandering Theory thus finds that highly popular and unpopular presidents do not engage in policy pandering. The only presidents who do so are marginally popular ones, and even they do not always pander. For example, given a sufficiently high probability that voters will learn before the election whether a policy choice succeeded, even marginally popular presidents want to exercise policy leadership. In this circumstance, voters will likely base their electoral decisions on the policy outcome, not the choice in and of itself. Presidents therefore want to endorse the option most likely to produce a good outcome.

10. It is worth underscoring that the initial configuration of presidential beliefs and public opinion influence voters' reactions to policy outcomes. Thus, for instance, a president can receive a larger boost in (personal) popularity from backing an unpopular policy that produces a good outcome than a popular one that does so.

It is only when voters are unlikely to learn before the election whether a policy choice succeeded that a marginally popular president will pander.[11] Under these circumstances, the increase in approval the incumbent receives from promoting a popular policy makes him likely to win reelection. The behavior still augments the possibility of a policy failure before the election and, in expectation, detracts from his historical legacy. However, because voters are unlikely to learn about the policy failure before they cast their ballots, the boost in popularity overwhelms these drawbacks. The president wants to pander now and hopefully create a favorable historical legacy in the next term.[12]

Employing again the example of a chief executive who faces public pressure for immigration restrictions that he believes would harm the economy, assume now that he is marginally popular. If the economic effects are unlikely to take hold before he faces a contest for reelection, the president has the incentive to pander to public opinion. Voters will approve of his policy choice immediately after he makes it, and they probably will not learn about the associated costs until after the ballots are cast. If instead, however, the economic effects are likely to occur immediately, the president's electoral incentive is to exercise policy leadership. If voters are likely to learn before the election that their interests have not been served by the immigration restrictions, he will want to avoid being associated with such a policy.

General Results

The description of the incentives suggests five general propositions about a president's likelihood of pandering to public opinion when he believes the mass public is misinformed about the optimal policy decision. These propositions are:

Proposition 1: Policy Leadership from Ahead. When a president is highly popular and believes the mass public misapprehends the optimal policy decision, his incentive is to exercise policy leadership.

Proposition 2: Policy Leadership from Behind. When a president is

11. In the formal model, even if a president is marginally popular and his policy options are unlikely to produce an outcome before the election, his optimal strategy is not to pander if he knows the optimal policy choice with certainty.

12. In the formal model, the strategy of pandering involves what game theorists call a "mixed strategy equilibrium." That is, the president panders with a given probability that is less than one and voters reelect him with a probability less than one. The reason that the president does not always pander is that he wants to give voters the impression he is not simply catering to current opinion but instead choosing the policy he believes will produce a good outcome for society.

unpopular and believes the mass public misapprehends the optimal policy decision, his incentive is to exercise policy leadership.

Proposition 3: Policy Leadership Early in Term. When voters are likely to learn before the next election whether a president's policy choice produced a good outcome and he believes the mass public misapprehends the optimal policy decision, his incentive is to exercise policy leadership.

Proposition 4: Policy Leadership Absent Electoral Motivations. When a president lacks electoral motivations and believes the mass public misapprehends the optimal policy decision, his incentive is to exercise policy leadership.

Proposition 5: Conditional Policy Pandering. When a president has electoral motivations, is marginally popular, and when voters are unlikely to learn before the next election whether his policy choice produced a good outcome, he has an incentive to pander to public opinion.

The propositions highlight that presidents can have incentives to cater to public opinion at the expense of pursuing good public policy but only under a restricted set of conditions. When a president is relatively popular or unpopular, when voters are likely to learn the outcome of an enacted policy before casting their ballots, and when a president lacks electoral motivations, his optimal policy behavior is to endorse the option he believes will succeed even if it lacks public support. Only if none of these conditions hold will a president have the incentive to pander to public opinion at the expense of citizens' interests.

These results offer some justification for the concern that presidents' monitoring of public opinion could encourage policymaking that places citizens' passions above their interests. Under routine conditions, a president's attention to current opinion gives him the incentive to appease citizens even though he believes they are misinformed about the optimal course of action. It is not the case, however, that he will categorically cater to public opinion. Under a multitude of circumstances, he is motivated to pursue the policies he believes will advance societal welfare even if they are not in line with public sentiments. Moreover, this willingness to buck current opinion is not exclusively a function of nonelectoral factors such as the president's desire for a strong historical legacy, his character, or an ability to craft public opinion. Electoral motivations induce a chief executive to exercise policy leadership under a variety of circumstances. For instance, when the president is highly popular or unpopular, and when voters are likely to learn whether his policy choice was a good one, his electoral incentive is to enact the policy most likely to be successful even if it lacks public support at the time.

The Conditional Pandering Theory not only generates predictions about presidents' incentives to pander to public opinion; it also generates predictions about variation in the overall amount of congruence between presidents' positions and public opinion. This overall policy congruence is akin to what is often characterized as "presidential responsiveness" in the literature. That is, the congruence reflects that an executive decision is aligned with current opinion. The president may simply agree with the public about the optimal course of action, or he may be pandering in the sense that the term is employed here.

The Conditional Pandering Theory predicts that whenever the president and public favor the same policy option, the president simply endorses this option. As a result, variation in the probability of policy congruence is entirely a function of variation in the probability of pandering. The following proposition summarizes this relationship.

Proposition 6: Policy Congruence and Policy Pandering. Variation in the probability of policy congruence between the president's position and public opinion is determined by variation in the probability of policy pandering.

The proposition implies that policy congruence should be most likely when the president is marginally popular, is running for reelection, and voters are unlikely to learn before the election whether his policy choice was a good one. Of course, because the president and citizens may simply agree about the optimal course of action, policy congruence can still occur if the president is not electorally motivated, if he is highly popular or unpopular, and if the electorate is likely to learn before voting whether his choice succeeded. Congruence should be less common in these circumstances, however, because pandering should not transpire.

RELATED LITERATURE

As mentioned at the start of the chapter, most work on presidential responsiveness to public opinion does not analyze the extent to which such responsiveness is in voters' interests. Still, a detailed comparison between the Conditional Pandering Theory and the literature is informative. First, the findings of the theory can be juxtaposed with the arguments of the few studies that explicitly address the possibility of a president's catering to current opinion at the expense of citizens' interests. In addition, the findings can be contrasted with prior predictions regarding the overall level of congruence between the president's positions and public opinion.

I classify the existing studies into five groups, which reflect five different perspectives on the relationship between presidential policy decisions and public opinion. The perspectives are entitled, respectively, Dynamic Representation, Need-Based Popularity, Lack of Substantive Responsiveness, Latent Opinion, and Electoral Cycle. In the interest of maintaining focus, I do not review the large literatures on congressional and judicial responsiveness except where they specifically concern one of the schools of thought.[13]

Dynamic Representation

Several recent studies suggest that presidents are highly responsive to public opinion. For instance, John Geer (1996) argues that scientific polling has enabled modern presidents to follow public opinion better than their predecessors could. This argument receives support from Erikson, MacKuen, and Stimson (2002a and 2002b; also Stimson, MacKuen, and Erikson 1995), who show that during the presidencies of Eisenhower through Clinton, change in the liberalism of the public mood was correlated with subsequent change in the presidents' positions over roll-call votes and Supreme Court cases.[14] Like the Conditional Pandering Theory, these studies imply that mass opinion plays an important role in presidential policymaking. However, unlike the theory, the studies are agnostic as to whether presidents follow public opinion when they believe doing so will harm society. Also unlike the theory, this research does not relate the likelihood of policy congruence to structural conditions such as the electoral cycle or the president's popularity.[15]

Need-Based Popularity

A few studies intimate that a president's responsiveness to public opinion is related to his popularity but not in the way predicted by the Conditional Pandering Theory. Specifically, existing research suggests

13. For an excellent review of research on the policy responsiveness of elected officials, including judges and legislators, see Manza and Cook (2002).

14. This result is consistent with Monroe (1979) and Page and Shapiro (1983), who find that change in public opinion on individual issues is systematically correlated with change in overall government policy. Notably, Page and Shapiro caution that this congruence may not reflect democratic responsiveness because the change in policy may have occurred independently of that in public opinion.

15. Thus whereas Geer argues that advances in polling have made presidents more likely to follow public opinion in general, the Conditional Pandering Theory indicates this increased sensitivity to mass opinion should be related to political conditions such as the electoral cycle and the president's popularity.

that the likelihood of policy congruence should be higher the less popular the president is. The president responds to public opinion on a "need basis." When his popularity is low, he tries to increase it by catering to public opinion, but when his approval is high he can afford to lose some of it by taking unpopular positions. Manza and Cook (2002) advance this perspective, supporting it with evidence from Douglas Hibbs's (1987) results on macroeconomic policymaking. Research on presidential popularity also comports with this school of thought. For instance, Douglas Rivers and Nancy Rose (1985) and Paul Brace and Barbara Hinckley (1992) show that a president takes more roll-call positions the higher his popularity, and this finding is interpreted to suggest that presidents capitalize on their public approval.[16]

This perspective that policy congruence is more likely the less popular is a president, which I call the Need-based Popularity perspective, differs critically from the Conditional Pandering Theory. The theory suggests that presidents will not pander when they are highly popular *and* when they are unpopular. Thus, the likelihood of pandering as well as overall policy congruence increases as a president's popularity increases from low to average popularity. In comparison, the Need-based Popularity perspective suggests that the likelihood of congruence will always decrease as the president's popularity rises. Other differences between the two schools of thought are also worth noting. The Conditional Pandering Theory predicts that early in a term a president's popularity will not affect the probability of pandering or congruence. The Need-based Popularity perspective, in contrast, applies equally across the president's term. Also unlike the Conditional Pandering Theory, the Need-based Popularity perspective is agnostic as to whether a president's willingness to follow public opinion is ultimately harmful to society.

Lack of Substantive Responsiveness and Crafting of Public Opinion

In contrast to the Dynamic Representation and Need-based Popularity perspectives, two recent and influential works advance the argument that presidents generally are not substantively responsive to public opinion. The first of these works, Cohen (1997), maintains that presidents will respond to public opinion through symbolic actions but not substantive policymaking. He observes that one reason for this behavior may be that

---

16. Research on legislative behavior provides further support for this perspective. Specifically, Figlio (2000) finds that a senator's margin of victory affects her ability to take unpopular positions without subsequently losing her seat; the higher her margin of victory, the more latitude she has to vote against public opinion in her state.

presidents care about producing good policy results. However, Cohen does not analyze whether the lack of substantive responsiveness is caused by presidential concern for expected policy consequences. Instead, he examines the degree of congruence between presidents' positions and public opinion.

Cohen's analysis of policy congruence has two main parts. The first involves quantitative examination of the effects of public opinion on the liberalism of presidents' roll-call positions and State of the Union addresses during the presidencies of Dwight Eisenhower through George H. W. Bush. The second part entails case studies of individual policy decisions. The quantitative analysis provides a good deal of support for Cohen's thesis. Except in the policy domain of civil rights, the liberalism of the mass public does not appear to influence presidents' overall liberalism. As Cohen admits, however, the case studies present more mixed evidence; in this analysis, at times presidents respond to public opinion and at other times they discount it. Cohen suggests this variation is a function of different degrees of presidential commitments to the policies. Therefore, unlike the Conditional Pandering Theory, Cohen does not argue that presidential pandering occurs routinely or that structural conditions influence variation in policy congruence between the president's position and public opinion.

Jacobs and Shapiro (2000; 2002a) similarly predict a low level of substantive responsiveness. Specifically, they contend that politicians do not respond to existing opinion but instead use modern tools of political communication to try to craft public support. To illustrate this point, Jacobs and Shapiro analyze Clinton's efforts to shape public sentiment over his proposal for nationalized health care and the Republican Party's endeavor to generate support for the Contract with America. The scholars allow that electoral proximity may generate some degree of responsiveness as politicians may lack the time to craft public opinion immediately before an election. Otherwise, however, the predictions on responsiveness are consistent with those of Cohen.

While Jacobs and Shapiro grant that a president's regard for citizens' long-run interests may on rare occasion influence his behavior, they attribute the general lack of responsiveness to ideological differences between politicians and the mass public. Thus unlike the Conditional Pandering Theory, Jacobs and Shapiro contend that the president will not routinely base his policy decisions on current opinion. Nor will these decisions be based on whether the president believes the policy results will enhance societal welfare.

Latent Opinion

Ideas closer to those of the Conditional Pandering Theory are presented in Zaller's (2003) call for a revival of scholarly attention to Key's concept of latent opinion. Following Key (1961), as well as Morris Fiorina (1981) and R. Douglas Arnold (1990), Zaller contends that voters are more concerned with policy results than initial policy decisions. Accordingly, he argues that a president will rationally ignore current opinion if he believes citizens are misinformed about how best to achieve desired policy outcomes and, moreover, can shape policymaking so that these outcomes will occur before the next election. When the president lacks the power to shape policymaking in this way, he will cater to current opinion, even if the citizenry is misinformed about their interests. Thus Zaller suggests that policy pandering may occur.

The Conditional Pandering Theory is certainly comparable to this line of reasoning. However, it differs in several key respects, which together suggest that pandering, and hence policy congruence, are less likely than Zaller's discussion implies. The theory predicts that a highly popular president does not pander to public opinion even if voters are unlikely to learn the outcome of his policy choice before the next election. In addition, the theory forecasts that unpopular incumbents do not pander. Zaller's logic thus applies only to the category of marginally popular presidents.

Electoral Cycle

Consistent with the argument that policy decisions are influenced by the likelihood voters learn the policy consequences before the next election, a range of work suggests electoral cycles affect politicians' behavior. For instance, various studies demonstrate that legislators take more moderate positions when they will soon be facing an electoral contest (e.g., Elling 1982; Kuklinski 1978; Thomas 1985; Wright and Berkman 1986).[17] Similarly, research on political economy establishes that as elections approach, politicians appropriate more funding (e.g., Kiewiet and McCubbins 1985; Levitt 1997) and expand the money supply (e.g.,

17. Except for Kuklinski, this work focuses on the behavior of U.S. senators. Kuklinski compares the voting behavior of California state senators, who are elected for four-year terms, with the voting behavior of California state assemblymen, who serve two-year terms. He finds that the senators become more reactive to constituency opinion in the second half of their terms, while the assemblymen are consistently responsive throughout their terms.

Lohmann 1999; Nordhaus 1975). Naturally, this work does not prove that executive policy decisions are influenced by the electoral cycle; it could be the case, for example, that legislators respond to the electoral cycle but presidents do not. In fact, the quantitative analysis of Cohen (1997) suggests that the imminence of elections does not affect presidents' (lack of) substantive responsiveness to public opinion.

Even so, the broader literature implies that the electoral cycle may affect presidential policy decisions, and this implication is consistent with the Conditional Pandering Theory. According to the theory, presidents have the incentive to pander to public opinion only when voters are unlikely to learn before the next election whether a policy succeeded. Thus the likelihood of pandering, and consequently the overall level of policy congruence, should increase as an election approaches. The theory still differs from prior work on electoral cycles in several ways, however. First, the prior research does not suggest that the electoral cycle should influence the likelihood of pandering, just the likelihood of policy congruence. Second, the work does not indicate that a president's popularity necessarily affects the probability of pandering or policy congruence.

CONCLUSION

The Conditional Pandering Theory offers a distinct perspective regarding presidential responsiveness to public opinion. Unlike most work on this subject, the theory analyzes a president's incentives to follow current opinion when he believes the public is misinformed. In analyzing this behavior, which is labeled policy pandering, the theory also provides predictions about variation in overall policy congruence between the president's positions and public opinion. The predictions about pandering and policy congruence contrast with those of the literature.

The president is found to lack the incentive to engage in policy pandering when he is highly popular, when he is unpopular, and when voters are likely to learn before the next election whether a policy succeeded. Only when the president is marginally popular and the mass public is unlikely to learn the outcome of a policy choice before an impending election does he have the incentive to pander to public opinion. Pandering thus occurs in a limited set of circumstances. Notably, this constrained amount of pandering is not a function of a public that is disengaged or a president who has purely altruistic motives; the Conditional Pandering Theory assumes that the public is attentive and that the president has electoral motivations. The theory thus suggests that presidents' monitoring of current opinion does not typically encourage demagogic policymaking.

The predictions regarding policy congruence are related to those regarding pandering. The theory implies that the likelihood of congruence decreases when a moderately popular president loses or gains public support. Furthermore, as an election nears, congruence becomes more likely, occurring most frequently for presidents who are marginally popular. Congruence between presidents' policy decisions and public opinion thus depends on structural conditions.

Of course, it remains possible that the Conditional Pandering Theory does not provide a realistic portrayal of presidential decision making. As of yet, I have not offered any empirical evidence for the theory. The following chapters assess its validity in two complementary ways. I begin by conducting three case studies and then proceed to analyze a larger data set of presidential policy decisions.

CHAPTER SIX

Examples of Policy Pandering and Leadership

Why did Jimmy Carter, a long-time proponent of expanding humanitarian assistance, suddenly propose to scale back the program? Why did Ronald Reagan, who was philosophically opposed to tax increases, recommend an unpopular one? And why did George H. W. Bush veto a bill extending unemployment benefits only to sign similar bills over the course of the following eight months?

For each of these presidential decisions, I assess whether the stylized facts fit the Conditional Pandering Theory and proceed to examine whether alternative accounts may also explain the president's policymaking. The analysis has two primary benefits. First, it establishes that the theory has explanatory power. In each case, a president's actions are inconsistent with his previous behavior, and the theory reconciles the apparent inconsistency. Second, by detailing presidents' beliefs, concerns, and actions over a few critical decisions, the analysis illustrates how the theory works in practice. In particular, the cases illustrate the behaviors of *policy pandering* and *policy leadership*. Pandering reflects circumstances in which a president supports a popular policy option despite the fact that he expects it to harm citizens' interests. Policy leadership, in comparison, occurs when a president endorses an unpopular option that he believes will advance societal welfare.

Because the case studies combine a "rational choice" theory with historical narrative, they contribute to the growing literature on the application of formal theory to the study of political history.[1] This literature is broad, and it is worth noting that the following analysis differs in purpose from some research in this vein. In particular, the "analytical narratives" research program of Robert Bates et al. (1998) uses historical case studies to motivate theories. Here, the theory is deductive and the cases illustrative. Such a use of narrative analysis is consistent with the research

1. For a discussion of this literature, see Cameron (2000).

program Charles Cameron (2000) terms "model-driven history." In particular, the theory serves as a framework for interpreting a sequence of historical events.

CASE SELECTION

The primary motivation for developing the Conditional Pandering Theory was to assess the incentives of the president to pander to public opinion when forced to choose between endorsing a popular course of action or one he believes will produce a good outcome for society. Given this substantive aim, I focus the narrative analysis on executive decisions for which the president's beliefs regarding the optimal policy choice differed from those of the mass public. As previously discussed, the concept of policy pandering does not require that a president's beliefs regarding the optimal course of action are necessarily correct. Accordingly, in the cases, the fact that a president deemed the mass citizenry to be misguided does not mean that the reader will necessarily agree with the president's assessment.

The need to ascertain the president's beliefs in relation to public opinion made the selection of cases contingent on the availability of historical evidence on these factors. Even so, I imposed a number of additional restrictions regarding the selection. First, to illustrate how the theoretical predictions vary according to the president's popularity relative to that of his likely competition, I ensured that one case concerned a president far ahead of his likely competition, one a president far behind, and one a president who could expect a tight race. Using the language of chapter 5, at least one case involved a highly popular president, one an unpopular chief executive, and one a marginally popular president. Thus, in the narratives, presidential approval ratings are often employed as a proxy for a chief executive's popularity relative to that of his potential competition. Prior research establishes that this factor is correlated with a president's likelihood of retaining office (e.g., Brody and Sigelman 1983; Sigelman 1979). By comparison, trial heats are not particularly accurate assessments of a president's electoral prospects until the final months of a race; indeed, trial heats are not even routinely available throughout a president's term.

The second restriction is that the universe of potential cases was limited to the decisions of presidents since Nixon. The literature suggests that these presidents have been more likely than their predecessors to involve the mass public in policymaking (e.g., Kernell 1997; Skowronek 1993); the restriction enables showing that the Conditional Pandering Theory is germane to these presidencies. Third, to demonstrate that the theory is not limited in applicability to a given administration or personality, I selected a different chief executive for each case. Fourth, I chose only policy decisions that were significant enough to receive coverage in the *Congressional Quarterly Almanac*. This restriction was inspired by a desire to establish that the theory is relevant to relatively important policy decisions. Finally, the selection was influenced by the fact that presidents can more easily change public opinion in foreign as compared with domestic affairs. Because of this asymmetry, one might suppose that presidential pandering would be uncommon in foreign affairs and common in domestic matters. To demonstrate the relevance of the Conditional Pandering Theory across both domains, I illustrate the behavior of policy pandering with decisions involving foreign affairs and the behavior of policy leadership with decisions on domestic matters.

A substantial portion of each narrative is devoted to describing why seemingly plausible alternative explanations do not explain the sequence of events. This attention to alternative explanations is partially a function of the fact that one would not necessarily anticipate truth revelation by presidents and their advisors. Chief executives are not likely to admit, even in retrospect, that they followed public opinion despite having evidence suggesting the action would produce harmful effects. (Nor are presidents particularly likely to state that electoral motivations were what lead them to take an unpopular position, as occurs in the Conditional Pandering Theory when first-term presidents exercise policy leadership.) The narratives accordingly do not revolve around "smoking guns" of admissions by presidents but, instead, careful attention to their long-standing beliefs, public opinion, and possible alternative accounts.

PRESIDENT CARTER AND FOREIGN AID: THE TRUSTEE PANDERS

Carter is reputed to have placed the public interest above other political objectives. For example, Erwin Hargrove (1988, 11) assesses in his biography of Carter: "The key of Carter's understanding of himself as a political leader was his belief that the essential responsibility of leadership was to articulate the good of the entire community rather than any part of it . . . Rather than being antipolitical or nonpolitical leadership, this was, for him, a different kind of leadership that eschewed the normal politician's preoccupation with representing private interests, bargaining, and short-term electoral goals." Similarly, Charles Jones (1988) characterizes Carter's regime as the "trusteeship presidency," in which the chief executive viewed himself as a trustee of the people and sought to enact policies he believed were in the public interest even when they were not politically expedient. Precisely because of this reputation, I illustrate the behavior of pandering with a case study that concerns President Carter. By establishing that the Conditional Pandering Theory has relevance for his policy decisions, I show it is applicable even to presidents who are not thought to cater to public opinion.

The case study focuses on Carter's budgetary proposal for the policy issue of humanitarian assistance in 1980, the year he ran for reelection. Upon taking office, Carter had pledged to switch U.S. policy toward communist containment in the Third World. Instead of responding militarily whenever conflicts over communism arose, Carter espoused a "preventive" approach. He sought to lessen the appeal of communism to the citizens of Third World nations by solving their underlying problems (e.g., Deibel 1987; Skidmore 1996). Development assistance comprised a key component of this preventive approach.

For the first three years of Carter's term, his proposals for humanitarian assistance, or economic aid, were consistent with this philosophy. In each year, Carter requested an increase and he invariably achieved one, even if not for the full amount he had requested. He pursued this expansion despite a lack of public support for the program; according to responses to the General Social Survey, throughout his administration over 65 percent of the populace believed the United States spent too much on foreign aid.[2]

Carter knew that his policy position was unpopular. He acknowledged as much during a call-in radio show he hosted during the first few months in office. Stating his policy stance to a caller, Carter began, "Well, John [the caller], I'm going to take a position that's not very popular, politically speaking."[3] Likewise, in a session with media representatives during the second year of the administration, Carter remarked, "I don't know of any issue that has less political support than that program itself, foreign aid in all its forms."[4]

2. The survey asked, "We are faced with many problems in this country, none of which can be solved easily or inexpensively. I'm going to name some of these problems, and for each one I'd like you to tell me whether you think we're spending too much money on it, too little money, or about the right amount. Are we spending too much money, too little money, or about the right amount on foreign aid?"

3. Jimmy Carter, "'Ask President Carter' Remarks During a Telephone Call-in Program on the CBS Radio Network," March 5, 1977, *Public Papers of the Presidents of the United States, 1977 Book 1* (Washington, DC: Government Printing Office, 1977).

4. Jimmy Carter, "Remarks and a Question-and-Answer Session with a Group of Editors and News Directors," May 19, 1978, *Public Papers of the Presidents of the United States, 1978 Book 1* (Washington, DC: Government Printing Office, 1978).

Carter's lack of pandering over foreign aid during his first three years in office is consistent with his reputation for placing the public interest above other, more political objectives. His behavior also, however, comports with the Conditional Pandering Theory. The theory suggests that a president will not pander to public opinion if he does not soon face a contest for reelection or if he is highly popular or unpopular. In the early months of 1977 and 1978, when Carter submitted his foreign aid proposals as a part of his annual budgetary requests, the presidential election was relatively distant. By the outset of 1979, when Carter offered his humanitarian aid proposal for the following fiscal year, the electoral race was approaching but Carter's popularity was weak. His public approval ratings for the past year had averaged 43 percent, a very low level by historical standards.[5] His decision to exercise policy leadership is thus consistent with the Conditional Pandering Theory.

Of course, that Carter's policymaking on foreign aid between 1977 and 1979 comports with the Conditional Pandering Theory does not eliminate the possibility that his actions were entirely the consequence of his character. For this reason, we focus on the humanitarian aid proposal Carter offered in 1980, when he reversed his previous position and recommended that the United States cut economic assistance. Specifically, in his budget of January 1980 (which was for fiscal year 1981), Carter proposed cutting economic assistance by 2 percent in nominal terms. The cut constituted a nominal decline of 26 percent relative to his recommendation in the previous budget.[6] Moreover, given the inflation rate predicted by the administration, his request signified a real reduction of 11 percent from the appropriations of last year and 39 percent from his earlier proposal.[7]

The descriptive summaries accompanying the numbers in Carter's budgets reflect the change in his policy position. The budget submitted in 1979 stated that it contained "increases in foreign aid with emphasis on long-term development of poor countries, and reducing widespread

5. The average annual approval rating of Presidents Kennedy through Ford was 54 percent. See Ragsdale (1998, 198).

6. The president's proposal for fiscal year 1981 was calculated from his 1981 budget, which was submitted on January 28 of 1980. See the *Budget of the United States Government, 1981* (Washington, DC: Government Printing Office, 1980). Also, this proposal is reflected in HR 7854 according to the *Congressional Quarterly Almanac,* vol. 36, 1980 (Washington, DC: Congressional Quarterly, Inc., 1981). The data on enacted appropriations and the president's proposal in the previous year are from the 1980 *Congressional Quarterly Almanac.*

7. See the *Economic Report of the President,* submitted January 30 of 1980 to Congress.

poverty."[8] In contrast, the budget submitted in 1980 characterized the proposals for foreign affairs as "designed to help meet the near-term challenges to stability."[9] This budget was also printed in the colors of Carter's reelection campaign, emphasizing the linkage between the document and election year politics (Hargrove 1988).

When Carter submitted his election-year budget, he had reason to believe the impending presidential race would be competitive. His approval ratings were respectable at 58 percent but not remarkably high by historical standards.[10] Moreover, economists were forecasting an imminent recession that would cause double-digit inflation and an increase in unemployment.[11] Carter knew that the recession, assuming it materialized, could cause him serious problems in his campaign for reelection. As a result, he very much wanted his budget to appeal to voters (Kaufman 1993, 168–69).

Carter's policy reversal on foreign aid helped to achieve this goal. By proposing a reduction in economic assistance, he ensured that his position on this program would be consonant with public opinion. According to a Roper survey taken the month before he submitted his budget, 72 percent of the population thought foreign assistance should be decreased.[12] Had Carter continued trying to expand economic aid, he would have handed challengers an easy issue on which to criticize him.

Thus consistent with the Conditional Pandering Theory, Carter switched his position in the direction of public opinion once he was marginally popular and soon faced a contest for reelection. He could reasonably expect that the effects of cutting economic assistance would not be known by voters before the election, particularly since appropriations bills are not typically enacted until summer at the earliest. Moreover, the anticipated competitiveness of the race meant that his policy choice might affect his likelihood of winning. As a result, Carter had an electoral incentive to take the popular position of cutting humanitarian

8. *Budget of the United States Government, 1980* (Washington, DC: Government Printing Office, 1979), p. 19.

9. *Budget of the United States Government, 1981,* p. 7.

10. As mentioned in footnote 5 of this chapter, the average annual approval rating of Presidents Kennedy through Ford was 54 percent. See Ragsdale (1998, 198).

11. For further details on the economic forecasts, see: Art Pine, "Cautious Economics: Good Politics this Year," *Washington Post,* January 13, 1980, G26. See also Art Pine, "A Year of Little Promise; If Anything, Economic Predictions about 1980 May Prove Worse," *Washington Post,* January 13, 1980, G1.

12. Survey conducted December 1–8, 1979. The question wording is identical to that in footnote 2 of this chapter.

assistance, even if he believed that increasing it was in America's long-term interest.

Among seemingly plausible alternative explanations, none receives support on careful examination. Perhaps the most natural justification, and one that would comport with Carter's reputation for pursuing the public interest, is that his beliefs about the value of humanitarian assistance had changed. In fact, as Michael Genovese (1994) observes, there is a good deal of evidence that Carter shifted from a "Wilsonian idealist" to a "Cold War confrontationist" as his term progressed. David Skidmore (1996) also describes this transformation in an analysis that is fittingly entitled *Reversing Course*. However, as these scholars acknowledge, the transformation began as early as 1978. Thus if the change in philosophy were the primary cause of Carter's policy reversal on foreign aid, the policy reversal should have occurred earlier.

Moreover, the budget that Carter proposed in his final month in office, after his electoral defeat, reiterated his commitment to a substantial growth in humanitarian assistance. He recommended increasing it by 26 percent in nominal terms, which, given the projected inflation rate, comprised a real increase of 12 percent. The justification Carter gave for this request in his Budget Message highlighted his continued belief in the importance of humanitarian assistance. He stated, "I believe in the need for higher levels of aid to achieve foreign policy objectives, promote economic growth, and help needy people abroad. Foreign aid is not politically popular and represents an easy target for budget reduction. But it is not a wise one." Carter's election-year proposal to decrease development assistance therefore cannot be attributed to a fundamental change in his convictions regarding the benefits of foreign aid.

Given that the policy shift cannot be ascribed to a change in Carter's convictions, I consider whether it can be attributed to factors specific to the time period in which it occurred. These alternative explanations include the macroeconomy, anticipated congressional behavior, and international events. I consider each in turn.

In January 1980, inflation was a major concern for President Carter and the public. During the past year, the consumer price index had increased by 12.4 percent and according to Gallup's Most Important Problem survey, 36 percent of citizens (a plurality of respondents) considered inflation to be the most important problem in the nation.[13] Carter accordingly designed his election-year budget with the goal of curbing

13. Survey conducted by the Gallup organization January 25–28, 1980. The survey asked the standard most important problem question, "What do you think is the most important problem in the nation today?" Responses were open-ended.

inflation (Hargrove 1988, 102–3; Kaufman 1993, 168–69). One could therefore argue that he proposed to cut humanitarian aid in order to help reduce inflation.

The key problem with this argument is that Carter's overall budget was not all that fiscally conservative. As Hargrove (1988, 103) assesses, the budget reflected that Carter was "not, in the final analysis, a conservative prepared to launch a period of austerity." In fact, Carter's budget entailed real increases in other, more popular programs. For example, Carter proposed conspicuous growth in funding for federal health programs and ground transportation, issues on which a majority of the public supported higher spending.[14] It is therefore difficult to conclude that Carter's desire to curb inflation was the primary determinant of his decision to recommend reducing humanitarian assistance.

A separate potential explanation for the policy shift involves Carter's congressional relations. In 1979, Congress failed to enact a Foreign Aid Appropriations Bill. The funding for international assistance programs came from continuing resolutions, which appropriated almost 20 percent less than the president had requested for the programs. Given these events, one might conjecture that Carter's policy reversal resulted from a change in his bargaining strategy.

The evidence suggests, however, that Carter's proposal to reduce international assistance did not reflect a general adjustment in his approach to budgetary negotiations. In fact, in the same budget he proposed expanding programs for which Congress had in the previous year appropriated far less than he had requested. For example, in 1979 Carter obtained 23 percent less funding than he had proposed for the District of Columbia, but in 1980 he still requested 9 percent more than he had in the previous budgetary cycle. Likewise, Congress appropriated 9 percent less than Carter recommended for agricultural spending in 1979, yet in 1980 the president recommended an increase of 20 percent relative to his proposal of the previous year. Carter thus did not system-

---

14. Carter proposed real increases of 9 percent in health programs and 4 percent in ground transportation. The public opinion data are from a Roper survey conducted December 1–8, 1979. Respondents were asked the (by-now familiar) question, "We are faced with many problems in this country, none of which can be solved easily or inexpensively. I'm going to name some of these problems, and for each one I'd like you to tell me whether you think we're spending too much money on it, too little money or about the right amount." For health, the question ended with "improving and protecting the nation's health" and for ground transportation, it ended with "improving the public transportation." The responses suggest that 59 percent of adults believed the government was spending too little on health and that 50 percent believed too little was being spent on public transportation.

atically lower his budgetary requests in response to previous failures to expand the programs.[15]

In keeping with this evidence that Carter's legislative negotiations differed by policy area, I consider as a final rationale for his policy shift an explanation particular to foreign aid. Specifically, I examine the possibility that an international event induced the president to desire a lower level of humanitarian assistance. In 1979 there were two major international incidents that affected U.S. interests: the abduction of American hostages in Iran in November 1979 and the Soviet invasion of Afghanistan in the following month. Ostensibly, these incidents could have affected Carter's beliefs concerning the value of bilateral assistance to the Soviet Union and Iran.

Regardless of the president's beliefs about such bilateral assistance, however, his proposal to reduce humanitarian aid could not be the consequence of them. As documented in the 1981 *Country Report on Human Rights Practices* prepared by the State Department, the United States offered no bilateral assistance to the Soviet Union or Iran in 1979.[16] Thus, Carter could not recommend cutting assistance to these countries.[17] A related possibility is that the Soviet invasion of Afghanistan and the Iranian hostage crisis induced the president to disfavor the use of humanitarian aid as a means of solving the problems of the Third World. Yet, as previously discussed, soon after the 1980 elections, Carter proposed a massive increase in humanitarian assistance. Thus the international events seem to have, if anything, strengthened the president's belief that humanitarian assistance would promote U.S. interests.[18]

In sum, Carter's policy reversal on foreign aid in 1980 cannot be attributed to a change in his belief system, the state of the economy, congressional relations, or to the major foreign events of the day. Nor is the shift consistent with his subsequent policy proposals on foreign aid. The decision does, however, comport with the Conditional Pandering Theory. When the election was distant or Carter's approval ratings were low, he

15. Jones's (1988) characterization of Carter's typical strategy for dealing with Congress also suggests that the president would not have altered his foreign aid proposal for the pure purpose of legislative bargaining. According to Jones (1998, 6–7), Carter "viewed himself as above the system of bargaining."

16. *Country Reports on Human Rights Practices,* report submitted to the Committee on Foreign Relations, U.S. Senate, and Committee on Foreign Affairs, U.S. House of Representatives, by the Department of State, February 2, 1981.

17. Carter did impose an embargo on the sale of grain to the Soviet Union, but this embargo did not affect appropriations for foreign assistance.

18. Nor did Carter shift his requests for humanitarian aid into security assistance; in nominal terms, Carter proposed a measly 0.002 percent increase in security aid.

pursued the course of action he believed to be in the public interest. Yet when the election was near and his public standing was such that he seemed likely to face a tight race, the president pandered to public opinion.

PRESIDENT BUSH AND UNEMPLOYMENT BENEFITS: POLICY LEADERSHIP FROM AHEAD AND PANDERING

Throughout the summer of 1991, President Bush looked likely to sail to reelection. His approval ratings had hit historically high levels in the wake of the Gulf War victory earlier that year and still hovered in the high 60s and low 70s.[19] Front-runners for the Democratic nomination decided one after another not to challenge the president. By September, Al Gore, Richard Gephardt, and Jay Rockefeller IV had all dropped out of the race. As Robert E. Denton and Mary E. Stuckey (1994, 19) surmise, "Bush simply seemed unbeatable."

This popularity was noteworthy given the lackluster economy over which the president was presiding. The gross national product (GNP) had increased only 0.4 percent during the second quarter of 1991, and this relatively meager growth followed nine months of GNP retraction.[20] As of June, the unemployment rate was approaching 7 percent.[21] Much of the unemployment involved middle-management workers who had been downsized by corporations. These managers were having a particularly difficult time finding alternative employment; many remained jobless at the time their unemployment benefits expired. The unemployment rate thus reflected a substantial number of workers who were not only out of work but also not receiving government assistance. For instance, in July 1991 unemployment compensation expired for 350,000 jobless Americans (Cohen 1997, 218).[22]

It was in this environment that Congress enacted a series of bills extending unemployment benefits. The first of these bills to reach Bush's desk was HR 3201, which arrived August 17. The legislation provided up to 20 weeks of extra benefits through July 1992 at an estimated cost of $5.3 billion. The legislation specified that for the compensation to be distributed, the president had to declare a state of emergency. Bush

19. Ragsdale (1998, 213).

20. Peter G. Gosselin, "Economy Rolling Again . . . But Slowly: Slight Gain in Gross National Product Worries Analysts," *Boston Globe,* July 27, 1991, 12.

21. U.S. Department of Labor, Bureau of Labor Statistics.

22. Cohen (1997) also analyzes Bush's policy decisions on unemployment benefits. Cohen does not, however, examine whether the decisions provide support for the Conditional Pandering Theory.

signed the bill but did not declare an emergency, thereby preventing the expenditure of the benefits.

The second unemployment bill to reach Bush's desk was S 1722, entitled the Emergency Unemployment Compensation Act of 1991. The bill, which was passed by Congress on October 1, again offered up to 20 weeks of extended benefits and had an estimated cost of $6.4 billion. Unlike the earlier legislation, S 1722 did not allow the president the option of signing the legislation without obligating the additional benefits. Bush could thus either veto the bill or enact the temporary extension.[23]

Surveys conducted around the time that Congress passed S 1722 suggest the bill was quite popular. A *Los Angeles Times* poll taken September 21 through 25 found that 63 percent of respondents favored the legislation strongly or at least somewhat, and only 33 percent opposed it.[24] Likewise, a Harris poll conducted September 27 through October 2 found that only 37 percent of respondents would rate the president's opposition to the bill as "excellent" or "pretty good."[25] These survey data suggest that to the extent Bush wished to placate the mass public, he had an incentive to endorse the legislation.

Bush's incentives were not straightforward, however, because he did not believe that the extension of unemployment benefits would promote a strong economy. As David Mervin (1996, 87) describes, the president was "particularly averse to government interference in the economy." This belief repeatedly put him in conflict with the Democratic-controlled Congress. Nicholas Calio, who was in charge of Bush's legislative relations, describes how the White House perceived congressional efforts to control the economy: "There were many things that, in our view, Congress got involved in [which] it really shouldn't—in micro managing markets . . . There were a lot of things we felt needed to be stopped."[26]

---

23. *Congressional Quarterly Almanac,* vol. 47 (1991), 304–8.

24. The question was: "Congress recently passed a bill to extend unemployment benefits beyond the regular 25-week period. To provide the 6.4 billion dollars needed to extend benefits, a budget emergency would have to be declared that President Bush says is not justified. Would you like to see Bush sign this bill into law, or do you think he should veto it?"

25. The question was: "Now let me ask you some specifics about President Bush. How would you rate him on . . . his opposition to a bill that would extend for 20 weeks unemployment insurance to unemployed workers whose benefits have run out . . . —excellent, pretty good, only fair or poor?" The responses of "only fair" and "poor" are reported jointly by Harris, with 59 percent of the population assigning Bush one of these ratings.

26. Quoted in Mervin (1996, 114).

The legislation S 1722, the Emergency Unemployment Compensation Act, was apparently one of those things. While the legislation was being considered, Bush openly referred to it as part of "a bunch of garbage" that the Democrats were sending his way.[27] In a news conference, he argued that the measure would ultimately harm taxpayers. Furthermore, he exhorted citizens to implore their representatives to "do something that the President can sign that will help us with unemployment benefits but will also protect the other taxpayer."[28] On October 11, Bush vetoed S 1722, declaring in an accompanying memorandum that it would "threaten economic recovery and its associated job creation." He continued, "the Congress has . . . ignored my call for passage of measures that will increase the nation's competitiveness, productivity and growth."[29]

For all of this strong language, Bush agreed to a measure quite similar to S 1722, HR 3575, less than two months later. HR 3575 extended unemployment benefits for up to 20 weeks through mid-June at an estimated cost of $5.3 billion. When the president signed the bill on November 15, his electoral vulnerability was much greater than it had been when he had vetoed S 1722. Headlines from the preceding weeks had declared "Democrats Find Bush Is Vulnerable" and "Democrat Hopefuls See Bush Weakness."[30] Correspondingly, his popularity ratings had dropped to 56 percent.[31]

The possibility that Bush switched his policy position for electoral reasons did not go unnoticed at the time. For example, Senator George Mitchell of Maine, referring to Bush's apparent reversal, asserted the president was in "panic city."[32] The administration rebuked such criticism and claimed the legislative negotiations had in fact culminated in a victory for the president over the details of how the unemployment benefits would be funded. According to the administration, the bill that Bush had originally vetoed would have increased the deficit and thus violated the

27. George Bush, "Remarks at a Republican Party Fundraising Dinner in East Brunswick, New Jersey," September 24, 1991, *Public Papers of the Presidents, 1991 Book 2* (Washington, DC: Government Printing Office, 1992).

28. George Bush, "The President's News Conference," October 4, 1991, *Public Papers of the Presidents, 1991 Book 2.*

29. George Bush, "Memorandum of Disapproval for the Emergency Unemployment Compensation Act of 1991," October 11, 1991, *Public Papers of the Presidents, 1991 Book 2.*

30. Andrew J. Glass, "Democrats Find Bush is Vulnerable," *Atlanta Journal and Constitution,* November 3, 1991, O5; Adam Pertman, "Democrat Hopefuls See Bush Weakness," *Boston Globe,* November 3, 1991, 213.

31. Ragsdale (1998), 213.

32. Michael Kranish, "Bush Bristles at Claims He Has Shifted," *Boston Globe,* November 17, 1991, 1.

1990 Budget Act, which required that any new program not add to the deficit. The bill he signed, in comparison, supposedly paid for itself through tax increases on the wealthy, the renewal of an employer tax, and a new policy of income confiscation from individuals who defaulted on school loans.[33]

Such a justification for Bush's action would have been more credible had the president not soon thereafter approved another temporary extension of unemployment benefits, HR 4095, which many believed would increase the deficit. Bush signed this subsequent legislation on February 7, 1992, after his popularity ratings had been hovering in the mid-40s for the past month.[34] HR 4095 provided an additional thirteen weeks of benefits, paying for them primarily through a "surplus" that the Office of Management and Budget (OMB) predicted would arise from 1991 tax bills.[35] The Congressional Budget Office (CBO) disputed the prediction of a surplus, and critics ridiculed the forecast.[36] For example, Representative Thomas J. Downey, a Democrat from Long Island, chided that "Only in the land of Oz could you take a $350 billion deficit and find $2 billion in savings."[37]

The claim that Bush did not switch his position seemed even more disingenuous in July 1992. On July 3, when the president was running neck-and-neck with Bill Clinton and Ross Perot in the pre-election polls, the president signed HR 5260, which permanently changed the unemployment system by allowing nonemergency benefits to take effect more easily during times of high unemployment.[38] As recently as April, Bush

33. *Congressional Quarterly Almanac,* vol. 48 (1992), 347–48.
34. Ragsdale (1998), 213.
35. *Congressional Quarterly Almanac,* vol. 48 (1992), 347.
36. Ibid.
37. To deal with the possibility that the additional unemployment compensation would add to the deficit, Congress voted to waive the 1990 Budget Act, which required that every new program pay for itself (*Congressional Quarterly Almanac,* vol. 48 [1992], 352).
38. For example, in a Gallup survey of the national adult population conducted on June 29, 32 percent of respondents supported Bush, 30 percent supported Clinton, and 28 percent supported Perot. In a Gallup survey of registered voters conducted between June 26 and July 1, 28 percent of the respondents supported Perot, 27 percent supported Bush, and 23 percent Clinton. The first survey asked, "Suppose the (1992) presidential election were being held today. If George Bush were the Republican candidate and Bill Clinton were the Democratic candidate and Ross Perot were an Independent candidate, who would you vote for? As of today, do you lean more to Bush, the Republican, to Clinton, the Democrat, or to Perot, the Independent?" The second survey asked, "Suppose the presidential election were being held today. If George Bush were the Republican candidate and Bill Clinton were the Democratic candidate and Ross Perot were an Independent candidate, who would you vote for?"

had opposed making such permanent changes to the system.[39] Even the day before signing HR 5260, the president had threatened to veto the permanent expansion.[40] The champion of the bill in Congress, Representative Thomas J. Downey, offered an explanation for Bush's actions during the brief House debate over the legislation. He predicted, "The President is going to sign this bill for two reasons. Unemployment is up, and his popularity is down."[41]

Does the variation in Bush's policy decisions over unemployment benefits correspond to the predictions of the Conditional Pandering Theory? The theory suggests that a president will endorse policies that he believes are in the public interest when he is quite popular relative to his likely electoral competition, when he is relatively unpopular, or when he does not soon face a contest for reelection. In this case, Bush supported an unpopular policy that he believed would advance a strong economy so long as his electoral prospects were strong. Once he seemed vulnerable, however, he changed course and issued popular decisions that did not reflect his belief that preventing government interference in the economy would harm it and, by consequence, societal welfare. This variation in executive behavior is exactly what the Conditional Pandering Theory would predict.

Some readers may take issue with the notion that Bush was trying to advance societal welfare by vetoing unemployment benefits. It is accordingly worth reemphasizing that the Conditional Pandering Theory does not require that a president is actually advancing citizens' interests, only that he believes he is doing so; the president can be wrong in this assessment. The preceding description of events documented that Bush believed economic recovery, as well as long-term growth, would be best advanced by limiting government interference in the macroeconomy. The question of whether these beliefs were accurate, or whether they are in part a function of ideological biases, is not paramount to analyzing the predicative power of the theory. In the concluding chapter of the book, I return to the issue of whether presidents are likely to have better information than citizens do about the expected consequences of policies. For now, I have a more precise goal, which is to show that the Conditional Pandering does a better job at predicting the variation in Bush's policy decisions than seemingly likely alternative explanations.

39. Adam Clymer, "Bush Fights Long-term Change in Jobless Benefits," *New York Times,* April 9, 1992, D20.

40. Adam Clymer, "Congress Passes Jobless Aid and Bush Says He Will Sign," *New York Times,* July 3, 1992, A13.

41. Ibid.

To realize this goal, four alternative rationales are evaluated, the last two of which are evaluated jointly. First, I examine whether Bush altered his policy beliefs in response to economic events. Second, the possibility that his claims of policy consistency were correct is considered. Third, I analyze executive-legislative negotiations that occurred after Clinton had taken a clear lead in order to assess whether Bush's likelihood of pandering was simply greater the sooner the election; and fourth, whether this likelihood was greater the lower his chances of retaining office.[42]

During the course of the executive-legislative negotiations over the extension of unemployment benefits, the unemployment rate itself varied noticeably. When the president vetoed an extension of benefits in October 1991, the Labor Department had just announced that the rate had dropped a tenth of a percentage point to 6.7 percent. A month later, when Bush approved a temporary extension, the rate had risen back up to 6.8 percent. Furthermore, at the subsequent bill signings in February and July, the rate was estimated to be 7.1 percent and 7.8 percent respectively.[43] It therefore seems plausible that changes in the economic situation caused Bush to believe greater government intervention in the economy was warranted.

Yet the evidence suggests otherwise. In June 1991 the unemployment rate was 6.9 percent and legislation temporarily extending compensation to the jobless was already making its way through Congress. Bush, who was enjoying approval ratings in the mid-70s, did not lend support to the bill.[44] Then in July 1992, Bush threatened to veto a permanent expansion

42. I also considered the possibility that an increase in public concern over unemployment caused Bush's policy shift. Survey data on the public's perception of the most important problem suggest such a causal relationship is highly unlikely. Soon before Bush issued his final veto regarding the unemployment compensation bills on October 11, 1991, 20 percent of respondents identified unemployment as the most important problem in a CBS poll that asked, "What do you think is the most important problem facing this country today?" (Poll conducted Oct. 5–7.) By comparison, the analogous CBS poll taken most immediately prior to Bush's extension of unemployment benefits in November had only 16 percent of respondents listing unemployment as the most important problem. (Poll conducted October 15–18.) Likewise, in the most problem series polls taken most immediately prior to Bush's later unemployment extensions of February and July of 1992, 22 percent and 10 percent, respectively, identified unemployment as the most significant problem. (Surveys conducted by the Wirthlin Group Feb. 3–5 and June 3–5. The surveys asked, "What would you say is the single most important problem facing the United States today, that is, the one that you, yourself, are most concerned about?")

43. See, for example, Cindy Richards, "Jobless Level Stays at 7.1%," *Chicago Sun-Times,* February 7, 1992, 8; Robert D. Hershey Jr., "Jobless Rate Jumps to 7.8%, Raising Doubts on Recovery," *New York Times,* July 3, 1992, A12.

44. For a discussion of the unemployment compensation bill already proposed in Congress by May 1991, see the *Congressional Quarterly Almanac,* vol. 47 (1991), 301–3.

of unemployment benefits even after the Labor Department had announced that the unemployment rate was 7.8 percent, the highest level in eight years.[45]

Finally, Bush never intimated that he reversed course because of changes in the economy. Instead, he consistently stated that his willingness to approve extensions of compensation depended on whether they would increase the deficit. For example, during a news conference in August 1991, he promoted Senator Dole's proposed extension of unemployment benefits, which was less expensive than the Democratic proposals, claiming that the Dole plan had "fiscal integrity."[46] At a fundraising luncheon in November, the president expounded his position further, declaring that:

> The Democratic leaders know that I've been ready since August to sign an extension, but to sign one as proposed by most of the Republicans in the Senate and House that lives within the budget agreement. We don't have to add to the ever-increasing deficit and still do what is compassionate and correct. They passed a bill. They wanted to embarrass me politically. I vetoed that bill . . . Unemployed workers deserve this kind of support, but we need a change in the Congress if we're going to do it in a way that lives within the budget agreement.[47]

These assertions comport with the ones Bush gave eight months later with regards to permanently extending unemployment compensation. When the president was asked by Congressman Robert H. Michel, the Minority Leader of the House, whether he might veto such legislation, Bush responded that he had a "certain custodianship for trying to support reasonable expenditures." He continued, "If [Democratic congressional members] send me something that we view and the leadership here views as too expensive, we'll have to send it back and urge them to get one down there that we can support."[48]

According to Ragsdale (1998, 213), Bush's approval ratings averaged 75 percent during May.

45. Jill Zuckman, "Bush Relents, Agrees to Sign Jobless Benefits Extension," *Congressional Quarterly Weekly,* July 4, 1992, 1961–62.

46. George Bush, "The President's News Conference," August 2, 1991, *Public Papers of the Presidents, 1991 Book 2.*

47. George Bush, "Remarks at a Bush-Quayle Fundraising Luncheon in New York City," November 12, 1991, *Public Papers of the Presidents, 1991 Book 2.*

48. George Bush, "Remarks and an Exchange with Reporters in a Meeting with the House Republican Conference on Health Care," July 2, 1992, *Public Papers of the Presidents, 1992–93 Book 1* (Washington, DC: Government Printing Office, 1993).

In sum, Bush's actions as well as rhetoric indicate that changes in the unemployment rate did not alter his fundamental beliefs about the appropriateness of extending benefits to the jobless. The president's rhetoric highlights a separate alternative explanation, however, which is that substantive differences among the assorted bills explain the variation in his willingness to sign them. The president's decisions could accordingly be construed as an example of what Cameron (2000) terms "veto bargaining." This rationale for the seemingly disparate decisions has some merit. In fact, had the legislative matter ended after Bush's approval of the extension of benefits in November 1991, it would be relatively straightforward to argue that his policy actions reflected an aversion to increasing the deficit.

The president's behavior in February 1992 suggests that this alternative explanation cannot completely account for his behavior, however. As discussed previously, the extension Bush approved in February paid for itself only under highly disputed assumptions about unexpected revenues. In fact, during a congressional hearing on the legislation, Republican House members recommended that the unemployment trust fund be taken off-budget so that it could not affect the official deficit.[49] Bush's ostensible fiscal restraint thus not only entailed questionable assumptions about unexpected surpluses but also coincided with Republicans recommending score-keeping changes in the accounting of unemployment benefits. Given these circumstances, Bush's supposed fiscal responsibility appears more superficial than substantial. His desire for restraint may well have been sincere, but this desire appears to have been superseded by an impetus to enact a popular policy once he was facing a competitive electoral contest.

The final alternative hypotheses I consider are that Bush was simply more likely to pander to public opinion as the election neared, independent of his popularity; and that he was simply more likely to pander as his popularity declined, and thus would have pandered even if the preelection polls had indicated he was quite likely to lose reelection. The events described thus far do not allow one to distinguish between these explanations and the Conditional Pandering Theory. However, subsequent events shed light on the matter.

Clinton took a substantial lead in the polls following the Democratic Party Convention in mid-July. Throughout the remainder of the race, Bush was consistently the underdog, trailing the competition by as much

---

49. Ways and Means Committee Subcommittee on Human Resources Hearing. "Extending Unemployment Benefits." Panel of Congressional Witnesses, B-318 Rayburn House Office Building, January 23, 1992.

as twenty-five points and sustaining approval ratings no higher than 40 percent.[50] While Congress did not enact other unemployment legislation during this period, the chambers did pass several bills that involved substantial government regulation of the private sector.

That legislation included the Family and Medical Leave Act of 1992 (S 5), which Congress enacted on September 10, and the Cable Television Consumer Protection and Competition Act of 1992 (S 12), which was sent to the president on September 22. The first bill granted workers up to twelve weeks of unpaid leave in order to care for a new baby or sick relative.[51] The second aided competitors to the cable industry, as well as bestowed the federal government with the power to set rates for the lowest-priced cable package.[52] Each of these bills appealed to popular sentiment. For instance, in a survey of registered voters, 63 percent of respondents stated that they would support a law requiring businesses to grant up to three months of unpaid leave for a new child or medical emergency, while only 31 percent opposed such a law.[53] Likewise, a Harris survey found that 87 percent of the national adult population believed most cable companies could overcharge customers owing to a lack of competition, and 70 percent favored allowing local telephone companies to provide cable services so that the cable industry would be more competitive.[54]

Despite the popularity of the policy issues, Bush vetoed the bills. In each case, his expressed rationale for doing so was consistent with his belief that government interference in the economy would harm it. The president professed that the Family and Medical Leave Act, if en-

50. The 1992 Gallup Poll Presidential Candidate Trial Heats are available in the Roper Center for Public Opinion Research database on polls and surveys (commonly referred to as RPOLL). For Bush's approval ratings, see Ragsdale (1998, 213–14).

51. Jill Zuckman. "Family Leave Act Falls Again: Veto Override Fails in House," *Congressional Quarterly Weekly,* October 3, 1992, 3059.

52. Mike Mills, "Bush Asks for a Sign of Loyalty: Congress Changes the Channel," *Congressional Quarterly Weekly,* October 10, 1992, 3149–51.

53. NBC News and Wall Street Journal Poll conducted September 12–15, 1992. The survey asked: "Congress has passed a law that would require companies to give employees up to three months of unpaid leave for the birth or adoption of a child, or to care for a seriously ill family member, while protecting their job. Would you favor or oppose this law, even if it means additional costs for business?"

54. Harris survey conducted March 19–24, 1992. The first question was, "Here are some statements people have made about the cable television industry in American today. For each one, please tell me whether you agree or disagree . . . Because most cable T.V. companies have local monopolies, they can charge too much for the service they provide." The second question was, "Would you favor or oppose changing the regulations so that your telephone company could provide cable television service in competition with the company that provides now?"

acted, would become a "government-dictated mandate that increases costs and loses jobs."[55] He predicted the cable bill would "cost the economy jobs, reduce consumer programming choices, and retard the deployment of growth-oriented investment critical to the future of our Nation's communications infrastructure."[56]

Bush issued each veto within seven weeks of the election, by which time Clinton held a convincing lead in the preelection polls. When Bush delivered the Family Leave veto on September 22, Clinton maintained a ten percentage point advantage according to the Gallup trial heat.[57] At the time of the Cable Bill veto, on October 3, Bush trailed by eleven to twelve percentage points.[58] That the president vetoed the bills under these conditions suggests that he did not continually pander to public opinion as the election approached or as his popularity declined relative to his electoral competition.

Instead, as predicted by the Conditional Pandering Theory, Bush endorsed the policies he believed to be the right ones when he was unpopular compared with his electoral opposition. In combination with his decisions on unemployment legislation, Bush's behavior illustrates the theoretically predicted relationship between the likelihood of pandering and presidential popularity. When he was highly popular or unpopular relative to his competition, he supported the policies he believed would produce the best outcomes for the nation, despite the proximity of the presidential election. Only when he was in the midst of a seemingly

55. George Bush, "Remarks and an Exchange with Reporters on Family Leave Legislation," September 16, 1992, *Public Papers of the Presidents, 1992–93 Book 2.*

56. George Bush, "Letter to Congressional Leaders on Cable Television Legislation," September 17, 1992, *Public Papers of the Presidents, 1992–93 Book 2.*

57. Each of the following trial heats, conducted September 17–20 of registered voters and those who could vote without having yet registered, gave Clinton a ten-point lead. The questions were "If the (1992) presidential election were being held today, would you vote for the Republican ticket of George Bush and Dan Quayle or for the Democratic ticket of Bill Clinton and Al Gore? (If Perot (vol.)/Other (vol.)/Don't know/Refused, ask:) As of today, do you lean more to Bush and Quayle, the Republicans, or to Clinton and Gore, the Democrats?" and "If the (1992) presidential election were being held today, would you vote for the Republican ticket of George Bush and Dan Quayle or for the Democratic ticket of Bill Clinton and Al Gore?" In the first case, Clinton received support from 50 percent of respondents, and in the second, he received support from 44 percent.

58. These trial heats were conducted by the Gallup Organization on October 1–3 using the questions in the format of footnote 55 of this chapter. The only difference in the questions is that Ross Perot was explicitly mentioned as a candidate, a result of the fact that he had reentered the race. In the survey that did not urge the leaners to make a choice, Clinton was favored by 47 percent of respondents and Bush by 35 percent. In the survey that pushed the leaners to choose a candidate, Clinton received support from 44 percent of the respondents and Bush from 33 percent.

tight race did he enact popular laws that he did not believe would ultimately advance citizens' interests.

REAGAN AND THE CONTINGENCY TAX PROPOSAL:
POLICY LEADERSHIP FROM BEHIND

In the beginning of 1983, Reagan's personal popularity was quite low.
Throughout the month of January, his approval ratings hovered in the
mid-30s.[59] This lack of popularity reflected the economic situation. In the
previous year, the GNP had fallen 1.8 percent, the largest annual reduction since 1946.[60] Unemployment stood at 10.8 percent, the highest level
since 1950.[61]

Many economists, including ones working in the executive branch,
believed the projection of large deficits for years to come was holding
back an economic recovery. As of January 1983, the projected deficits for
the next five years were in the range of $185 to $300 billion, approximately 7 percent of GNP. In comparison, the deficit of the last full year
before Reagan entered office was $60 billion, around 2 percent of GNP.[62]
Paul Volcker, the Chairman of the Federal Reserve, publicly expressed his
concerns about the projected deficits in January. He observed, "We are
exposed to fears of 'out-of-control' structural deficits, and the result is
upward pressure on interest rates."[63] Martin Feldstein, chairman of the
Council of Economic Advisors, agreed with Volcker that the projection of
large deficits was boosting interest rates and therefore impeding an economic recovery, particularly in sectors dependent on borrowing, such as
housing and automobiles.[64] Indeed, interest rates were quite high; the
prime rate was 11 percent and the rate for a conventional home loan was
13.25 percent.[65]

Reagan was deeply concerned about the economy and, moreover, real-

59. Ragsdale (1998, 210).

60. Anantole Kaletsky, "GNP in U.S. Fell 1.8% Last Year," *Financial Times* (London
ed.), January 20, 1983, I1.

61. "Unemployment Claims Rose at End of the Year," *New York Times*, January 14,
1983, D15.

62. Jonathan Fuerbringer, "Do Deficits Impede Recovery?" *New York Times*, January
20, 1983, D1.

63. Volcker's statement was made at a meeting of the American Council for Capital
Formation. Kenneth B. Noble, "Deficits Criticized by Volcker," *New York Times*, January
21, 1983, D3.

64. Fuerbringer, "Do Deficits Impede Recovery?"

65. "Current Interest Rates," *New York Times*, January 10, 1983, D7; Kenneth R.
Harney, "Interest Rates May Rise Along with Economy," *Washington Post*, January 15,
1983, F1.

ized that he would not win reelection in 1984 unless conditions improved. He acknowledged that if his administration could not move the country into a recovery it "obviously . . . would be a sign" that he should retire after one term.[66] Reagan also recognized the projected deficits as a problem. For example, in an administration briefing in May 1982, he claimed that "the only thing that's keeping the interest rates up and preventing a speedier recovery is the lack of confidence on the part of the private sector that government will stay the course" by progressing toward a balanced budget.[67]

Curbing the deficit was not a simple matter for the president, however. He desired significant increases in defense spending and the preservation of his recently enacted income tax cuts (e.g., Dallek 1984, 105; Feldstein 1994, 26 and 36–37). Furthermore, Reagan did not want to obtain the needed reductions through changes to Medicare, Social Security, or federal employee retirement programs, which together constituted a majority of the budget (Dallek 1984, 72–73).[68] The president was willing, indeed wanted, to decrease spending on social welfare programs (e.g., Hogan 1990, 225), but congressional leaders had indicated that they would be unwilling to curtail these programs substantially.[69]

It was in this setting that Reagan proposed standby taxes that would be triggered in a couple of years if the deficit did not decline by then; specifically, the taxes were scheduled to take effect on October 1, 1985, if the estimated deficit for fiscal year 1986 turned out to be greater than $2\frac{1}{2}$ percent of the gross national product and Congress had approved the president's spending cuts. The taxes included an excise fee on oil of approximately five dollars a barrel as well as an increase in corporate and personal income tax payments of approximately 1 percent of taxable income.[70] Reagan promoted this proposal in his State of the Union address, a radio address, and several targeted addresses during the first two months of 1983.[71]

66. Rich Jaroslovsky, "Economic Upturn Aids President's Popularity, but It Is Not Panacea," *Wall Street Journal*, April 28, 1983, 1. Cited in Kernell (1997, 224).

67. Ronald Reagan, "Meeting with Editors from the Midwestern Region," May 10, 1982, *Public Papers of the Presidents, 1982 Book 1* (Washington, DC: Government Printing Office, 1983).

68. Reagan supported the recommendations of the National Commission on Social Security Reform, and these reforms helped to keep the program solvent (Dallek 1984, 103). However, they did not eliminate the prospect of high deficits into the mid-1980s.

69. Hedrick Smith, "Deficit in the $185 Billion Range Expected in 1984 Reagan Budget," *New York Times*, January 18, 1983, A1.

70. Robert D. Hershey Jr., "President to Seek Contingent Taxes," *New York Times*, January 26, 1983, A15.

71. These addresses include the State of the Union on January 25, a national radio address entitled "Fiscal Year 1984 Budget" on January 29, "Remarks and a

The evidence suggests that Reagan believed the policy was in citizens' interests because it would help to control the deficit and thereby improve the economy by reducing interest rates. Martin Feldstein, who helped to design the plan along with Reagan's domestic policy adviser Ed Harper, describes how the president came to espouse the idea. Feldstein recounts that the president supported the policy over the objections of others within the White House because, ultimately, he "recognized the need to project declining deficits and an eventual budget balance" (Feldstein 1994, 28). The president's statements support this assertion. For example, in remarks to the St. Louis Regional Commerce and Growth Association on February 1, the president promoted the standby tax proposal by claiming that "it will reassure many of those out in the money markets today that we do mean to control inflation and interest rates."[72]

Despite Reagan's public espousal of the policy, it was quite unpopular. In fact, survey data suggest it was even less popular than the option of eliminating Reagan's income tax reductions. When citizens were asked whether they would support "a standby program of increased personal and business taxes—as well as a special tax on oil" for the years 1986–88 in order to reduce the budget deficit, 60 percent opposed the proposal.[73] In comparison, only 39 percent of the population believed that "July's tax cut should be put into effect despite the size of the government deficit."[74]

Reagan's promotion of the contingency tax proposal is thus not a case of a president following public opinion. Instead, consistent with the Conditional Pandering Theory, Reagan advocated a policy he believed would serve the public interest even though it was unpopular. As docu-

---

Question-and-Answer Session at the St. Louis Regional Commerce and Growth Association" on February 1, "Remarks and a Question-and-Answer Session via Satellite to the Young Presidents Organization" on February 14. All of these addresses are in the *Public Papers of the Presidents, 1983 Book 1* (Washington, DC: Government Printing Office, 1984).

72. Ibid.

73. Cambridge Reports, Research International survey conducted in January of 1983. The full question was "Last month, in his State of the Union and Budget Messages to Congress, President (Ronald) Reagan proposed the following actions as ways of reducing these budget deficits for the next few years. Please tell me whether you would favor or oppose each of them. . . . Putting in effect a standby program of increased personal and business taxes—as well as a special tax on oil—for the years 1986–88."

74. Roper survey conducted January 8–22, 1983. The full question was, "A 5% cut in income taxes took effect in October 1981, and another 10% cut in income taxes took effect this past July. An additional 10% cut in income taxes is due to take effect this coming July. Do you think next July's tax cut should be put into effect despite the size of the government deficit, or do you think next July's tax cut should be cancelled to help reduce the deficit?"

mented earlier, the president knew that without an economic recovery, he would be unlikely to win reelection. He believed that the standby taxes, if enacted, would help the economy and thereby increase his likelihood of winning the upcoming race. His electoral incentive was therefore to promote the proposal despite its lack of popular support.

Of course, it remains plausible that Reagan's behavior was consistent with the Conditional Pandering Theory but that he promoted the proposal for other reasons. I discuss three plausible alternative explanations: that Reagan had a propensity to follow his policy beliefs regardless of the political circumstances; that the president was somehow catering to his conservative base; and that he was playing blame-game politics with the Democrats over who was responsible for the budget deficit. None of these explanations is corroborated under scrutiny.

A seemingly credible rationale for Reagan's behavior is that he generally advocated policies he thought were in the public interest, regardless of their popularity. Indeed, this claim receives some support from officials who worked for him. For example, Edwin Meese III, Reagan's attorney general from February 1985 through August 1988, observes that "Reagan was remarkably steadfast when pursuing his key objectives" (Meese 1992, 330). Martin Anderson, the chief domestic and policy adviser to the president in 1981 and 1982, similarly assesses that Reagan would "never alter his course" when he felt strongly about a decision (Pemberton 1997, 110).

Notwithstanding Reagan's dedication to his beliefs, there is evidence that he was not above catering to public opinion. For example, he was more than willing to fire agency heads who became unpopular while following his agenda. William Pemberton (1997, 121) notes that after the White House pressured Ann Gorsuch Burford to resign her post as head of the Environmental Protection Agency, she "felt betrayed" by the president because he had "abandoned her when she came under fire for carrying out his policy." Likewise, when James Watt, Reagan's first Secretary of Interior, told the president that he probably have to fire Watt at some point because of the unpopular agenda Watt would be implementing, "Reagan, eyes sparkling with laughter, replied, 'I will'" (Pemberton 1997, 119).

Robert Dallek (1984, 33) reconciles the apparent tension between Reagan's faithfulness to his beliefs and capacity to make tactical modifications. "If Goldwater was ready to stand or fall on principle," Dallek observes, "Reagan, in his determination to be liked and to gain his personal goals, will compromise." As this assessment and Reagan's dealings with his officials imply, the president's support for the contingency taxes cannot be attributed to a universal unwillingness to take positions for purely political reasons.

Another potential explanation for Reagan's endorsement of the standby taxes is that he wanted to appeal to his conservative base. The problem with this explanation is that tax increases were anathema to conservatives at that time, and in fact, conservatives had criticized Reagan after he had agreed to tax hikes the previous summer (Dallek 1984, 109). The contingency tax proposal similarly put the president on the defensive. Even before Reagan promoted the policy in his State of the Union address, it faced opposition from leading Republicans, including the Senate Majority Leader Howard H. Baker, Jr., and Bob Dole, who was then Chairman of the Senate Finance Committee.[75]

Reagan acknowledged the lack of conservative support for the proposal. When discussing it with the Conservative Political Action Conference, he stated, "I know that some of you have been disturbed by the notion of standby tax increases in the so-called out years. Well, I wasn't wild about the idea myself." He continued, "But the economy is getting better, and I believe these improvements are only the beginning. And with some luck, and if the American people respond with the kind of energy and initiative they've always shown in the past, well, maybe it's time we started thinking about some standby tax cuts, too."[76] Reagan thus did not promote the contingency tax proposal in an effort to appeal to his conservative base.

A third alternative explanation for the president's behavior is that he proposed the taxes with the hope that Congress would reject them and thereby allow him to blame the projected deficits on the legislature. This interpretation arguably has a good deal of merit. The proposal was in fact never enacted, and Reagan had reason to believe this might occur. The taxes would have increased the price of gasoline by approximately twelve cents per gallon, and just a few years beforehand Congress had rejected a comparable, noncontingent gasoline fee proposed by President Carter. Also supporting this interpretation is the fact that the president could benefit from voters blaming the Democratic-controlled legislature for the budgetary problems.

Still, Reagan could not be certain that his proposal would indeed be dead on arrival. It had some influential congressional supporters, including the Chairman of the Senate Budget Committee Pete Domenici (R-NM).[77] Furthermore, media reports in the days immediately following the

75. Jonathan Fuerbringer, "Baker Opposes Contingency Tax: Reagan Doubts Restructuring Soon," *New York Times,* January 24, 1983, A1.

76. Ronald Reagan, "Conservative Political Action Conference, Remarks at the 10th Annual Conference Dinner," February 18, 1983, *Public Papers of the Presidents, 1983 Book 1.*

77. Jonathan Fuerbringer, "Baker Opposes Contingency Tax: Reagan Doubts Restructuring Soon," *New York Times,* January 24, 1983, A1.

president's State of the Union address, in which he promoted the policy, indicate that it was at least initially on the legislative agenda. For example, the *New York Times* stated that while some Republican leaders opposed the proposal, it had "a reasonable chance of passage."[78] The *Washington Post* similarly assessed that the chambers would consider the proposal and predicted the gasoline fee would "divide Congress along regional lines between producing and consuming states."[79] These appraisals indicate that it was conceivable Congress would enact Reagan's contingency tax proposal, or at least an amended version of it. Thus even if the proposal was attractive to Reagan in part because it would facilitate his blaming Congress for the projected deficits if it failed to enact the policy, the president could not presume that the legislature would grant him this opportunity.

Moreover, if blame-game politics were the primary goal of the proposal, Reagan easily could have chosen to recommend more popular contingency taxes. The standard nature of blame-game politics between the president and Congress is that one of the actors offers a *popular* proposal the other will not accept (e.g., Groseclose and McCarty 2001). Here, as already discussed, Reagan's standby taxes on personal income and gasoline were quite unpopular. In comparison, citizens were favorable toward other tax increases that would decrease the deficit, such as ones on cigarettes and alcohol.[80]

In sum, Reagan's behavior surrounding his 1983 contingency tax proposal supports the predictions of the Conditional Pandering Theory. When the president was highly unpopular, he promoted a policy he believed was in voters' interests even though it lacked public support and he soon faced a race for reelection. Plausible alternative explanations for this behavior, including Reagan's character, a desire to appeal to his conservative base, and blame-game politics, do not hold up under scru-

78. Robert D. Hershey Jr., "President to Seek Contingent Taxes," *New York Times,* January 26, 1983, A15.

79. David Hoffman, "President's Deficit Remedy Calls for Standby Tax Rise," *Washington Post,* January 26, 1983, A1.

80. For example, 63 percent of respondents favored increasing cigarette taxes when asked, "Do you think federal taxes on cigarettes should be raised, or don't you think so?" (NBC News poll conducted January 18–19). Similarly, 58 percent of respondents in a Cambridge Reports survey conducted in April 1983 favored increasing taxes on tobacco, liquor, airplane tickets, and telephone calls when asked, "To help reduce federal budget deficits in the next few years, the Reagan Administration and Congress have been trying to develop a compromise economic plan they can all support. Here is a list of some actions that have been proposed as ways of reducing these budget deficits for the next few years. Please tell me whether you favor or oppose each of them . . . Increase federal taxes on items like tobacco products, liquor, airplane tickets, and telephone calls."

tiny. Instead, the analysis indicates that Reagan exercised policy leadership for the reasons identified by the Conditional Pandering Theory.

CONCLUSION

The narratives on Carter's humanitarian assistance proposals, Bush's policy decisions on unemployment compensation, and Reagan's proposal for standby taxes establish that the Conditional Pandering Theory has explanatory power. In all of these analyses, the predictions of the theory were consistent with the president's policy decisions. Furthermore, the theory made sense of seemingly puzzling events; in each case a president switched positions and/or supported policies counter to his ideological leanings. In contrast, conventional explanations of presidential decision making—character, inside the beltway bargaining, and the appeasement of core constituencies, for example—did not account for the executive behavior.

Overall, the analysis of the first six chapters has suggested that a president will cater his public appeals to mass opinion but not follow it more generally. That is, while his speeches could give the misimpression he is some sort of plebiscite, in fact he typically does not support popular policies that he believes would harm society. Indeed, he will only support such policies when he is marginally popular and soon faces a contest for reelection. These findings on policy pandering indicate that the results of the first half of the book present less nefarious implications for policymaking than many observers of American politics have feared. Specifically, while a president's involvement of the mass public increases the likelihood that current opinion dictates policy, most of the time this effect will not entail the enactment of policies that the president believes counter citizens' interests.

The obvious limitation of the foregoing analysis is that the Conditional Pandering Theory has been evaluated by only a few presidential decisions. The narrative analysis has established the empirical relevance of the theory, but the question remains as to whether it is more widely applicable. The following chapter addresses this issue, examining predictions of the theory on a larger set of presidential decisions.

CHAPTER SEVEN

Patterns of Presidential Decisions

With Kenneth W. Shotts

The case studies of chapter 6 established that the Conditional Pandering Theory has empirical applicability. When the theory predicted that a president should pander to public opinion, in the sense of supporting a popular policy he believed would produce a bad outcome if implemented, the presidents in the case studies pandered. Likewise, when the theory predicted a president should exercise policy leadership by supporting an unpopular policy he believed would produce a good outcome, this behavior occurred. What the case studies have left open is the possibility that the theory does not explain broad patterns of presidential policy decisions.

To address this issue, Ken Shotts and I amassed a larger data set of presidential decisions on which we tested the predictions of the theory regarding "policy congruence," or congruence between the president's position and current opinion. An advantage of testing the predictions on policy congruence is that they do not require distinguishing pandering from basic concurrence between the president and public about the optimal course of action. The analysis can thus include observations for which such differentiation would not be readily feasible. A second asset of examining the predictions on congruence is that the literature offers a myriad of competing hypotheses. The ability of the Conditional Pandering Theory to explain presidential decision making can accordingly be assessed relative to that of other schools of thought.

The following analysis of policy congruence is valuable not only in terms of evaluating the Conditional Pandering Theory but also for providing insight into how a variety of political factors affect a president's likelihood of supporting a popular policy. These various factors include the key theoretical ones of presidential popularity and the electoral cycle, as well as other variables, such as the president's ideological leanings, the intensity of public concern, and whether an issue involves foreign affairs. The testing also evaluates whether some presidents, owing to their personalities or other personal traits, are more apt than other ones to follow public opinion.[1]

The chapter proceeds in four sections: a brief review of the predictions on policy congruence from the Conditional Pandering Theory and previous literature; a description of the data; a presentation of the technical details of the testing; and a discussion of the results.

PREDICTIONS

The predictions on policy congruence from the Conditional Pandering Theory follow from the general theoretical propositions of chapter 5. That chapter provided a detailed description of the logic generating them. Here, in outlining the predictions, this logic is briefly sketched.

Recall that in the Conditional Pandering Theory, the president always supports a popular policy if he believes it will produce a good outcome. As a result, and as Proposition 6 summarizes, variation in the probability of policy congruence depends entirely on variation in the likelihood a president will pander to public opinion by supporting a popular option he believes is not in voters' long-term interests. In other words, policy congruence would not vary systematically if the president never pandered. Thus by testing the predictions on congruence, we are indirectly testing for the existence of pandering.

The variation in policy congruence that is predicted by the theory concerns only presidents who are seeking reelection. As stated in Proposition 4, presidents who are not electorally motivated simply choose the policy they believe will produce a good outcome; they are not worried about placating current opinion but are, instead, driven by a desire to secure a strong historical legacy. Of course, in moving from the theory to empirical analysis, we recognize that second-term presidents of the United States may behave as if they are seeking reelection. For example, they may want to help their vice-president or another party member be elected. Accordingly, this chapter assesses whether in fact presidents' decision making differs systematically between first and second terms. In doing so, we examine whether the theoretically predicted patterns of policy congruence for the first term hold more generally.

In the Conditional Pandering Theory, two main factors influence variation in the likelihood first-term presidents will choose a popular policy:

---

1. The testing in this chapter is based on, yet differs from, Canes-Wrone and Shotts (2004). For instance, the set of control variables differs here in order to provide more consistency throughout the book. The econometric models are dissimilar in other ways as well.

(1) the probability that the policy options will produce noticeable results before the next election; and (2) the president's relative popularity, which refers to voters' evaluation of the president's competence relative to their estimation of the competence of the presumed challenger. The first of these variables naturally corresponds to the electoral cycle. Late in a term, the policies a president enacts are unlikely to produce outcomes before the election. Consequently, voters' decisions will be influenced more by the president's choices than by the consequences of those choices. Conversely, early in the term, the probability is much higher that a president's decisions will produce outcomes before the next election.

This reasoning implies that the Conditional Pandering Theory offers a prediction regarding the relationship between the electoral cycle and policy congruence.

Prediction 7.1: Electoral Proximity. Policy congruence between a president's positions and public opinion should be more likely the sooner the president faces a contest for reelection.

The prediction asserts that the likelihood of policy congruence should increase as the president's term proceeds. Late in the term, congruence should be significantly more likely than early in the term.

A second testable hypothesis concerns the other factor the Conditional Pandering Theory suggests will cause variation in policy congruence, namely, the president's relative popularity. In the theory, a president's relative popularity reflects the likelihood he would win reelection if a contest were held imminently; highly popular presidents would quite likely defeat the presumed challenger, while less popular ones would likely lose to him or her. As mentioned in the previous chapter, reliable trial heats are not conducted routinely throughout presidents' terms. Job approval ratings, in contrast, are assessed regularly, and research shows these ratings are highly correlated with a president's likelihood of winning reelection (e.g., Brody and Sigelman 1983; Sigelman 1979). We therefore use the ratings to test the implications of the Conditional Pandering Theory regarding presidential popularity. The following hypothesis summarizes these implications.

Prediction 7.2: Conditional Pandering Theory Popularity. The prediction has three parts: (1) when the next election is distant, the likelihood that the president chooses a popular policy is unrelated to his personal popularity; (2) when the next election is soon and the president's popularity is below average, the likelihood he chooses a popular policy increases as his personal popularity increases; and (3) when the next election is soon and the president's popularity is above average, the likelihood he chooses a popular policy decreases as his personal popularity increases.

Figure 7.1 Conditional Pandering Theory Popularity Prediction

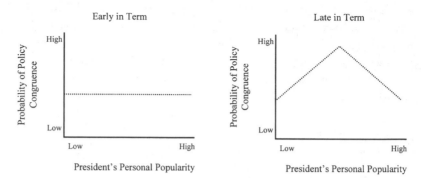

Figure 7.1 depicts this hypothesis. The prediction reflects that the president's policy choice should affect his popularity differently in the short term versus the long term. The Conditional Pandering Theory suggests that after a president makes a policy choice, it initially has a small effect, which is determined entirely by whether the decision corresponded to public opinion. However, once citizens can observe whether the choice was a good one, it is the outcome and not the initial choice that drives their opinion of the president. Accordingly, when the election is far away, the president has an incentive to enact the policy he believes is most likely to be successful. The left-hand panel of figure 7.1 exhibits this policy incentive by showing that early in the term the probability of policy congruence is not related to the president's popularity.

The right-hand panel displays the theoretical predictions for the later portion of the term. The probability of policy congruence is generally higher in the right-hand than the left-hand panel owing to the Electoral Proximity prediction, which states that congruence is more likely as the next election nears. Even when the election is soon, however, policy congruence does not always occur. Highly popular presidents only choose a popular option if they believe it is in the public interest. Likewise, unpopular presidents lack the incentive to support a popular policy if their information suggests it will not produce a good outcome; the theory suggests that the best way for an unpopular president to win is to produce a policy success. By comparison, when marginally popular presidents will soon face a contest for reelection, they have an incentive to enact policies that are popular even if these policies will likely fail. Voters are unlikely to learn about the failure prior to the election, and the small boost in popularity may be pivotal to reelection. Consequently, policy congruence is more likely for marginally popular presidents than for unpopular or highly popular ones. This relationship translates into the testable predic-

Table 7.1 Competing Predictions on Policy Congruence

Theory/School of Thought	Personal Popularity	Electoral Cycle	Other Implications
Dynamic Representation (E.g., Erikson, MacKuen, Stimson; Geer)	—	—	Overall level of congruence should be high
Need-based Popularity (E.g., Manza and Cook; research on popularity as resource)	Congruence more likely as popularity decreases	—	—
Lack of Substantive Responsiveness (Cohen)	Finds no monotonic relationship	Finds no relationship	—
Crafting of Public Opinion (Jacobs and Shapiro)	—	Congruence more likely as election nears	President's own preferences typically dictate his policy choices
Latent Opinion (E.g., Key; Zaller)	—	Congruence more likely as election nears	—
Electoral Cycle (E.g., Kuklinski; Wright and Berkman)	—	Congruence more likely as election nears	—

tion that when a president will soon face a contest for reelection, policy congruence becomes more likely as his popularity increases from low to average levels and decreases as his popularity increases from average to high levels.

Differing from the predictions of the Conditional Pandering Theory are alternative hypotheses from other theories or perspectives in the literature. Given that I reviewed this work in detail in chapter 5, I describe it only briefly here. Table 7.1 summarizes the competing schools of thought. As the table highlights, the Conditional Pandering Theory Popularity prediction is not suggested by any of the other schools, and only some support the Electoral Proximity prediction.

The first perspective, what I call the Dynamic Representation perspective, implies that change in public opinion will significantly influence a president's policy positions, causing the overall level of congruence between his stances and public opinion to be high (e.g., Erikson, MacKuen, and Stimson 2002a and 2002b; Geer 1996; Stimson, MacKuen, and Erikson

1995). This research does not consider the possibility that responsiveness may be a function of structural factors such as the electoral cycle or presidential popularity. Accordingly, the perspective allows that these factors may not affect the likelihood of policy congruence.

The second school of thought encompasses work that indicates policy congruence should be more likely the less popular the president is. The Need-based Popularity perspective appears in work on political responsiveness (e.g., Manza and Cook 2002) and is consistent with research that characterizes presidential popularity as a resource presidents can expend to achieve policy goals (e.g., Brace and Hinckley 1992; Rivers and Rose 1985).[2] The perspective contrasts with the Conditional Pandering Theory given that the latter implies the probability of policy congruence *decreases* as the president's popularity shifts from average to low levels. Also, unlike the Need-based Popularity perspective, the Conditional Pandering Theory predicts that personal popularity should not affect the probability of policy congruence early in a president's term.[3]

Yet a third school of thought supports neither of the predictions on policy congruence from the Conditional Pandering Theory. The lack of substantive responsiveness perspective, represented by Jeffrey Cohen (1997), indicates that American presidents' policy choices are not influenced by citizens' policy positions. Lawrence Jacobs and Robert Shapiro (2000; 2002a) also predict a low level of responsiveness. However, their Crafting of Public Opinion perspective, which argues that presidents try to shape public opinion, incorporates that an impending election temporarily increases the level of responsiveness. The latter school of thought is thus consistent with the Electoral Proximity Hypothesis.

The remaining perspectives—the Latent Opinion and Electoral Cycle perspectives—also suggest that the electoral cycle, but not a president's

2. Stokes's (2001) analysis of Latin American presidents' willingness to take unpopular campaign positions on neoliberal reform is also consistent with this logic. In particular, Stokes argues that candidates who are far ahead of their competition will be more likely to advocate unpopular neoliberal reform than candidates who are facing tight races.

3. Fiorina (1974) and Powell (1982) suggest that in order to receive additional funding and support from party activists, a congressional member will be less likely to take popular positions the more competitive his district is. Notably, this prediction suggests that if presidents face the same incentives, the Conditional Pandering Theory Popularity hypothesis should not be supported; indeed one interpretation of Fiorina and Powell is that we should expect policy congruence to become less likely as the president's popularity decreases from high to average or increases from low to average. Because of the differences in public financing between presidential and congressional races, we do not characterize our test as an examination of the Fiorina and Powell argument but simply highlight that research on party activism indicates a different pattern of decision making than does the Conditional Pandering Theory.

popularity, should affect the likelihood of policy congruence. The Latent Opinion perspective derives from V. O. Key's (1961) concept, which bears this name, where the opinion is "latent" because it reflects preferences that will be realized only after the results of policies are known. Applying this concept to the presidency, John Zaller (2003) observes that a president will base his policy decisions on latent opinion if voters are likely to observe the ensuing policy results before the next election; when voters will not, the president will care only about current opinion.[4] Zaller's argument, while developed independently of the Conditional Pandering Theory, mirrors the logic of the Electoral Proximity hypothesis.

This hypothesis is also consistent with studies that find the approach of an election causes ideological moderation in the position-taking of federal and state legislators (e.g., Elling 1982; Kuklinski 1978; Thomas 1985; Wright and Berkman 1986). In these works, ideological moderation is interpreted to reflect the legislators' greater responsiveness to public opinion. Accordingly, policy congruence is most likely when an election is imminent. The Latent Opinion, Electoral Cycle, and Crafting of Public Opinion perspectives are thus indistinguishable from the Conditional Pandering Theory in terms of the predicted relationship between policy congruence and the electoral cycle. These other schools of thought do not, however, predict any sort of relationship between congruence and the president's personal popularity.

In sum, the literature offers a myriad of alternative perspectives that challenge the implications of the Conditional Pandering Theory. No other school of thought supports the Conditional Pandering Theory Popularity prediction, and several perspectives suggest the Electoral Proximity hypothesis may be incorrect. The remainder of the chapter examines the various predictions with a data set of presidential policy decisions. To the extent that this analysis supports the Conditional Pandering Theory, it will suggest that the theory provides a more comprehensive understanding of presidential decision making than do the other perspectives.

DATA

The data set revolves around annual observations of presidential proposals and public opinion for a set of eleven budgetary issues during the

4. This logic is also expressed in Stokes's (2001) analysis of whether Latin American presidents, during their first six months in office, are willing to enact unpopular neoliberal reform that they believe will aid their countries. In particular, Stokes finds that the presidents often enact neoliberal reform under these conditions and attributes this willingness to the fact that the presidents (and their parties) will be rewarded in the next election if the policies have produced good economic outcomes.

Nixon through Clinton administrations.[5] The issues concern many of the most significant domestic and foreign policy matters of the past thirty years. For example, government services for the poor, defense spending, and environmental protection are all included. The complete set includes crime, defense, education, the environment, foreign aid, ground transportation, health, national parks, social security, space, and welfare.

Each issue has been the subject of a recurring survey question conducted by the National Opinion Research Center (NORC) and Roper Organization since 1972. The question is the same one employed in the other analyses of budgetary data in the book: "We are faced with many problems in this country, none of which can be solved easily or inexpensively. I'm going to name some of the problems, and for each one I'd like you to tell me whether you think we're spending too much money, too little money, or about the right amount on [the particular problem]."[6] It is worth observing that respondents did not uniformly support higher spending.[7] In fact, for over one-third of the observations there were more respondents who wanted to decrease spending than wanted to increase it.

We matched each of the eleven issues to the U.S. federal budget at the level of function codes, which concern all spending within a given policy area. The purpose of conducting the analysis at the function level was to create as close a fit as possible between the budgetary data and survey questions. Thus, for example, the survey question on the environment asks about government spending on "improving and protecting the environment," and the budgetary data concern all federal spending on environmental matters. For each policy issue, we have an annual observation of the budgetary authority proposed by the president and that enacted in the previous year.

Just as budgetary data were valuable for analyzing public appeals, they offer many advantages here for the purpose of examining presidential decision making. On many types of executive decisions, including most roll-call votes, a president can avoid publicly stating a policy position.

5. See Achen (1978) for a discussion on the benefits of analyzing representation at the level of individual policy issues.

6. The National Opinion Research Center data are from the General Social Survey (GSS). The question ends as follows for each issue. Crime: ". . . halting the rising crime rate?" Defense: ". . . the military, armaments and defense?" Education: ". . . improving the nation's education system?" Environment: ". . . improving and protecting the environment?" Foreign Aid: ". . . foreign aid?" Ground Transportation: ". . . highways and bridges?" Health: ". . . improving and protecting the nation's health?" Parks: ". . . parks and recreation?" Social Security: ". . . social security?" Space: ". . . the space exploration program?" Welfare: ". . . welfare?"

7. See Hansen (1998) for a review and critique of research that suggests citizens always support higher spending.

This avoidance is more likely the less popular a president's stance (e.g., Covington 1987). Consequently, data based on noncompulsory positions may be biased toward finding policy congruence where it does not exist. Because the Budget and Accounting Act of 1921 requires presidents to submit an annual budget to Congress, budgetary data avoid this problem. A related asset is that the annual recurrence of the executive proposals creates a panel data set. The policy issue can therefore be held constant when evaluating the various determinants of congruence. Finally, the data cover a wide range of policy areas and yet are readily comparable.

Key Variables

Four key variables are identified by the predictions: policy congruence, presidential popularity, the electoral cycle, and the presidential term. This section describes the measurement of these factors as well as summarizes relationships among them.

The dependent variable *Policy Congruence* links the presidential budgetary proposals with the previously described NORC and Roper survey responses about spending. In keeping with the fact that the theoretical predictions concern a dichotomy between the existence of congruence and a lack thereof, the variable is dichotomous, with one representing policy congruence and zero a lack of it. Whenever the president proposes an increase in budgetary authority from the previous year and more respondents prefer an increase than prefer a decrease, the variable equals one.[8] Likewise, it equals one if the president proposes to cut spending and the number of respondents who prefer to decrease spending is greater than the number who prefer to increase it. The variable equals zero otherwise.[9]

In total, we have 235 observations of *Policy Congruence*. The data include all observations for which the National Opinion Research Center or the Roper Center conducted the survey during the prior year. Unfortunately, an observation is not available for every policy issue and year. Since the survey question was initiated in 1972, the question was not asked in some years and in others it was asked about only a subset of the policy issues.

8. If Roper and the National Opinion Research Center conducted a survey on the issue in the year prior to the president's proposal, the variable is based on the average results of the two surveys. If only one organization conducted a survey on the policy issue that year, the factor is based on these responses alone.

9. The analysis has also been conducted under the assumption that *Policy Congruence* equals one if and only if the percentage of respondents favoring a change in the direction of the president's proposal was at least ten points higher than the percentage desiring a change in the opposite direction. All substantive results hold with this assumption.

Of the 235 observations of *Policy Congruence,* the variable equals one for 51 percent of them. This overall level seems surprisingly low at first glance but becomes more understandable when considering the lower level of congruence for certain policy issues. For example, within the data set, congruence occurs for less than 10 percent of the observations on space policy. Citizens routinely express an interest in cutting spending on the space program, yet presidents typically propose to expand the program. Likewise, congruence is uncommon for the foreign policy issues, where presidents again are more apt than the public to support an increase in spending. Among the observations on foreign and defense spending, presidents' positions are in line with public opinion only 32 percent of the time.[10]

Simply by removing the observations on foreign and space policy, the proportion of congruent observations jumps to 63 percent. It rises even higher, to 68 percent, if the issue of national parks is removed. The president's proposal corresponds to public opinion on only 15 percent of these observations. Unlike the aforementioned issues for which congruence is the exception, on national parks the public consistently desires higher spending and presidents still commonly propose to cut expenditures in this area.

These statistics highlight the wide variation that exists in policy congruence across the various policy issues. For some, such as national parks and space policy, congruence is the exception rather than the norm. In contrast, for other issues, congruence is the norm. In education policy, for example, congruence occurs for 56 percent of the observations, and it occurs for 92 percent of the observations on crime policy. Because of such variation, the subsequent testing accounts for the possibility that even after other factors are accounted for, presidents may simply be less likely to take popular positions on individual policy issues. Before proceeding to this testing, however, descriptive statistics on other potential sources of variation in policy congruence are presented. In particular, we examine the sources implied by the Conditional Pandering Theory: presidential popularity, the electoral cycle, and the presidential term.

The first of these factors, *Presidential Popularity,* is measured with the familiar Gallup poll that asks, "Do you approve or disapprove of the way [the current president] is handling his job as president?" The variable

10. Individually as well, defense and foreign aid spending each have congruence rates of 32 percent. Page (2002) points out that Erikson, MacKuen, and Stimson (2002a; 2002b) remove issues that do not fit well on the traditional liberal-conservative spectrum. This difference in the set of issues examined may be one reason that the data here suggest a lower overall level of responsiveness than the work of Erikson, MacKuen, and Stimson would predict.

Table 7.2 Proportion of Observations Reflecting Policy Congruence, by Key Theoretical Variables

	Term 1 (*n* = 160)		Term 2 (*n* = 75)	
Presidential Popularity	1st Half (*n* = 74)	2nd Half (*n* = 86)	1st Half (*n* = 42)	2nd Half (*n* = 33)
<50 (*n* = 102)	0.33	0.53	0.33	0.55
≥50, <60 (*n* = 56)	0.47	0.77	No observations	No observations
≥60 (*n* = 77)	0.45	0.55	0.61	0.64

equals the percentage of respondents who approve of the president's performance in the poll taken most immediately prior to the president's submission of his budgetary proposal. Within the data, the average level of presidential popularity is 55 percent.

The other key factors, *2nd Half* and *2nd Term*, are based on the electoral institutions of the U.S. presidency. The variable *2nd Half*, which equals one if the president offered his proposal during the last two years of the term and zero otherwise, accounts for the possibility that a president's behavior may differ according to the proximity of the next presidential election. The binary division of the president's term into two-year portions is consistent with research that shows U.S. senators and state legislators take more moderate positions during the two years before an electoral race (e.g., Elling 1982; Kuklinski 1978; Thomas 1985; Wright and Berkman 1986). The remaining key factor, *2nd Term*, allows that first- and second-term presidents may make different types of policy decisions. Accordingly, the variable equals one if the president is serving a second term and zero otherwise. As discussed previously, the predictions on policy congruence from the Conditional Pandering Theory are based on the assumption that the president has electoral motivations. Given that second-term presidents may or may not behave as if they are seeking reelection, we analyze their behavior separately from that of first-term administrations.

Table 7.2 summarizes the basic relationships between policy congruence and the other key variables. The president's approval ratings are divided into three ranges: below 50 percent, at least 60 percent, and between these boundaries. The categories represent, respectively, an "average" level of popularity, an above average level and a below average one, with these ranges crudely approximating the theoretical categories of marginally popular, highly popular, and unpopular presidents. The groupings are based on the fact that the average approval rating is 55 percent. Such justification for the cutoff points notwithstanding, they are naturally somewhat arbitrary. For this reason, the testing that follows does not divide presidential popularity into ranges but instead analyzes how marginal changes in the factor affect the probability of policy congruence. Here the categories help expose the basic relationships of the raw data.

As the table shows, the summary statistics are generally consistent with the predictions of the Conditional Pandering Theory. For example, during the first term, policy congruence is more likely during the second half of the administration. In fact, for each level of presidential popularity, the percentage of congruent observations is at least 10 points higher during the latter two years. The raw data thus support the Electoral Proximity prediction that policy congruence is more likely when the president is running for reelection in the near future.

The summary statistics are also consistent with the Conditional Pandering Theory Popularity hypothesis. As expected, policy congruence occurs most frequently when the president is marginally popular and soon faces an electoral contest. During the second half of the first term, the proportion of observations reflecting an occurrence of policy congruence is 0.77 for marginally popular presidents. In comparison, during that period the proportions for highly popular and unpopular presidents are, respectively, only 0.53 and 0.55. For presidents in the early part of the first term, the proportion for marginally popular presidents is only 0.47. Thus, for first-term presidents, the summary statistics on policy congruence vary exactly as the Conditional Pandering Theory would predict.

The smaller number of observations on second-term administrations makes inference about them more difficult. This lack of data derives from the fact that during the time series only Nixon, Reagan, and Clinton served a second term, and Nixon's lasted less than two years. Still, a few patterns of presidential decision making can still be gleaned. Consistent with the Conditional Pandering Theory, the policymaking of second-term presidents appears to differ from that of first-term ones. In particular, the consistently large proportion of congruent decisions by highly popular second-term presidents suggests that the proximity of the next election may not have a large effect on these presidents' decision making. Obviously, the lack of data for the middle range of presidential popularity limits the strength of this conclusion. In the subsequent testing, where we examine marginal changes in popularity, more specific inferences can be drawn.

Control Variables

The testing involves not only the four key variables described above but also a set of control variables, which encompass a variety of factors the literature suggests may affect presidential decision making. The variables are defined as follows.

President's Ideological Congruence

Previous work establishes that a president's ideological preferences affect his policy decisions (e.g., Stimson, MacKuen, and Erikson 1995; Cohen 1997). To account for the influence of this factor on policy congruence, we include a variable that reflects the degree to which a president's ideology corresponds to citizens' preferences as measured by the General Social Survey and Roper surveys. We expect that the higher the congruence between presidential ideology and public opinion, the more likely that the president's policy stance will be consistent with public opinion.

The measurement of presidential ideology is based on Keith Poole's (1998) common space (CS) scores that estimate ideology as a function of presidents' roll-call positions.[11] The scores range from −1 to +1, with a higher score representing a more conservative preference. The coding of *President's Ideological Congruence* incorporates that liberals tend to prefer higher domestic and lower foreign and defense spending while conservatives typically have the reverse preferences.[12] Specifically, the factor equals:

−1 × CS Score   if the issue is domestic and the number of respondents who prefer an increase is greater than the number who prefer a decrease in spending;

CS Score   if the issue is domestic and more respondents prefer a decrease in spending;

CS Score   if the issue is foreign or defense and more respondents prefer an increase in spending;

−1 × CS Score   if the issue is foreign or defense and more respondents prefer a decrease in spending.

---

11. These common space scores derive from the McCarty and Poole (1995) presidential ideology scores.

12. As Jacoby (1994) demonstrates, certain policy issues fit the ideological spectrum better than others. For instance, welfare spending corresponds more closely to the traditional left-right spectrum than spending on crime prevention. For the data of this chapter, bivariate regression results suggest that liberalism (in terms of the CS scores) is positively correlated with a preference for higher spending on the domestic issues and negatively correlated with a preference for higher spending on the foreign and defense issues. Still, we have conducted the testing of the Conditional Pandering Theory under a variety of alternative assumptions about how ideology relates to preferences over spending and found substantively similar results.

Thus if the survey responses suggest that the public desires more spending on a foreign or defense issue, *President's Ideological Congruence* assumes a high value for a conservative president and a low value for a liberal one. If the responses support more spending on a domestic issue, the variable takes on a low value for a conservative president and high value for a liberal one.

Congress's Ideological Congruence

Congruence between congressional ideology and public opinion may affect presidents' policy decisions in two countervailing ways. The first concerns what Timothy Groseclose and Nolan McCarty (2001) call "blame-game" politics, where the president and Congress seek to blame one another for legislative gridlock. In examining this phenomenon, Groseclose and McCarty show that a president's popularity increases when citizens learn that their policy preferences are closer to those of the president than those of Congress. A president may accordingly have greater incentives to take popular positions when congressional preferences are out of step with public opinion. On the other hand, when congressional preferences are in step with public opinion, a president's desire to appear successful in the legislative arena could cause him to support policies consistent with these preferences. Given the counteracting influences, we have no expectation about the sign of the effect of congressional ideological congruence.

The measurement of the variable follows the measurement of the president's ideological congruence. For domestic issues, the variable equals the median CS score of the House if more survey respondents prefer a decrease than prefer an increase in spending and the negative inverse of this score if more respondents prefer a growth in spending.[13] For defense and foreign issues, the coding is similar except that it assumes a member will want less spending the more liberal she is.

Foreign Affairs

The variable equals one for the issues of defense and foreign aid and zero for the domestic issues. Part 1 emphasized that the relationship between presidential policymaking and public opinion differs between foreign and

---

13. We use the median preference of the House because collinearity prevents including variables for both the House and Senate, and research suggests that the median House preference will typically determine legislative outcomes for budgetary issues in this chamber (e.g., Brady and Volden 1998; Krehbiel 1998).

domestic affairs, with presidents having a greater ability to alter citizens' preferences on the former types of issues. Also, presidents have greater unilateral authority in the realm of foreign policy (Howell 2003), making them less beholden to Congress to achieve their foreign policy goals. We accordingly account for the possibility that congruence between the president's policy positions and public opinion may be less likely for foreign and defense matters.

Public Concern

This variable controls for the possibility that public concern about an issue could affect a president's propensity to take a popular position. For instance, a president could be more likely to take a popular position if the issue were at the top of the public agenda. The Conditional Pandering Theory does not offer a prediction on this factor, and Cohen (1997) finds it does not significantly affect the substance of presidents' statements in State of the Union addresses. Still, we control for *Public Concern* to ensure that the results are not a function of excluding it. As in chapter 3, the variable is measured with responses to the Gallup Organization's recurring Most Important Problem survey, which asks, "What do you think is the most important problem facing this country today?"[14] In chapter 3, many of the issues analyzed were unlikely to be salient, and public concern was accordingly measured as a function of whether an issue was at all given as a response to the Most Important Problem survey. Here, because all of the policy issues examined are relatively salient, we adopt a more nuanced accounting of the factor. Specifically, *Public Concern* equals the percentage of responses that cite the given policy issue in the survey taken most immediately prior to the date the president submitted his budgetary proposal.[15]

President Indicators

Fred Greenstein (2000) and Richard Neustadt (1990 [1960]), among others, argue that a chief executive's personal qualities affect his role in the policy process. To account for the possibility that personal qualities influence the likelihood a president will take popular policy positions, we include a set of dummy variables, each of which equals one for the given president's years in office and zero otherwise.

14. We use the Most Important Problem surveys that do not constrain the set of responses.

15. If, instead, the analysis is conducted with a measure of *Public Concern* like the one in chapter 3, all substantive results still hold.

SPECIFICATION AND ESTIMATION

The following model tests for each policy issue i and year t the various predictions on policy congruence:

(7.1)   Policy Congruence$_{it}$ = $f$$\{\beta_0 + \beta_1$2nd Half$_t$ + 2nd Half$_t$
[β_2(Pop$_t$ − Mean Pop) × (1 − Above Avg Pop$_t$) +
β_3(Pop$_t$ − Mean Pop) × (Above Avg Pop$_t$) + γ_1 President's
Ideological Congruence$_{it}$ + γ_2 Congress's Ideological
Congruence$_{it}$ + γ_3 Foreign Policy$_{it}$ + γ_4 Public Concern$_{it}$]
+ 1st Half$_t$[β_4(Pop$_t$ − Mean Pop) × (1 − Above Avg Pop$_t$)
+ β_5(Pop$_t$ − Mean Pop) × (Above Avg Pop$_t$) + γ_5 President's
Ideological Congruence$_{it}$ + γ_6 Congress's Ideological
Congruence$_{it}$ + γ_7 Foreign Policy$_{it}$ + γ_8 Public Concern$_{it}$]
+ κ President Indicators$_t$ +α_i},

where *Pop* represents the president's personal popularity, *Mean Pop* is the mean of presidential popularity across all observations, *Above Avg Pop* is an indicator for whether the president's popularity is above this mean (equaling one when popularity is greater than the mean and zero otherwise), *1st Half* equals (1 − *2nd Half*), and α is a set of time-invariant effects for the eleven policy issues.[16]

The specification is simpler than it may appear at first glance. For each half of the term, the model estimates how the likelihood of policy congruence is influenced by the president's personal popularity, his ideology, congressional ideology, whether the given issue involves foreign affairs and public concern for the issue. In addition, the specification accounts for the impact of each individual president and policy issue.

The key coefficients are β_1 through β_5, which assess the predictions about policy congruence and the electoral cycle. The first of the parameters, β_1, estimates the difference in the average level of policy congruence between the halves of the term. According to the Conditional Pandering Theory, as well as the Crafting of Public Opinion, Electoral Cycle, and Latent Opinion perspectives, congruence should be more likely as a presidential election nears. The coefficient is therefore expected to be positive.

The other key coefficients, β_2 though β_5, estimate the impact of presidential popularity on the likelihood of policy congruence. The dummy

16. It is worth noting that all substantive findings also hold if the data is analyzed with all observations aggregated by year. The dependent variable in that case is the annual percentage of issues for which the president's position is congruent with public opinion. Even with this aggregation, the signs and significance levels of the key variables support the Electoral Proximity hypothesis and the Conditional Pandering Theory Popularity prediction.

variables *Above Avg Pop* and ($1 - $ *Above Avg Pop*) capture that the impact may differ according to whether the president's approval ratings are above or below average, and the difference (*Pop* $-$ *Mean Pop*) captures changes in presidential popularity relative to the mean of this factor. Accordingly, the coefficient β_2 estimates the effect of a marginal change in a president's popularity when he has below average ratings and is in the second half of his term. Similarly, the parameter β_3 evaluates the impact of a marginal change in a president's popularity if it is above average and he is running for reelection within two years. The effects for the first half of the term follow analogously. The coefficient β_4 estimates the impact of a change in presidential popularity for a president whose approval is initially below average, and β_5 estimates this impact for a president whose approval is initially above average.

The various perspectives have different predictions about the signs of these effects. Take, for example, β_2, which estimates the impact of a change in the president's personal popularity when it is initially below average and the president is in the last two years of his term. The Conditional Pandering Theory suggests this effect should be significantly positive, the Need-based Popularity perspective indicates it should be significantly negative, while the other perspectives imply it should not have a significant impact. According to the Conditional Pandering Theory Popularity prediction, a president with below average approval ratings late in the term will be more likely to take a popular position if his approval ratings rise. In contrast, the Need-based Popularity perspective suggests that throughout a president's term, he should be more likely to take popular positions the less popular he is. The other theoretical perspectives—the Crafting of Public Opinion, Electoral Cycle, Latent Opinion, Dynamic Representation, and Lack of Substantive Responsiveness perspectives—all indicate that a president's popularity is inconsequential in terms of his likelihood of catering to public opinion.

The Conditional Pandering Theory also diverges from the other perspectives in terms of the expected effects of β_3, β_4, and β_5. The schools of thought that imply a president's popularity will not affect the probability of policy congruence naturally indicate that all three of these coefficients should be insignificant. The Need-based Popularity perspective suggests that they should be significantly negative. By comparison, the Conditional Pandering Theory Popularity prediction implies that β_3 should be significantly negative, β_4 insignificant, and β_5 insignificant as well. According to the theory, a president with above average popularity in the second half of his term should be less likely to cater to public opinion the higher are his approval ratings. During the first half of his term, however, the ratings should not significantly affect the likelihood of policy congruence.

The coefficients β_1 through β_5 thus compare the empirical validity of the Conditional Pandering Theory with that of the competing perspectives. The other coefficients of equation (7.1) identify the effects of the control variables. These variables, except for the president indicators, are separated according to the half of the term. This specification is employed because if a president's popularity has a smaller (larger) effect when he does not face an election within the next two years, other factors may presumably have larger (smaller) effects. The indicators for the individual presidents are not divided across the term because doing so would prohibit testing the Electoral Proximity prediction, which implies a single temporal effect, not a separate one for each president.[17]

We employ what is called a random-effects probit model to estimate the equation. An advantage of this specification is that it controls for the impact of the individual issues; each "unit," which in this case is a policy issue, is allowed to have a separate intercept.[18] Thus, the testing accounts for the possibility that the politics of presidential decision making differs systematically across the policy domains. Technically, we assume that the issue effects α_i are random disturbances distributed normally and independently (Greene 1993, 469–79). A probit specification is assumed because the dependent variable is dichotomous.[19]

RESULTS

First-Term Presidents

We begin with the results for first term presidents. Table 7.3 describes the findings. Overall, the table strongly corroborates the Conditional Pan-

17. If the model is estimated with the president dummies separated by term, the signs and significance levels of the effects on presidential popularity remain substantively similar to those presented. The effect of *2nd Half* depends on which president indicator is omitted, making the result incomparable to the one presented.

18. Fixed-effects models also maintain this assumption. A key distinction between fixed- and random-effects models is that the latter presume the units in the data are a random sample from a larger population of units. We have also analyzed the data with a fixed-effects model and received substantively similar results. The fixed-effects model can only be estimated for a portion of the data regarding first-term presidents given that three of the policy issues perfectly predict the dependent variable. In particular, for first-term presidents, policy congruence always occurs for social security and never occurs for space or parks.

19. Following the approach of Beck, Katz, and Tucker (1998), we have also tested for whether individual year effects should be included and found no evidence that they should be. Specifically, when we include them in a basic probit model with fixed effects for the individual issues, the year effects are jointly insignificant ($p = 0.332$).

Table 7.3 Determinants of Policy Congruence, First-term Presidents

Independent Variables	Probit Coefficient (Standard Error)	
2nd Half	1.612 (0.708)	
	2nd Half	**1st Half**
(Popularity − Mean Popularity) × (1 − Above Average Popularity)	0.106 (0.045)	0.043 (0.089)
(Popularity − Mean Popularity) × (Above Average Popularity)	−0.068 (0.032)	−0.002 (0.032)
President's Ideological Congruence	−0.013 (0.037)	1.473 (0.486)
Congress' Ideological Congruence	2.400 (2.679)	1.280 (3.518)
Foreign Policy	−0.893 (0.502)	−1.113 (0.522)
Public Concern	−0.069 (0.041)	−0.012 (0.032)
Richard Nixon	−1.271 (0.816)	
Jimmy Carter	−0.106 (0.574)	
Ronald Reagan	−0.030 (0.626)	
George H. W. Bush	0.795 (1.059)	
Clinton	−0.484 (0.634)	
Constant	−0.293 (0.742)	
Number of Observations	160	
Log Likelihood	−75.017	
LR Test for Random Effects	$\chi^2_{(1)} = 37.909$ ($p = 0.000$)	

Note: The dependent variable is Pr (Policy Congruence = 1). The results in the separate columns for the first and second terms regard the variables that are estimated separately by the half of the term. Ford is the omitted president indicator.

dering Theory. Both the Electoral Proximity prediction and the Conditional Pandering Theory Popularity prediction receive strong support.

The first of these predictions, which is that a president will be more likely to take popular positions when he will soon face a contest for reelection, is validated by the coefficient on *2nd Half*. The effect is positive and highly significant ($p < 0.05$, two-tailed). Thus during the first term, policy congruence is significantly more likely in the latter two years. This finding supports not only the Conditional Pandering Theory but also the Latent Opinion, Electoral Cycle, and Crafting of Public Opinion perspectives given that they all imply electoral proximity should increase the likelihood of policy congruence.

Interpreting the magnitude of the impact is less straightforward than doing so for ordinary least squares models because, as discussed in previous chapters, the size of an effect in a logit or probit model depends on the values of the independent variables. Commonly one assumes that the other variables are at their means. Under this assumption, the findings suggest that the likelihood of policy congruence is 10 percent higher in the second half of the term. The Electoral Proximity prediction thus receives support not only from the statistical significance of the effect of the electoral cycle but also from the magnitude of this effect.

The results on presidential popularity also comport with the Conditional Pandering Theory. As predicted, presidential popularity only affects the likelihood of policy congruence during the second half of the term; the coefficients on the popularity variables for the first half are not significant at any conventional level. Also as predicted, later in the term personal approval has a significantly negative effect for presidents with below average ratings and a significantly positive effect for ones with above average ratings. These results are shown in the column of results labeled "2nd Half." The coefficient on *(Popularity − Mean Popularity) × (1 − Above Average Popularity)*, which represents the impact of a change in popularity for a president whose popularity is below average, is positive with a p value of 0.019.[20] Likewise, the effect on *(Popularity − Mean Popularity) × (Above Average Popularity)*, which represents the effect for a president with above average approval, is negative with a p value of 0.031.

To interpret the magnitudes of these findings, we again assume that the control variables are at their means. At these parameter values, when a president's popularity is five points below average in the second half of the term, a ten-point decline in his approval ratings decreases the likelihood of his taking a popular position by 22 percent. In comparison, when

20. We considered the possibility that this result is driven by the behavior of presidents with extraordinarily low popularity. (Our concern was that a president may be more likely to follow public opinion the lower his personal popularity except when it is so low that he believes he simply cannot win reelection.) Specifically, we reestimated the model excluding the 20 observations for which the president's personal popularity was less than 40 percent. The signs and significance of the key coefficients all hold under this alternative estimation.

his popularity is five points above average during this time, the analogous increase in approval depresses the likelihood he follows public opinion by 38 percent. Popularity thus has a substantively important as well as statistically significant impact on whether a president's decisions correspond to public opinion.

These estimates establish that the Conditional Pandering Theory provides a more accurate description of presidential policymaking than the competing perspectives do. Most of them, including the Dynamic Representation, Lack of Substantive Responsiveness, Crafting of Public Opinion, Electoral Cycle, and Latent Opinion perspectives, indicate that the effect of popularity should be insignificant. The only other perspective implying a significant impact is the Need-based Popularity perspective, and it suggests that all four of the popularity variables should have negative effects. The results on presidential popularity thus provide strong support for the Conditional Pandering Theory over other schools of thought.

The results for the control variables are also largely consistent with expectations. The first control, *President's Ideological Congruence,* has a significant impact in the first half of the term. During these years, the greater the correlation between a president's ideology and citizens' preferences, the more likely the president is to take a popular position. In the second half of the term, the factor does not have a significant effect. The estimates thus suggest that reelection-seeking chief executives tend to pursue a more ideological agenda in their first two years and then refocus the agenda toward the goal of reelection during the latter two.

The other control variables that have significant effects include the indicators for foreign policy and the individual presidents. As predicted, in each half of the term policy congruence is less likely for the foreign policy issues. This result comports with presidents' greater capacity to change public opinion and take unilateral action on foreign policy issues. Together with the findings of chapters 2 and 4, the negative impact suggests that presidents are less concerned with current opinion on matters of foreign affairs.

The effects of the individual presidents imply that personal differences explain some, but not a great deal, of variation in presidential policymaking across administrations. In particular, the findings indicate that, once one accounts for structural factors, Richard Nixon was less likely than Gerald Ford or George H. W. Bush to take popular positions and Bill Clinton also less likely to do so than Bush. The lower degree of responsiveness by Clinton is in one sense surprising given his reputation for following public opinion.[21] The finding, however, is consistent with Jacobs

---

21. See, for instance, Morris (1997).

and Shapiro (2000), who argue that Clinton did not design his policies to cater to public opinion but instead tried to craft opinion to support his agenda.

The remaining control variables, which represent congressional ideology and public concern, do not have significant effects on the likelihood of policy congruence. The negligible impact of congressional ideology is not surprising given that, as discussed at the outset, blame-game politics and the president's desire to appear successful in the legislative arena could have countervailing effects. The result regarding public concern is also not terribly surprising given that Cohen (1997) similarly finds it does not affect presidential policy decisions once one controls for other factors.

Second-Term Presidents

All in all, table 7.3 is consistent with expectations. The results on the key variables as well as the control factors are generally in line with predicted effects. Most significantly, the analysis upholds the Electoral Proximity and Conditional Pandering Theory Popularity predictions. In doing so, it supports the Conditional Pandering Theory and challenges competing perspectives. We have therefore validated the theory with regards to the policy decisions of presidents running for reelection.

We still have not, however, examined the behavior of second-term presidents. The theory suggests that these presidents will endorse those policies most likely to establish a favorable historical legacy. Thus from a theoretical standpoint, the Electoral Proximity and Conditional Pandering Theory Popularity predictions do not concern the policymaking of second-term presidents. It is possible, however, that these predictions are relevant to second-term administrations. For example, to the extent that a second-term president wants a particular candidate, e.g., his vice-president or another member of his party, to win the office, he may behave as if running for reelection.

This subsection assesses whether in fact the policy decisions of second-term presidents differ from those of first-term presidents. At the outset, three types of findings are possible. First, the electoral cycle and personal popularity may influence a chief executive's policy decisions similarly in the first and second terms. Second, we could find that a second-term president's likelihood of taking a popular position is unrelated to the electoral cycle or his personal approval ratings. Such a result would accord not only with the Conditional Pandering Theory but also with the Dynamic Representation and Lack of Substantive Responsiveness perspectives. These latter perspectives suggest that regardless of whether a president is running for reelection, the factors should not affect executive policymaking.

A third possibility is that presidential popularity and/or the electoral cycle could affect the likelihood of policy congruence but not in the way the factors do during the first term. For instance, the results could indicate that the Need-based Popularity perspective holds during second terms; that is, we could find that presidents who are not running for reelection are more likely to take popular positions the lower their personal approval ratings are. Naturally, we could also uncover a pattern of policymaking distinct from any of the perspectives thus far introduced.

Unfortunately, the testing on second-term presidential behavior is more limited in scope than the analysis of first-term behavior. Within the years of the survey data, the only second-term administrations include those of Nixon (prior to his resignation), Reagan, and Clinton. Moreover, during two of these administrations, presidents faced a threat of impeachment, which may have given them the incentive to behave as if they were running for reelection. For these reasons, the conclusions about second-term presidents are necessarily more tentative than those about first-term ones.

The more limited scope of the data requires eliminating at least two of the control variables from the earlier analysis. We chose to exclude the president indicators since the likelihood of policy congruence did not significantly differ among Nixon, Reagan, and Clinton during the first term. There are also insufficient degrees of freedom to estimate separate effects for both presidential and congressional ideology by the half of the term. In the preceding analysis, congressional ideology had an insignificant impact in each half, while the effect of presidential ideology was significant only in the first half. We accordingly estimate one effect of congressional ideology for the entire second term. Table 7.4 presents the findings.

It is immediately apparent that presidents' decision making differs between the first and second terms. The effect of the electoral cycle is not at all significant and is even negative. Also, unlike the results for first-term presidents, personal popularity does not appear to influence the likelihood of policy congruence during the latter two years of the second term.

Interestingly, the coefficients on popularity for the first two years are marginally significant and follow the pattern for first-term presidents who will run for reelection within two years.[22] This result is arguably an

---

22. The effect for presidents with below-average popularity is positive with a two-tailed p value of 0.07 while the effect for presidents with above-average ratings is negative with a two-tailed p value of 0.11.

Table 7.4 Determinants of Policy Congruence, Second-term Presidents

Independent Variables	Probit Coefficient (Standard Error)	
2nd Half	−1.432 (2.811)	
	2nd Half	1st Half
(Popularity − Mean Popularity) × (1 − Above Average Popularity)	−0.009 (0.345)	0.117 (0.065)
(Popularity − Mean Popularity) × (Above Average Popularity)	−0.019 (0.179)	−0.278 (0.175)
President's Ideological Congruence	2.811 (1.409)	1.901 (1.175)
Foreign Policy	−1.926 (2.273)	−0.110 (1.024)
Public Concern	−0.048 (0.089)	−0.070 (0.109)
Congress' Ideological Congruence	7.916 (6.690)	
Constant	2.655 (1.688)	
Number of Observations	75	
Log Likelihood	−38.868	
LR Test for Random Effects	$\chi^2_{(1)} = 9.942$ ($p = 0.002$)	

Note: The dependent variable is Pr (Policy Congruence = 1). The results in the separate columns for the first and second terms regard the variables that are estimated separately by the half of the term. Ford is the omitted president indicator.

artifact of the impeachment threats Nixon and Clinton faced during the first two years of their second terms. In May of 1973 the Senate Watergate Committee began its nationally televised hearings, while during 1997 and 1998 the Monica Lewinsky scandal was unfolding. The threat of losing office may accordingly have caused Nixon and Clinton to behave like presidents soon facing a contest for reelection.

Among the control variables, only presidential ideology appears to affect the likelihood of policy congruence. In each half of the term, the effect is positive and at least marginally significant ($p \leq 0.1$, two-tailed). This result differs from the findings regarding first-term behavior, where presidential ideology did not have a substantial impact on policy congruence during the second half of the term. The discrepancy is consistent with the argument that second-term presidents are less motivated than first-term ones by electoral motivations.

The results on the other control variables in table 7.4 are consistent with the analogous ones of table 7.3 except for the parameter estimates regarding foreign policy. While these coefficients remain negative, they are no longer significant at conventional levels. A possible explanation for this discrepancy relates to the argument that second-term presidents are primarily concerned with establishing an historical legacy. Given that principal motivation, a president may simply want to enact the foreign and domestic policies that will advance his legacy, thus causing there to be no discernible discrepancy between the domains in his likelihood of taking popular positions.

Overall, the findings provide additional support for the Conditional Pandering Theory. As it predicts, a second-term president does not become more likely to support popular policies as the election nears. Also, a second-term president's personal popularity appears to influence his decision making only when he faces the threat of losing office through impeachment, a situation that arguably creates incentives similar to when he is running for reelection. Presidents' decision making thus differs substantially between first and second terms and in ways that are consistent with the Conditional Pandering Theory.

CAVEATS

The two major caveats of chapter 7 are ones that have been identified elsewhere but are worth underscoring. First, some readers may be uncomfortable with the idea of examining the Conditional Pandering Theory with data on congruence. As we have taken pains to explain, the analysis of this chapter concerns predictions of the theory that *specifically regard congruence;* thus we have *direct* evidence on the verisimilitude of the theory, if only, through this corroboration, indirect evidence on pandering. Of course, this test like all others is subject to the criticism that alternative explanations may account for the observed patterns in the data. We have accordingly taken pains to account for possible alternative explanations, highlighting where, if at all, each overlaps with the theory as well as where each differs.

The other major qualification is that the testing relies on budgetary data, a reliance that raises questions about the generalizability of the results. For instance, the fact that budgetary issues are relatively salient allows for the possibility that the findings are limited to salient legislation. While this feature of the data does not pose a problem for purposes of testing the Conditional Pandering Theory (recall that the theory concerns only policy decisions the public is likely to learn about), the empirical patterns should not be presumed to hold for more obscure legislation. Other questions about generalizability may be less specific but simply spring from the fact that the analysis lacks a larger set of (salient) policy decisions. Obviously, in an ideal world, we would have examined even more decisions than the 235 of this chapter. Having said as much, we emphasize that these 235 observations have numerous features that indicate the results should indeed be more broadly applicable. The data encompass a range of substantive domains, presidencies, and political contexts. Moreover, because presidents legally cannot avoid stating a budgetary proposal, our data lack the typical bias toward responsiveness that most data on presidential policy decisions possess.

CONCLUSION

This chapter has examined predictions that the Conditional Pandering Theory generated about the likelihood of congruence between a president's policy decisions and public opinion. The predictions have concerned how the electoral cycle, a president's personal popularity, and the presidential term affect the likelihood of congruence. The analysis also controlled for a variety of other factors, including the ideological leanings of the president and Congress, differences among individual chief executives, and the intensity of public concern. Even accounting for these factors, the Conditional Pandering Theory received a great deal of support. Indeed, compared with the other major schools of thought, the theory better explained the patterns of presidential decision making.

As expected, the president was found to be most likely to take a popular position when he would soon be facing a contest for reelection and had average approval ratings. When the approval ratings of such a president dropped so that he was relatively unpopular, or when they rose so that he was highly popular, his likelihood of supporting policies favored by the public declined. The likelihood of his taking a popular position was also lower in the earlier part of the term. Finally, as predicted by the Conditional Pandering Theory, these effects of presidential popularity and the electoral cycle held only for presidents running for reelection. During the second term, the electoral cycle had no effect, and a president's popularity seemed to affect his behavior only when he faced a threat of losing office through impeachment proceedings.

In the Conditional Pandering Theory, all of this variation is predicted as a function of presidents' incentives to pander to public opinion; in the theory, the likelihood of congruence is constant whenever the president agrees with the mass public about the optimal course of action. Furthermore, other schools of thought do not predict the same patterns of variation in congruence. Consequently, the results of this chapter, in supporting the Conditional Pandering Theory, provide indirect evidence for the existence of pandering.

Considering these results together with those of earlier chapters, they suggest that presidents will pander to public opinion but only under a limited set of conditions. In particular, when a president is marginally popular and will soon face a contest for reelection, he has an incentive to placate current opinion even if doing so entails supporting a policy he believes will not advance societal welfare. Otherwise, he will not want to pander to current opinion.

Of course, the fact that American presidents are not constantly pandering to the public does not imply that they are constantly making policy decisions that advance societal welfare. Indeed, the Conditional Pandering Theory highlights how the president's competence, or ability to assess the likely effects of policies, is critical to the enactment of good policies. To the extent presidents have low levels of competence, it is far from heartening that they commonly have incentives to ignore mass opinion. The concluding chapter discusses this issue in more detail, as well as other implications regarding the ability of the American political system to produce policies in the long-term interest of the nation.

CHAPTER EIGHT

Chief Executives, Policymaking, and the Public

This book has established that presidents' involvement of the mass public significantly affects policymaking in Washington. More specifically, presidents' arousing and monitoring of mass opinion have been shown to move executive and legislative decisions in the direction of majority sentiment. This impact does not, however, entail citizens leading the policy process. Instead, it tends to involve the passage of policies that the president as well as the general public supports.

Part 1 showed how presidents' public appeals advance the enactment of such policies. I found that presidents increase their prospects for legislative success by publicizing popular initiatives Congress is not initially disposed toward enacting. Particularly for domestic affairs, the legislative impact of an appeal depends on the initial popularity of the proposal. When a president publicly advocates a domestic initiative that comports with citizens' preferences, he pressures congressional members to support it. In contrast, by going public about an unpopular domestic proposal, he actually loses legislative influence.

On issues of foreign affairs, the impact of an appeal is less dependent on citizens' initial support for the position the president is advocating because he has a greater ability to alter their predispositions. Still, a chief executive cannot simply obtain any foreign policy proposal he wants by promoting it over the airwaves. If the initiative is highly unpopular, publicizing it will likely harm rather than aid his prospects for legislative success. As a result, even though the president will at times go public about foreign policy proposals that are somewhat unpopular, in general he will not make appeals about initiatives that face mass opposition.

This finding that the policy impact of an appeal depends on current opinion suggests presidents may have the incentive to pander to the citizenry on salient issues. Yet part 2 established that, in fact, presidents do not invariably have the incentive to follow current opinion on salient issues. Instead, the president is typically motivated to pursue the policies he believes will promote societal welfare, regardless of whether they are popular. This is the case even during his first term. A president will only want to pander to public opinion, in the sense of supporting a popular policy he believes is not in voters' interests, if he expects to confront a very competitive electoral race in the near future. In contrast, when the president is highly popular or unpopular, when the election is distant, and when he is not seeking reelection, he will enact policies he deems likely to produce good outcomes for society.[1]

In sum, the results imply that much of the time a president is prone to take unpopular positions, but he will not advocate them to the citizenry. Because his appeals are focused on popular domestic proposals and foreign policy ones that do not face strong public opposition, the speeches may give the misimpression that he is a plebiscite who endorses whatever the current stances of the public are. In reality, however, the president is typically publicizing policies that he would have supported had they not been popular. Furthermore, on salient issues in general, the president will not simply follow mass opinion.

These findings diverge from the two recurring themes of the literature that have appeared throughout the book. The first, that presidents' involvement of the public does not increase the extent to which current opinion influences policymaking, emerges in studies that claim public appeals are merely grandstanding (e.g., Clinton et al. 2004), ones that argue congressional members are not pressured by appeals (e.g., Polsby 1978), and ones that suggest presidents are not substantively responsive to public opinion (e.g., Cohen 1997; Jacobs and Shapiro 2000). In contrast with this theme, the analysis here has shown that presidents' involvement of the public does shift policy toward current opinion. By appealing to the mass citizenry, a president increases the likelihood that relatively popular initiatives are enacted. Furthermore, on salient issues, a chief executive who will soon face a tight electoral race may pander by supporting popular initiatives independent of his beliefs about the merits of the initiatives.

The fact that such policy pandering is restricted to when the chief executive faces an imminent, competitive electoral contest suggests presi-

1. It is worth noting that the results on pandering suggest House members face greater incentives to pander to public opinion than is the case for presidents. House elections occur every two years, and most members face a race that is sufficiently competitive that they cannot take unpopular positions on salient issues without incurring electoral risk (e.g., Canes-Wrone, Brady, and Cogan 2002). In fact, according to the findings of part 2, most House members perpetually face the same electoral context in which a president has the incentive to pander to public opinion on salient issues. These congressional motivations arguably contribute to presidents' incentive to focus public appeals on relatively popular initiatives.

dents' incentives for demagogic policymaking are quite limited. The book thus diverges from the second recurring theme of the literature, which is that a president's involvement of the mass public, on balance, disserves citizens because it causes him to disregard their long-term welfare. As documented previously, this theme has appeared in recent scholarly research (e.g., Bessette 1994; Tulis 1998) as well as early philosophical analyses of the U.S. political system (e.g., *Federalist Papers* 1987 [1788]; Mill 1958 [1861]). In contrast to these works, this study suggests presidents typically do not follow mass opinion if they believe it is misguided or misinformed.

PRESIDENTIAL (IN?)COMPETENCE AND UNRESPONSIVENESS

Of course, whether a president's propensity to disregard current opinion is in fact beneficial to society depends on the extent to which the chief executive is better informed than the mass public. This section discusses how the results pertain to situations in which the president is not in fact more knowledgeable.

The Conditional Pandering Theory described in chapter 5 allows that presidents may be wrong and the mass public correct in their assessments about the likely consequences of policies. In the theory, a president's ability at obtaining policy expertise is captured by his level of competence; the more competent the chief executive, the more capable he is at ascertaining likely outcomes of policies. When a president endorses an initiative that produces a bad outcome, this error costs him reelection if voters learn about it before casting their ballots. Thus while the Conditional Pandering Theory finds that presidents can usually disregard current opinion, it does not indicate that they can enact whatever policy they want without concern for voters' evaluations. Instead, the analysis suggests that presidents who make incompetent decisions are likely to be voted out of office.

This implication may still not make the theory, as well as the empirical findings supporting it, entirely heartening to those who hold that a chief executive almost never has more expertise than the public does; to the extent this is the case, the book indicates the American electorate might be better off with a political system that motivated presidents to pander to public opinion more consistently. An even wider range of readers may be dismayed by the fact that the empirics do not uncover a high level of popular responsiveness given that, clearly, responsiveness has many virtues. For example, it ensures leaders do not pursue a course of action that benefits them over the populace and encourages citizens to be engaged with the political process. It is my hope that nothing in this book has left the impression that I believe such assets of popular responsiveness are non-existent. At the same time, the assets do not negate the possibility that responsiveness can also have problematic consequences. My purpose in focusing on the issues of demagoguery and pandering has been to say something novel, and precise, about this set of potentially problematic consequences.

Moreover, for all who like to see high levels of popular responsiveness, the book offers a combination of good news and ammunition for arguing that fears of demagoguery have been overblown. The good news is the finding that presidents' success from appealing to the public is dependent on promoting relatively popular proposals; in other words, speechmaking is not (successfully) employed to propel the enactment of unpopular legislation. The ammunition, by comparison, is the finding that presidents will often not want to pander to public opinion. According to the preceding chapters, there are a wide set of conditions when we can observe a president taking a popular position and need not be concerned that he is disregarding information about how to further societal welfare.

IMPLICATIONS/SPECULATION ABOUT ALTERNATIVE POLITICAL SYSTEMS

While the book has focused on national American politics, the question of how a chief executive's arousing and monitoring of current opinion may alter policymaking is naturally not limited to this context. Indeed, the quote of Aristotle at the start of the Preface underscores the applicability of the question to democratic governance more generally. An in-depth comparative study of how presidents' involvement of the mass public affects policymaking in other contexts, or given certain reforms to the American system, would clearly be beyond the parameters of this analysis. However, as a preliminary effort in this vein, I speculate about some implications for alternative electoral institutions. Because the primary normative finding of the book concerns presidents' incentives to pander to mass opinion, the following discussion is focused on these incentives.

It is worth emphasizing that even within this limited subject matter, the discussion is in no way meant to be a thorough inquiry. Instead, this section has two related aims. It attempts to offer insights on what the preceding chapters can (and, equally important, cannot) say about the benefits of the various electoral institutions, and second, hopes to provoke future research that may evaluate these insights.[2]

---

2. See Rockman (1998) for a more general call for comparative research regarding the U.S. presidency in relation to other executive institutions.

A Longer Presidential Term

The book suggests that a president will not pander to public opinion unless he will soon be running for reelection, where "soon" was measured by the final two years in office. Consequently, one might suppose that the analysis supports a long presidential term. Indeed, the Conditional Pandering Theory implies that, all else equal, lengthening a chief executive's term would decrease the amount of policy pandering.[3] The theory does not, however, suggest that such an institution would necessarily improve societal welfare. In particular, this welfare is highly dependent on the ability of the chief executive to assess the likely consequences of policies. Citizens thus have a strong interest in quickly replacing presidents whose skills at policymaking prove lacking.

Relating this logic to the United States, assume the length of the presidential term was extended to six years. During the first term, less pandering would occur because the president would only have the incentive to engage in this behavior toward the end of the six years. However, if the president showed himself to be an incompetent policymaker during the first few years, the public could not soon replace him with a more competent leader. The American populace may accordingly be worse off than if his term were only four years, even with the reduction in pandering.

By this same logic, neither the Conditional Pandering Theory nor any other part of the analysis recommends a benign dictatorship. While the theory suggests that a dictator appointed for life would lack incentives to pander to public opinion, it also incorporates that she would not be removable after issuing incompetent decisions. The public may accordingly be far worse off with a benign dictator than with a succession of presidents running for reelection. In the latter situation, the chief executives would at times pander to public opinion. However, much of the time they would try to enhance citizens' long-term interests, and whenever one of these executives was incompetent at doing so, the electorate could simply replace her.

A Limit of One Term

A separate electoral institution that could alter the policy incentives of chief executives would be to prohibit them from seeking reelection. This

---

3. This implication is consistent with Chappell and Keech (1983), who show through a series of simulation experiments that American presidents would take a longer-term perspective toward macroeconomic policy, and thus better promote citizens' welfare, if they served a six-year rather than a four-year term.

restriction is present in the presidential systems of Colombia, Costa Rica, Ecuador, El Salvador, Guatemala, Honduras, Mexico, and Sri Lanka (Shugart and Carey 1992, 88). The analysis of the preceding chapters suggests that a president in such a system should lack any incentive to pander to public opinion.[4] In particular, the Conditional Pandering Theory finds that presidents who do not face electoral pressures are more concerned with the expected outcomes of policies than the initial popularity of them.

The theory does not imply, however, that a limit of one term would necessarily improve a citizenry's well-being relative to what it would be given a limit of two terms, such as exists in the United States. With a limit of one term, voters would never be able to assess a presidential candidate's competence on the basis of his behavior in office. Their ability to evaluate the candidates would consequently decline, potentially causing the election of less capable leaders. The benefits to citizens from the reduction in pandering could accordingly be offset by the lower competence of the elected executives.

A limit of one term could also influence the types of individuals who would run for office. If a president could never seek reelection, highly qualified individuals who would be interested in the position given the possibility of serving multiple terms might no longer be interested in pursuing it. Such an effect could reduce the typical level of executive competence and thus further offset the benefits the restriction would generate in terms of reducing the incentives for pandering.

An Interim Term

The final electoral institution I speculate about is the requirement of an interim term, by which I mean that a president may run for reelection but cannot do so while still in office. This institution is not merely theoretical. At certain points, Argentina, Panama, Peru, and Venezuela have had laws specifying that the president can seek reelection only after an interim term or terms have passed (Shugart and Carey 1992, 88). Also, within the United States, Virginia requires an interim term before a governor can run for reelection.

---

4. Stokes (2001) finds that term limits do not alter the likelihood Latin American presidents will choose unpopular neoliberal reforms during the first six months in office. Given that the findings in part 2 also suggest pandering is unlikely in the beginning of a president's term, they are consistent with Stokes's result, which should not be interpreted to suggest that term limits would not affect pandering or responsiveness later in a president's term.

The logic of the Conditional Pandering Theory implies that this electoral institution should provide fewer incentives for pandering than a system like that of the United States. Given a requisite interim term, the president is never running for reelection while in office. By the time he does seek to serve again, voters will have likely learned the outcomes of most policies he enacted. Consequently, compared with a system in which a president can seek immediate reelection, chief executives should be more concerned with the expected outcomes of policies and less with current opinion.

A mandatory interim term does not entail some of the negative consequences inherent to the previously discussed reforms. Unlike lengthening the presidential term, a requisite interim term does not force voters to suffer incompetent presidents for a longer period of time. Also, unlike a limit of one term, an interim term does not eliminate the possibility that a president's behavior could affect voters' assessments on whether to grant him another period of service. Still, the institution has potentially negative consequences. For instance, as with the limit of one term, a prohibition on consecutive terms could affect the type of individual willing to run for office; some highly capable aspirants might be dissuaded from seeking the position if they could not serve consecutive terms.

Furthermore, as documented in Martha Joynt Kumar et al. (2000), presidential transitions impose costs on society. Summarizing some of these costs, Democratic political advisor Harrison Wellford observes that during a transition "You have a series of action-forcing deadlines that come up against you like freight trains. There are a lot of things that happen right there and for a brand new administration that hasn't done any of this before, these are intimidating challenges" (Kumar et al. 2000, 754). Obviously, such issues are beyond the scope of this study. For our purposes, it is simply worth underscoring that a requisite interim term should give presidents less incentive to pander to public opinion but that the electoral institution may have other, negative effects on societal welfare.

PRESIDENTS, POLITICAL INSTITUTIONS AND THE MASS PUBLIC

The literature on how presidents affect policymaking has been dominated by research that all but ignores mass opinion. A great deal of work has been conducted on formal powers like the veto and executive orders, on presidents' ability to bargain with Congress, and on their personal qualities. Among studies that consider the impact of public opinion, most have examined presidents' personal popularity or prestige. The policy preferences of the mass citizenry, in contrast, have not often been the focus of scholarly inquiry.

The preceding analysis implies that this lack of attention is not justified. Citizens' policy preferences have a substantial impact on the president's role in policymaking, both in terms of executive power and decision making. When Congress is likely to reject a popular executive proposal, a president may appeal to the public about his position and thereby pressure members to enact it. Moreover, mass opinion can affect a president's likelihood of supporting an initiative. Future analysis of the president's role in the policy process should accordingly incorporate that the involvement of the mass public affects this role.

This implication is not limited to the American context or even to existing democracies. In nations undergoing democratization, the optimal design of executive institutions is a practical matter. The findings of this book underscore that the relationship between a chief executive and his or her public can significantly affect the ways in which formal institutions operate in practice. Constitutional scholars and architects should therefore consider this relationship when evaluating how a political system will likely function.

References

Achen, Christopher H. 1978. "Measuring Representation." *American Journal of Political Science* 22: 475–510.

Aldrich, John H. 1995. *Why Parties? The Origin and Transformation of Party Politics in America.* Chicago: University of Chicago Press.

Amemiya, Takeshi. 1978. "The Estimation of a Simultaneous Equation Generalized Probit Model." *Econometrica* 46: 1193–1205.

Ansolabehere, Stephen, Roy Behr, and Shanto Iyengar. 1993. *The Media Game: American Politics in the Television Age.* New York: Macmillan.

Aristotle. 1988 [350 B.C.E.]. *The Politics.* Ed. Stephen Everson. Cambridge, UK: Cambridge University Press.

Arnold, R. Douglas. 1990. *The Logic of Congressional Action.* New Haven, CT: Yale University Press.

Austen-Smith, David, and Jeffrey S. Banks. 2000. "Cheap Talk and Burned Money." *Journal of Economic Theory* 91: 1–16.

Barber, James David. 1977. *The Presidential Character: Predicting Performance in the White House,* 2nd ed. Englewood Cliffs, NJ: Prentice-Hall, Inc.

Baron, David P. 2003. *Business and Its Environment,* 4th ed. Upper Saddle River, NJ: Prentice Hall.

Barrett, Andrew W. 2000. "Gone Public: The Impact of Presidential Rhetoric in Congress." Ph.D. diss., Texas A&M University.

Bartels, Larry M. 1991. "Constituency Opinion and Congressional Policy Making: The Reagan Defense Buildup." *American Political Science Review* 85: 429–56.

Bates, Robert, Avner Greif, Margaret Levi, Jean-Laurent Rosenthal, and Barry Weingast. 1998. *Analytical Narratives.* Princeton, NJ: Princeton University Press.

Baum, Matthew A., and Samuel Kernell. 1999. "Has Cable Ended the Golden Age of Presidential Television?" *American Political Science Review* 93: 99–114.

Bawn, Kathleen. 1995. "Political Control versus Expertise: Congressional Choices about Administrative Procedures." *American Political Science Review* 89: 62–73.

Beck, Nathaniel, Jonathan N. Katz, and Richard Tucker. 1998. "Taking Time Seriously: Time-Series-Cross-Section Analysis with a Binary Dependent Variable." *American Journal of Political Science* 42: 1260–88.

Behr, Roy, and Shanto Iyengar. 1985. "Television News, Real-World Cues, and Changes in the Public Agenda." *Public Opinion Quarterly* 49: 38–57.

Bessette, Joseph M. 1994. *The Mild Voice of Reason: Deliberative Democracy and American National Government.* Chicago: University of Chicago Press.

Bond, Jon R., and Richard Fleisher. 1990. *The President in the Legislative Arena.* Chicago: University of Chicago Press.

Brace, Paul, and Barbara Hinckley. 1992. *Follow the Leader: Opinion Polls and the Modern Presidents.* New York: Basic Books.

Brady, David W., and Craig Volden. 1998. *Revolving Gridlock.* Boulder, CO: Westview Press.

Brody, Richard A. 1991. *Assessing the President: The Media, Elite Opinion, and Public Support.* Stanford: Stanford University Press.

Brody, Richard A., and Lee Sigelman. 1983. "Presidential Popularity and Presidential Elections: An Update and Extension." *Public Opinion Quarterly* 47: 325–28.

Budget of the United States Government. Washington, DC: Government Printing Office, fiscal years 1958–2001. Individual volumes within this range of years have been consulted for this study.

Caldeira, Gregory A., and John R. Wright. 1998. "Lobbying for Justice: Organized Interests, Supreme Court Nominations, and the United States Senate." *American Journal of Political Science* 42: 499–523.

Cameron, Charles M. 2000. *Veto Bargaining: President and the Politics of Negative Power.* Cambridge, UK: Cambridge University Press.

Cameron, Charles M., and Rebecca R. Morton. 2002. "Formal Theory Meets Data." In *State of the Discipline, Volume 3,* ed. Ira Katznelson and Helen V. Milner, 787–804. New York: W. W. Norton and Co.

Campbell, Kathryn Kohrs, and Kathleen Hall Jamieson. 1990. *Deeds Done in Words: Presidential Rhetoric and the Genres of Governance.* Chicago: University of Chicago Press.

Canes-Wrone, Brandice. 2001a. "The President's Legislative Influence from Public Appeals." *American Journal of Political Science* 45: 313–29.

———. 2001b. "A Theory of Presidents' Public Agenda-setting." *Journal of Theoretical Politics* 13: 183–208.

Canes-Wrone, Brandice, David W. Brady, and John F. Cogan. 2002. "Out of Step, Out of Office: Electoral Accountability and House Members' Voting." *American Political Science Review* 96: 127–40.

Canes-Wrone, Brandice, and Scott de Marchi. 2002. "Presidential Approval and Legislative Success." *Journal of Politics* 64: 491–509.

Canes-Wrone, Brandice, Michael C. Herron, and Kenneth W. Shotts. 2001. "Leadership and Pandering: A Theory of Executive Policymaking." *American Journal of Political Science* 45: 532–50.

Canes-Wrone, Brandice, and Kenneth W. Shotts. 2004. "The Conditional Nature of Presidential Responsiveness to Public Opinion." *American Journal of Political Science* 48: 690–706.

Chang, Kelly. 2003. *Appointing Central Bankers.* Cambridge, UK: Cambridge University Press.

Chappell, Henry W., and William R. Keech. 1983. "Welfare Consequences of the Six-Year Presidential Term Evaluated in the Context of a Model of the U.S. Economy." *American Political Science Review* 77: 75–91.

Chong, Dennis. 1991. *Collective Action and the Civil Rights Movement.* Chicago: University of Chicago Press.

Clinton, Joshua D., David E. Lewis, Stephanie K. Riegg, and Barry R. Weingast. 2004. "Strategically Speaking: A New Analysis of the President's Going Public." Princeton University. Typescript.

Cohen, Jeffrey E. 1995. "Presidential Rhetoric and the Public Agenda." *American Journal of Political Science* 39: 87–107.

———. 1997. *Presidential Responsiveness and Public Policy-Making: The Public and the Policies that Presidents Choose.* Ann Arbor: University of Michigan Press.

Congressional Quarterly Almanacs. Washington, DC: Congressional Quarterly, Inc., 1945–2004. Individual volumes within this range of publication years have been consulted for this study.

Conley, Patricia Heidotting. 2001. *Presidential Mandates: How Elections Shape the National Agenda.* Chicago: University of Chicago Press.

Cornwell, Elmer E., Jr. 1965. *Presidential Leadership of Public Opinion.* Bloomington: Indiana University Press.

Covington, Cary R. 1987. " 'Staying Private': Gaining Congressional Support for Unpublicized Presidential Preferences on Roll-Call Votes." *Journal of Politics* 49: 737–55.

Covington, Cary R., and Rhonda Kinney. 1999. "Enacting the President's Agenda in the House of Representatives: The Determinants and Impact of Presidential Agenda-setting Success." Paper presented at the Midwest Political Science Association Meetings, Chicago, IL.

Crawford, Vincent P., and Joel Sobel. 1982. "Strategic Information Transmission." *Econometrica* 50: 1431–51.

Dahl, Robert A. 1950. *Congress and Foreign Policy.* New York: Harcourt Brace.

———. 1961. *Who Governs? Democracy and Power in an American City.* New Haven, CT: Yale University Press.

Dallek, Robert. 1984. *Ronald Reagan: The Politics of Symbolism.* Cambridge, MA: Harvard University Press.

———. 1998. *Flawed Giant: Lyndon Johnson and His Times, 1961–1973.* New York: Oxford University Press.

Deibel, Terry L. 1987. *Presidents, Public Opinion, and Power: The Nixon, Carter and Reagan Years.* New York: Foreign Policy Association.

de Marchi, Scott, and Terry Sullivan. 1997. "Modeling Presidential Persuasion: Constitutional Position, Bargaining and Dead Ducks." Paper presented at the American Political Science Association Meetings, Washington, DC.

Denton, Robert E., Jr., and Mary E. Stuckey. 1994. "A Communication Model of Presidential Campaigns: A 1992 Overview." In *The 1992 Presidential Campaign: A Communication Perspective,* ed. Robert E. Denton, Jr., 1–42. Westport, CT: Praeger.

Derthick, Martha, and Paul J. Quirk. 1985. *The Politics of Deregulation.* Washington, DC: Brookings Institution.

Diamond, Martin. 1987. "The Federalist." In *History of Political Philosophy,* 3rd ed., ed. Leo Strauss and Joseph Cropsey, 659–79. Chicago: University of Chicago Press.

Downs, Anthony. 1957. *An Economic Theory of Democracy.* New York: HarperCollins.

Edwards, George C., III. 1982. "Presidential Manipulation of Public Opinion." In *Rethinking the Presidency,* ed. Thomas E. Cronin. Boston: Little, Brown and Company.

———. 1983. *The Public Presidency: The Pursuit of Popular Support.* New York: St. Martin's Press.

———. 2003. *On Deaf Ears: The Limits of the Bully Pulpit.* New Haven, CT: Yale University Press.

Edwards, George, and B. Dan Wood. 1999. "Who Influences Whom?: The President and the Public Agenda." *American Political Science Review* 93: 327–44.

Eisinger, Robert M. 2003. *The Evolution of Presidential Polling.* New York: Cambridge University Press.

Elling, Richard C. 1982. "Ideological Change in the United States Senate: Time and Electoral Responsiveness." *Legislative Studies Quarterly* 7: 75–92.

Ellis, Richard, ed. 1998. *Speaking to the People: The Rhetorical Presidency in Historical Perspective.* Amherst: University of Massachusetts Press.

Epstein, David, and Sharyn O'Halloran. 2000. *Delegating Powers: A Transaction Cost Politics Approach to Policy Making under Separate Powers.* Cambridge, UK: Cambridge University Press.

Erikson, Robert S., Michael B. MacKuen, and James A. Stimson. 2002a. *The Macro Polity.* Cambridge, UK: Cambridge University Press.

———. 2002b. "Public Opinion and Policy: Causal Flow in a Macro System Model." In *Navigating Public Opinion: Polls, Policy, and the Future of American Democracy,* ed. Jeff Manza, Fay Lomax Cook, and Benjamin I. Page, 33–53. Oxford: Oxford University Press.

Fearon, James D. 1999. "Electoral Accountability and the Control of Politicians: Selecting Good Types versus Sanctioning Poor Performance." In *Democracy, Accountability, and Representation,* ed. Bernard Manin, Susan Stokes, and Adam Przeworski, 55–97. Cambridge, UK: Cambridge University Press.

The Federalist Papers. 1987 [1788]. New York: Penguin Books.

Feldstein, Martin. 1994. Introductory chapter of *American Economic Policy in the 1980s,* ed. Martin Feldstein, 1–79. Chicago: University of Chicago Press.

Fenno, Richard F., Jr. 1973. *Congressmen in Committees.* Boston: Little, Brown.

Ferejohn, John. 1986. "Incumbent Performance in Office." *Public Choice* 50: 1–26.

Ferejohn, John, and Keith Krehbiel. 1987. "The Budget Process and the Size of the Budget." *American Journal of Political Science* 31: 296–320.

Ferejohn, John, and Debra Satz. 1995. "Unification, Universalism, and Rational Choice Theory." *Critical Review* 9: 71–84.

Fett, Patrick J. 1994. "Presidential Legislative Priorities and Legislators' Voting Decisions: An Exploratory Analysis." *Journal of Politics* 56: 502–12.

Figlio, David N. 2000. "Political Shirking, Opponent Quality, and Electoral Support." *Public Choice* 103: 271–84.

Fiorina, Morris P. 1974. *Representatives, Roll Calls, and Constituencies.* Lexington, MA: Lexington Books.

———. 1981. *Retrospective Voting in American National Elections.* New Haven, CT: Yale University Press.

Fisher, Louis. 1975. *Presidential Spending Power.* Princeton, NJ: Princeton University Press.

Gamm, Gerald, and Renee M. Smith. 1998. "Presidents, Parties, and the Public: Evolving Patterns of Interaction, 1977–1929." In *Speaking to the People: The Rhetorical Presidency in Historical Perspective,* ed. Richard Ellis, 87–111. Amherst: University of Massachusetts Press.

Geer, John G. 1996. *From Tea Leaves to Opinion Polls.* New York: Columbia University Press.

Genovese, Michael A. 1994. "Jimmy Carter and the Age of Limits: Presidential Power in a Time of Decline and Diffusion." In *The Presidency and Domestic Politics of Jimmy Carter,* ed. Herbert D. Rosenbaum and Alexej Ugrinsky, 187–221. Westport, CT: Greenwood Press.

Gilligan, Thomas W., and Keith Krehbiel. 1987. "Collective Decisionmaking and Standing Committees: An Informational Rationale for Restrictive Amendment Procedures." *Journal of Law, Economics and Organization* 3: 287–335.

Green, Donald P., and Ian Shapiro. 1994. *The Pathologies of Rational Choice*. New Haven, CT: Yale University Press.

Greene, William H. 1993. *Econometric Analysis*, 2nd ed. New York: Macmillan Publishing Company.

Greenstein, Fred I. 2000. *The Presidential Difference: Style and Character in the Oval Office from FDR to Bill Clinton*. New York: Free Press.

Groseclose, Timothy, and Nolan McCarty. 2001. "The Politics of Blame: Bargaining before an Audience." *American Journal of Political Science* 45: 100–119.

Grossman, Michael Baruch, and Martha Joynt Kumar. 1981. *Portraying the President: the White House and the News Media*. Baltimore: Johns Hopkins University Press.

Hacker, Jacob S. 1999. *The Road to Nowhere: The Genesis of President Clinton's Plan for Health Security*. Princeton, NJ: Princeton University Press.

Hager, Gregory L., and Terry Sullivan. 1994. "President-centered and Presidency-centered Explanations of Presidential Public Activity." *American Journal of Political Science* 38: 1079–1103.

Hall, Richard L, and Frank W. Wayman. 1990. "Buying Time: Moneyed Interests and the Mobilization of Bias in Congressional Committees." *American Political Science Review* 84: 797–820.

Hammond, Thomas H., and Jack H. Knott. 1996. "Who Controls the Bureaucracy?: Presidential Power, Congressional Dominance, Legal Constraints, and Bureaucratic Autonomy in a Model of Multi-Institutional Policymaking." *Journal of Law, Economics, and Organization* 12: 121–68.

Hansen, John Mark. 1998. "Individuals, Institutions, and Public Preferences over Public Finance." *American Political Science Reivew* 92: 513–34.

Hargrove, Erwin C. 1988. *Jimmy Carter as President: Leadership and the Politics of the Public Good*. Baton Rouge: Louisiana State University Press.

Hart, Roderick P. 1987. *The Sound of Leadership: Presidential Communication in the Modern Age*. Chicago: University of Chicago Press.

Hartmann, Robert Trowbridge. 1980. *Palace Politics: An Inside Account of the Ford Years*. New York: McGraw Hill.

Heckman, James J. 1978. "Dummy Endogenous Variables in a Simultaneous Equation System." *Econometrica* 46: 931–59.

Herbst, Susan. 1993. *Numbered Voices: How Opinion Poplling Has Shaped American Politics*. Chicago: University of Chicago Press.

———. 1998. *Reading Public Opinion: How Political Actors View the Democratic Process*. Chicago: University of Chicago Press.

Hibbs, Douglas. 1987. *The American Political Economy: Macroeconomics and Electoral Politics*. Cambridge, MA: Harvard University Press.

Hill, Kim Quaile. 1998. "The Policy Agendas of the President and the Mass Public: A Research Validation and Extension." *American Journal of Political Science* 42: 1328–34.

Hogan, Joseph. 1990. *The Reagan Years: The Record in Presidential Leadership*. Ed. Joseph Hogan. Manchester, NY: Manchester University Press.

Howell, William. 2003. *Power without Persuasion: A Theory of Unilateral Action*. Princeton, NJ: Princeton University Press.

Howell, William, Scott Adler, Charles Cameron, and Scott Riemann. 2000. "Divided Government and the Legislative Productivity of Congress, 1945–94." *Legislative Studies Quarterly* 25: 285–312.

Huffington, Arianna. 2000. *How to Overthrow the Government*. New York: Regan Books.

Huntington, Samuel. 1961. *The Common Defense.* New York: Columbia University Press.

Hutchings, Vincent L. 1998. "Issue Salience and Support for Civil Rights Legislation among Southern Democrats." *Legislative Studies Quarterly* 23: 521–44.

Ingberman, Daniel, and Dennis Yao. 1991a. "Circumventing Formal Structure through Commitment: Presidential Influence and Agenda Control." *Public Choice* 70: 151–79.

———. 1991b. "Presidential Commitment and the Veto." *American Journal of Political Science* 35: 351–89.

Jacobs, Lawrence R. 1993. *The Health of Nations: Public Opinion and the Making of American and British Health Policy.* Ithaca, NY: Cornell University Press.

Jacobs, Lawrence R., and Robert Y. Shapiro. 2000. *Politicians Don't Pander: Political Manipulation and the Loss of Democratic Responsiveness.* Chicago: University of Chicago Press.

———. 2002a. "Politics and Policymaking in the Real World: Crafted Talk and the Loss of Democratic Responsiveness." In *Navigating Public Opinion: Polls, Policy, and the Future of American Democracy,* ed. Jeff Manza, Fay Lomax Cook, and Benjamin I. Page, 54–75. Oxford: Oxford University Press.

———. 2002b. "Public Opinon, Foreign Policy, and Democracy: How Presidents Use Public Opinion." In *Navigating Public Opinion: Polls, Policy, and the Future of American Democracy,* ed. Jeff Manza, Fay Lomax Cook, and Benjamin I. Page, 184–200. Oxford: Oxford University Press.

Jacoby, William C. 1994. "Public Attitudes Toward Government Spending." *American Journal of Political Science* 38: 336–61.

Jones, Charles O. 1988. *The Trusteeship Presidency: Jimmy Carter the United States Congress.* Baton Rouge: Louisiana State University Press.

Kaufman, Burton Ira. 1993. *The Presidency of James Earl Carter, Jr.* Lawrence: University Press of Kansas.

Kennan, George F. 1951. *American Diplomacy, 1900–1950.* Chicago: University of Chicago Press.

Kennedy, Peter. 1989. *A Guide to Econometrics,* 2nd ed. Cambridge, MA: MIT Press.

Kernell, Samuel. 1976. "The Truman Doctrine Speech: A Case Study of the Dynamics of Presidential Opinion Leadership." *Social Science History* 1: 20–44.

———. 1997. *Going Public: New Strategies of Presidential Leadership,* 3rd ed. Washington, DC: Congressional Quarterly Press.

Ketcham, Ralph. 1986. "Republicanism in the 1780s." In *The Anti-Federalist Papers and the Constitutional Convention Debates,* ed. Ralph Ketcham, 6–7. New York: Mentor.

Key, V. O., Jr. 1961. *Public Opinion and American Democracy.* New York: Alfred Knopf.

Key, V. O., Jr., with the assistance of Milton C. Cummings, Jr. 1966. *The Responsible Electorate: Rationality in Presidential Voting, 1936–1960.* Cambridge, MA: Harvard University Press.

Kiewiet, D. Roderick, and Keith Krehbiel. 2002. "Domestic Discretionary Appropriation, 1950–1999: Here's the President. Where's the Party?" *Leviathan* 30: 115–37.

Kiewiet, D. Roderick, and Mathew D. McCubbins. 1985. "Congressional Appropriations and the Electoral Connection." *Journal of Politics* 47: 59–82.

———. 1988. "Presidential Influence on Congressional Appropriations Decisions." *American Journal of Political Science* 32: 713–36.

———. 1991. *The Logic of Delegation: Congressional Parties and the Appropriations Process.* Chicago: University of Chicago Press.

Kingdon, John W. 1977. "Models of Legislative Voting." *Journal of Politics* 39: 563–95.

Kollman, Ken. 1998. *Outside Lobbying: Public Opinion and Interest Group Strategies.* Princeton, NJ: Princeton University Press.

Kumar, Martha Joynt, George C. Edwards III, James P. Pfiffner, and Terry Sullivan. 2000. "Meeting the Freight Train Head On: Planning for the Presidential Transition." *Presidential Studies Quarterly* 30: 754–69.

Krehbiel, Keith. 1998. *Pivotal Politics.* Chicago: University of Chicago Press.

Kuklinski, James H. 1978. "Representativeness and Elections: A Policy Analysis." *American Political Science Review* 72: 165–77.

Lawrence, Alan B. 2003. "What Presidents Say and Why It Matters: The Influence of Presidential Rhetoric on the Public Agenda, 1946–2002." Paper presented at the Midwest Political Science Association Meetings. Chicago, IL.

Levitt, Steven D. 1997. "Using Electoral Cycles in Police Hiring to Estimate the Effect of Police on Crime." *American Economic Review* 87: 270–90.

Lewis, David A. 1997. "The Two Rhetorical Presidencies: An Analysis of Televised Presidential Speeches, 1947–1991." *American Politics Quarterly* 25: 380–95.

Lewis, David E. 2003. *Presidents and the Politics of Agency Design: Political Insulation in the United States Government Bureaucracy, 1946–1997.* Stanford, CA: Stanford University Press.

Lippmann, Walter. 1922. *Public Opinion.* New York: Harcourt, Brace and Company.

Lodge, Milton, Kathleen M. McGraw, and Patrick Stroh. 1989. "An Impression-Driven Model of Candidate Evaluation." *American Political Science Review* 83: 399–419.

Lohmann, Susanne. 1999. "What Price Accountability? The Lucas Island Model and the Politics of Monetary Policy." *American Journal of Political Science* 43: 396–430.

Lowi, Theodore J. 1985. *The Personal President: Power Invested, Promise Unfulfilled.* Ithaca, NY: Cornell University Press.

Lunch, William L., and Peter Sperlich. 1979. "American Public Opinion and the War in Vietnam." *Western Political Quarterly* 32: 21–44.

Lupia, Arthur. 1994. "Shortcuts versus Encyclopedias: Information and Voting Behavior in California Insurance Reform Elections." *American Political Science Review* 88: 63–76.

Maltzman, Forrest. 1999. *Competing Principals: Committees, Parties and the Organization of Congress.* Ann Arbor: University of Michigan Press.

Manza, Jeff, and Fay Lomax Cook. 2002. "The Impact of Public Opinion on Public Policy: The State of the Debate." In *Navigating Public Opinion: Polls, Policy and the Future of American Democracy,* ed. Jeff Manza, Fay Lomax Cook and Benjamin I. Page, 17–32. Oxford: Oxford University Press.

Maskin, Eric, and Jean Tirole. 2004. "The Politician and the Judge: Accountability in Government." *American Economic Review* 94: 1034–54.

Matthews, Steven A. 1989. "Veto Threats: Rhetoric in a Bargaining Game." *Quarterly Journal of Economics* 104: 347–69.

Mayer, Kenneth R. 2001. *With the Stroke of a Pen: Executive Orders and Presidential Power.* Princeton, NJ: Princeton University Press.

Mayhew, David R. 1974. *Congress: The Electoral Connection.* New Haven, CT: Yale University Press.

McCarty, Nolan M. 1997. "Reputation and the Veto." *Economics and Politics* 9: 1–26.

McCarty, Nolan M., and Keith T. Poole. 1995. "Veto Power and Legislation: An Empirical Analysis of Executive and Legislative Bargaining from 1961–1986." *Journal of Law, Economics, and Organization* 11: 282–312.

Meernik, James, and Michael Ault. 2001. "Public Opinion and Support for U.S. Presidents' Foreign Policies." *American Politics Research* 29: 352–73.

Meese, Edwin III. 1992. *With Reagan: The Inside Story.* Washington, DC: Regnery Gateway.

Mervin, David. 1996. *George Bush and the Guardianship Presidency.* New York: St. Martin's Press.

Milkis, Sidney M. 1998. "The Presidency and Political Parties." In *The Presidency and the Political System,* ed. Michael Nelson, 374–407. Washington, DC: Congressional Quarterly.

Mill, John Stuart. 1958 [1861]. *Considerations on Representative Government.* New York: The Liberal Arts Press.

Miller, Gary J. 1993. "Formal Theory and the Presidency." In *Researching the Presidency: Vital Questions, New Approaches,* ed. George C. Edwards III, John H. Kessel, and Bert A. Rockman, 289–336. Pittsburgh, PA: University of Pittsburgh Press.

Miroff, Bruce. 1982. "Monopolizing the Public Space: The President as a Problem for Democratic Politics." In *Rethinking the Presidency,* ed. Thomas E. Cronin, 218–32. Boston: Little, Brown and Company.

Modigliani, Andre, and Franco Modigliani. 1987. "The Growth of the Federal Deficit and the Role of Public Attitudes." *Public Opinion Quarterly* 51: 459–80.

Moe, Terry M. 1985. "The Politicized Presidency." In *The New Directions in American Politics,* ed. John E. Chubb and Paul E. Peterson, 235–71. Washington, DC: Brookings Institution.

Moe, Terry M., and William Howell. 1999. "A Theory of Unilateral Action." *Presidential Studies Quarterly* 29: 850–72.

Monroe, Alan D. 1979. "Consistency between Public Preferences and National Policy Decisions." *American Politics Quarterly* 7: 3–19.

Morgenthau, Hans J. 1948. *Politics among Nations: The Struggle for Power and Peace.* New York: A. A. Knopf.

Morris, Dick. 1997. *Behind the Oval Office: Winning the Presidency in the Nineties.* New York: Random House.

Morton, Rebecca B. 1999. *Models and Methods: A Guide to the Empirical Analysis of Formal Models in Political Science.* Cambridge, UK: Cambridge University Press.

Mouw, Calvin J., and Michael B. MacKuen. 1992. "The Strategic Agenda in Legislative Politics." *American Political Science, Review* 86: 87–105.

Mueller, John E. 1973. *War, Presidents, and Public Opinion.* New York: Wiley.

Neustadt, Richard E. 1990 [1960]. *Presidential Power and the Modern Presidents: The Politics of Leadership from Roosevelt to Reagan.* New York: The Free Press.

Nordhaus, William D. 1975. "The Political Business Cycle." *Review of Economic Studies* 42: 169–90.

Oldfield, Duane M., and Aaron Wildavsky. 1991. "Reconsidering the Two Presidencies." In *The Two Presidencies: A Quarter Century Assessment,* ed. Steve A. Shull, 181–90. Chicago: Nelson-Hall Publishers.

Ostrom, Charles W., Jr., and Dennis M. Simon. 1985. "Promise and Performance: A Dynamic Model of Presidential Popularity." *American Political Science Review* 79: 334–58.

Page, Benjamin I., 1978. *Choices and Echoes in Presidential Elections: Rational Man and Electoral Democracy.* Chicago: University of Chicago Press.

———. 2002. "The Semi-Sovereign Public." In *Navigating Public Opinion: Polls, Policy and the Future of American Democracy,* ed. Jeff Manza, Fay Lomax Cook and Benjamin I. Page, 3–16. Oxford: Oxford University Press.

Page, Benjamin I., and Jason Barabas. 2000. "Foreign Policy Gaps between Citizens and Leaders." *International Studies Quarterly* 44: 339-64.

Page, Benjamin I., and Robert Y. Shapiro. 1983. "Effects of Public Opinion on Policy." *American Political Science Review* 77: 175-90.

———. 1984. "Presidents as Opinion Leaders: Some New Evidence." *Policy Studies Journal* 12: 649-61.

———. 1992. *The Rational Public: Fifty Years of Trends in Americans' Policy Preferences.* Chicago: University of Chicago Press.

Page, Benjamin I., Robert Y. Shapiro, and Glenn R. Dempsey. 1987. "What Moves Public Opinion?" *American Political Science Review* 81: 23-43.

The Papers of Thomas Jefferson Volume 31, 1799-1800. 2004. Princeton, NJ: Princeton University Press.

Peltzman, Sam. 1976. "Toward a More General Theory of Regulation." *Journal of Law and Economics* 19: 211-40.

Pemberton, William E. 1997. *Exit with Honor: The Life and Presidency of Ronald Reagan.* Armonk, NY: M. E. Sharpe.

Persson, Torsten, and Guido Tabellini. 1990. *Macroeconomic Policy, Credibility, and Politics.* New York: Harwood Academic Publishers.

Peterson, Mark A. 1990. *Legislating Together: The White House and Capitol Hill from Eisenhower to Reagan.* Cambridge, UK: Cambridge University Press.

Peterson, Paul E. 1994. "The President's Dominance in Foreign Policy Making." *Political Science Quarterly* 109: 215-34.

Polsby, Nelson. 1978. "Interest Groups and the Presidency: Trends in Political Intermediation in America." In *American Politics and Public Policy,* ed. Walter Dean Burnham and Martha Wagner Weinbey, 41-54. Cambridge, MA: MIT Press.

Poole, Keith T. 1998. "Estimating a Basic Space from a Set of Issue Scales." *American Journal of Political Science* 42: 954-93.

Popkin, Samuel. 1991. *The Reasoning Voter: Communication and Persuasion in Presidential Campaigns.* Chicago: University of Chicago Press.

———. 1994. *The Reasoning Voter,* 2nd ed. Chicago: University of Chicago Press.

Powell, Lynda. 1982. "Issue Representation in Congress." *Journal of Politics* 44: 658-78.

Public Papers of the Presidents of the United States. Washington, DC: Government Printing Office, 1936-2003. Individual volumes within this range of publication years have been consulted for this study.

Quirk, Paul J., and Joseph Hinchliffe. 1998. "The Rising Hegemony of Mass Opinion." *Journal of Policy History* 10: 19-50.

Ragsdale, Lyn. 1998. *Vital Statistics on the Presidency: Washington to Clinton.* Washington, DC: Congressional Quarterly, Inc.

Riker, William H. 1982. *Liberalism against Populism: A Confrontation between the Theory of Democracy and the Theory of Social Choice.* San Francisco, CA: Freeman.

———. 1996. *The Strategy of Rhetoric: Campaigning for the American Constitution.* New Haven, CT: Yale University Press.

Rivers, Douglas, and Nancy L. Rose. 1985. "Passing the President's Program: Public Opinion and Presidential Influence in Congress." *American Journal of Political Science* 29: 183-96.

Rockman, Bert A. 1998. "The American Presidency in Comparative Perspective: Systems, Situations, and Leaders." In *The Presidency and the Political System,* ed. Michael Nelson, 62-90. Washington, DC: Congressional Quarterly Press.

Rohde, David W. 1991. *Parties and Leaders in the Postreform House*. Chicago: University of Chicago Press.

Romer, Thomas, and Howard Rosenthal. 1978. "Political Resource Allocation, Controlled Agendas, and the Status Quo." *Public Choice* 33: 27–43.

Schattschneider, E. E. 1960. *The Semisovereign People: A Realist's View of Democracy in America*. New York: Holt.

Schick, Allen. 1995. *The Federal Budget: Politics, Policy, Process*. Washington, DC: Brookings Institution.

Schlesinger, Arthur Meier. 1965. *A Thousand Days: John F. Kennedy in the White House*. Boston: Houghton Mifflin.

Sheldon, Garrett Ward. 1991. *The Political Philosophy of Thomas Jefferson*. Baltimore, MD: Johns Hopkins University Press.

Shepsle, Kenneth A., and Barry R. Weingast. 1987. "The Institutional Foundations of Committee Power." *American Political Science Review* 81: 85–104.

Shugart, Matthew Soberg, and John M. Carey. 1992. *Presidents and Assemblies: Constitutional Design and Electoral Dynamics*. New York: Cambridge University Press.

Shull, Steven A., ed. 1991. *The Two Presidencies: A Quarter Century Assessment*. Chicago: Nelson-Hall.

Sigelman, Lee. 1979. "Presidential Popularity and Presidential Elections." *Public Opinion Quarterly* 43: 532–34.

Sinclair, Barbara. 1983. *Majority Leadership in the U.S. House*. Baltimore, MD: Johns Hopkins University Press.

Skidmore, David. 1996. *Reversing Course: Carter's Foreign Policy, Domestic Politics, and the Failure of Reform*. Nashville, TN: Vanderbilt University Press.

Skocpol, Theda. 1996. *Boomerang: Clinton's Health Security Effort and the Turn Against Government in U.S. Politics*. New York: Norton.

Skowronek, Stephen. 1993. *The Politics Presidents Make: Leadership from John Adams to George Bush*. Cambridge, MA: Harvard University Press.

Smith, Mark A. 2000. *American Business and Political Power: Public Opinion, Elections, and Democracy*. Chicago: University of Chicago Press.

Sniderman, Paul M., Richard A. Brody, and Philip E. Tetlock. 1991. *Reasoning and Choice: Explorations in Political Psychology*. New York: Cambridge University Press.

Snyder, James M., and Tim Groseclose. 2000. "Estimating Party Influence on Congressional Roll-Call Voting." *American Journal of Political Science* 44: 193–211.

Sobel, Richard. 1993. "What Have We Learned about Public Opinion in U.S. Foreign Policy?" In *Public Opinion in U.S. Foreign Policy: The Controversy over Contra Aid*, ed. Richard Sobel, 269–78. Lanham, MD: Rowman & Littlefield.

Stigler, George J. 1971. "The Regulation of Industry." *Bell Journal of Economics and Management Science* 2: 3–21.

Stimson, James A., Michael B. MacKuen, and Robert S. Erikson. 1995. "Dynamic Representation." *American Political Science Review* 89: 543–65.

Stokes, Susan C. 2001. *Mandates and Democracy: Neoliberalism by Surprise in Latin America*. Cambridge, UK: Cambridge University Press.

Su, Tsai-Tsu, Mark S. Kamlet, and David C. Mowery. 1993. "Modeling U.S. Budgetary and Fiscal Policy Outcomes: A Disaggregated, Systemwide Perspective." *American Journal of Political Science* 37: 213–45.

Sullivan, Terry. 1990. "Bargaining with the President: A Simple Game and New Evidence." *American Political Science Review* 84: 1167–96.

————. 1991. "A Matter of Fact: The 'Two Presidencies' Thesis Revitalized." In *The "Two Presidencies": A Quarter Century Assessment,* ed. Steven A. Shull, 143–57. Chicago: Nelson-Hall.

Thomas, Martin. 1985. "Electoral Proximity and Senatorial Roll Call Voting." *American Journal of Political Science* 29: 96–111.

Tocqueville, Alexis de. 1945 [1835]. *Democracy in America.* 2 Vols. Ed. Phillips Bradley. New York: Vintage Books.

Truman, David. 1951. "The Governmental Process: Political Interests and Public Opinion." New York: Knopf.

Tulis, Jeffrey K. 1987. *The Rhetorical Presidency.* Princeton, NJ: Princeton University Press.

————. 1998. "The Two Constitutional Presidencies." In *The Presidency and the Political System,* ed. Michael Nelson, 91–123. Washington, DC: Congressional Quarterly Press.

Volden, Craig. 2002. "A Formal Model of the Politics of Delegation in a Separation of Powers System." *American Journal of Political Science* 46: 111–33.

Waldman, Michael. 2000. *POTUS Speaks: Finding the Words that Defined the Clinton Presidency.* New York: Simon and Schuster.

Waldron, Jeremy. 1995. "The Wisdom of the Multitude: Some Reflections on Book 3, Chapter 11 of Aristotle's *Politics.*" *Political Theory* 23: 563–84.

Wayne, Stephen J. 1978. *The Legislative Presidency.* New York: Harper & Row.

Weissberg, Robert. 2001. "Why Policymaking Should Ignore Public Opinion Polls." *Policy Analysis,* No. 402. Washington, DC: Cato Institute.

White, Joseph. 1995. "Almost Nothing New Under the Sun: Why the Work of Budgeting Remains Incremental." In *Budgeting, Policy, Politics: An Appreciation of Aaron Wildavsky,* ed. Naomi Caiden and Joseph White, 111–32. New Brunswick, NJ: Transaction Publishers.

Wildavsky, Aaron. 1966. "The Two Presidencies." *Trans-Action* 4: 7–14.

————. 1992. *The New Politics of the Budgetary Process.* New York: HarperCollins.

Wilson, James Q. 1989. *Bureaucracy: What Government Agencies Do and Why They Do It.* New York: Basic Books.

Wlezien, Christopher. 1995. "The Public as Thermostat: Dynamics of Preferences for Spending." *American Journal of Political Science* 39: 981–1000.

Wright, Gerald C., and Michael Berkman. 1986. "Candidates and Policy in United States Elections." *American Political Science Review* 80: 567–90.

Zaller, John R. 1992. *The Nature and Origins of Mass Opinion.* New York: Cambridge University Press.

————. 2003. "Coming to Grips with V. O. Key's Concept of Latent Opinion." In *Electoral Democracy,* ed. Michael MacKuen and George Rabinowitz, 311–36. Ann Arbor: University of Michigan Press.

Name Index

Achen, Christopher H., 164n. 5
Aldrich, John H., 22
Amemiya, Takeshi, 65, 65n. 23
Ansolabehere, Stephen, 23n. 14
Arnold, R. Douglas, 22, 111n. 1, 127
Ault, Michael, 31, 35, 96
Austen-Smith, David, 31

Babcok, Charles R., 44n. 50
Banks, Jeffrey S., 31
Barabas, Jason, 109
Barber, James David, 108
Baron, David P., 104n. 2
Barrett, Andrew, 36–37n. 36
Barshay, Jill, 1n. 1
Bartels, Larry M., 89
Bates, Robert, 131
Baum, Matthew A., 30n. 21
Bawn, Kathleen, 23n. 13, 108
Beck, Nathaniel, 174n. 19
Behr, Peter, 44n. 50
Behr, Roy, 23n. 14
Berkman, Michael, 127, 161, 163, 167
Bessette, Joseph M., 7, 8, 8n. 22, 39, 40, 44n. 48, 80, 103, 109, 187
Bettelheim, Adriel, 1n. 1, 2n. 7
Bond, Jon, 35–36n. 34, 64, 76, 77
Brace, Paul, 7n. 20, 125
Brady, David W., 6n. 18, 11n. 25, 22, 25n. 16, 60, 67–68n. 26, 186n. 1
Brody, Richard A., 29, 55, 68, 69n. 28, 115n. 5, 132
Byron, Beverly, 43–44

Caldeira, Gregory A., 22
Cameron, Charles M., 6n. 18, 11nn. 24, 25, 26, 12, 12n. 28, 131n. 1, 132, 147
Campbell, Kathryn Kohrs, 38n. 41
Canes-Wrone, Brandice, 7n. 20, 21n. 9, 22, 24n. 15, 59n. 14, 69n. 28, 78n. 39, 112, 112n. 2, 116n. 8, 158n. 1, 186n. 1
Cannon, Lou, 20n. 5, 43n. 45
Carey, John M., 190
Chang, Kelly, 11n. 25
Chappell, Henry W., 189n. 3
Chong, Dennis, 12n. 27
Clinton, Joshua, 41, 51, 80, 186
Clymer, Adam, 144nn. 39, 40
Cogan, John F., 22, 186n. 1
Cohen, Jeffrey E., 9, 23, 62n. 18, 106n. 7, 111, 125–26, 128, 140n. 22, 161, 162, 171, 178, 186
Conley, Patricia Heidottig, 11n. 25
Cook, Fay Lomax, 111, 112, 124n. 13, 125, 161, 162
Cornwell, Elmer E., Jr., 7n. 21, 23, 38, 39, 51, 80
Covington, Cary R., 37–38, 60, 77–78, 165
Crawford, Vincent P., 31, 32

Dahl, Robert A., 10, 34, 96
Dairymple, Mary, 3n. 11
Dallek, Robert, 68n. 27, 151, 153, 154
de Marchi, Scott, 7n. 20, 11n. 25, 69n. 28, 78n. 39
Dempsey, Glenn R., 23
Denton, Robert E., 140
Derthick, Martha, 104n. 2

Diamond, Martin, xi
Downs, Anthony, 8

Edsall, Thomas B., 43n. 45
Edwards, George C., III, 7, 23, 30n. 22,
    31, 31n. 24, 35, 35n. 32, 38n. 41, 40,
    95, 96, 114n. 4
Eisinger, Robert M., 4
Eland, Ivan, 1, 1n. 3
Elling, Richard C., 127, 163, 167
Ellis, Richard, 7n. 21
Epstein, David, 11n. 25
Erikson, Robert S., 9, 77, 89, 106n. 7,
    111, 124, 161, 166n. 10

Fearon, James D., 115
Feldstein, Martin, 150, 151, 152
Fenno, Richard F., Jr., 22, 34, 96
Ferejohn, John, 12, 22, 63
Figlio, David N., 125n. 16
Fiorina, Morris P., 22, 111n. 1, 127, 162n. 3
Firestone, David, 3n. 9
Fisher, Louis, 90
Fiske, Edward B., 44n. 51
Fleisher, Richard, 35–36n. 34, 64, 76, 77
Fuerbringer, Jonathan, 150nn. 60, 62,
    154nn. 75, 77

Gamm, Gerald, 7n. 21, 13nn. 30, 33, 16n. 5
Geer, John G., 9, 11n. 25, 13n. 30, 16n. 5,
    105n. 6, 124, 124n. 15, 161
Genovese, Michael A., 137
Gilligan, Thomas W., 31, 108
Glass, Andrew J., 142n. 30
Gosselin, Peter G., 140n. 20
Green, Donald P., 12
Greene, William H., 64n. 22, 66nn. 24, 25
Greenstein, Fred I., 74, 77, 97, 108, 115,
    171
Groseclose, Timothy, 22, 155, 170
Grossman, Michael Baruch, 23n. 14

Hacker, Jacob S., 52
Hager, Gregory L., 7n. 21, 70n. 31
Hall, Richard L., 22
Hammond, Thomas H., 11n. 25
Hansen, John Mark, 164n. 7
Hargrove, Erwin C., 108, 133, 136, 138
Harney, Kenneth R., 150n. 65

Hart, Roderick P., 41, 51
Hartmann, Robert Trowbridge, 68n. 27
Heckman, James J., 66n. 24
Herbst, Susan, 53n. 4
Herron, Michael, 112, 112n. 2, 116n. 8
Hershey, Robert D., Jr., 145n. 43, 151n.
    70, 155n. 78
Hibbs, Douglas, 125
Hill, Kim Quaile, 23
Hinchcliffe, Joseph, 9, 103
Hinckley, Barbara, 7n. 20, 125
Hoffman, David, 155n. 79
Hogan, Joseph, 151
Howell, William, 6n. 18, 11nn. 24, 25, 48,
    171
Huntington, Samuel, 7n. 19, 34, 96
Hutchings, Vincent, 23

Ingberman, Daniel, 8
Iyengar, Shanto, 23n. 14

Jacobs, Lawrence, 4, 9, 30n. 22, 31, 52,
    56, 87, 88, 104nn. 2, 5, 106n. 7, 111,
    114n. 4, 126, 161, 177, 186
Jacoby, William C., 62n. 19, 169n. 12
Jamieson, Kathleen Hall, 38n. 41
Jaroslavsky, Rich, 151n. 66
Jones, Charles O., 108, 133–34, 138n. 15

Kaletsky, Anatole, 150n. 60
Kamlet, Mark S., 60
Katz, Jonathan N., 174n. 19
Kaufman, Burton Ira, 136, 138
Keech, William R., 189n. 3
Kennan, George F., 9, 103n. 1, 109
Kennedy, Peter, 64n. 22
Kernell, Samuel, 7, 7n. 21, 8, 13n. 30, 14,
    16n. 5, 29, 30n. 21, 37, 37n. 40, 40,
    51, 69, 79, 132
Ketcham, Ralph, 3–4
Key, V. O., xiii, 8, 10–11, 12n. 27, 25,
    111, 116, 127, 161, 163
Kiewiet, D. Roderick, 6n. 18, 11n. 25,
    60–61, 61n. 17, 63, 67n. 25, 76, 127
Kingdon, John W., 22–23
Kinney, Rhonda, 77–78
Knott, Jack H., 11n. 25
Kollman, Ken, 23
Kranish, Michael, 142n. 32

Krehbiel, Keith, 6n. 18, 11nn. 24, 25,
   25n. 16, 31, 60, 63, 67n. 25, 67–68n.
   26, 108
Kuklinski, James H., 127, 127n. 17, 161,
   163, 167
Kumar, Martha Joynt, 23n. 14, 191

Lawrence, Alan B., 23
Levitt, Steven D., 127
Lewis, David A., 40
Lewis, David E., 11nn. 24, 25
Lippmann, Walter, 9, 103n. 1, 109
Lodge, Milton, 23
Lohmann, Susanne, 128
Lowi, Theodore J., 7n. 21, 13nn. 30, 31,
   33, 16n. 5, 38n. 41
Lunch, William L., 97
Lupia, Arthur, 115n. 5

MacKuen, Michael B., 8, 9, 52, 77, 89,
   106n. 7, 111, 124, 161, 166n. 10
Maltzman, Forrest, 22
Manza, Jeff, 111, 112, 124n. 13, 125, 161,
   162
Maskin, Eric, 104n. 5, 115n. 6
Matthews, Steven A., 11n. 25, 22, 31
Mayer, Kenneth R., 6n. 18
Mayhew, David R., 22
McCarty, Nolan M., 6n. 18, 11n. 25, 22,
   155, 169n. 11, 170
McCubbins, Matthew D., 6n. 18, 11n. 25,
   60–61, 61n. 16, 63, 76, 127
McGraw, Kathleen M., 23
McGregor, Deborah, 3n. 10
McGrory, Mary, 48n. 58
Meernik, James, 31, 35, 96
Mervin, David, 141
Milkis, Sidney M., 7n. 21, 13n. 30, 16n.
   5, 101
Miller, Gary J., 8, 11n. 25, 26, 36–37, 40,
   51, 79
Milligan, Susan, 2n. 4
Mills, Mike, 148n. 52
Miroff, Bruce, 25
Moe, Terry M., 6n. 18, 12, 114
Monroe, Alan D., 8, 124n. 14
Morgenthau, Hans, 9, 103n. 1, 109
Morris, Dick, 83, 177n. 21
Morton, Rebecca B., 12n. 28

Mouw, Calvin J., 8, 52
Mowery, David C., 60
Mueller, John E., 35n. 31

Neustadt, Richard, 7, 13, 77, 97, 108, 171
Noble, Kenneth B., 150n. 60
Nordhaus, William D., 128

O'Halloran, Sharyn, 11n. 25
Oldfield, Duane M., 7n. 19, 34, 97n. 10
Ostrom, Charles W., Jr., 7n. 20

Page, Benjamin I., 8, 12n. 27, 23, 23n. 12,
   30, 35, 77, 89, 109, 124n. 14, 166n.
   10
Peltzman, Sam, 104n. 2
Pemberton, William, 153
Persson, Torsten, 115
Pertman, Adam, 142n. 30
Peterson, Mark A., 58n. 13
Peterson, Paul E., 7n. 19, 34, 96
Pine, Art, 136n. 11
Polsby, Nelson, 7n. 21, 37n. 40, 38n. 42,
   38–39, 40, 51, 80, 186
Poole, Keith T., 6n. 18, 11n. 25, 169,
   169n. 11
Popkin, Samuel, 23, 115n. 5
Powell, Lynda, 162n. 3
Purdum, Todd S., 2n. 8

Quirk, Paul J., 9, 103, 104n. 2

Ragsdale, Lyn, 4, 90, 92n. 5, 135n. 5,
   136n. 10, 140n. 19, 142n. 31, 143n.
   34, 146n. 44, 150n. 59
Raum, Tom, 44n. 47
Richards, Cindy, 145n. 43
Riker, William H., 23n. 12, 104n. 3
Rivers, Douglas, 7n. 20, 125
Roedor, Bill (journalist), 19, 19n. 3
Rohde, David W., 22
Romer, Thomas, 27n. 19
Rose, Nancy L., 7n. 20, 125
Rosenbaum, David E., 2n. 8
Rosenthal, Howard, 27n. 19

Satz, Debra, 12
Schattschneider, E. E., 10, 22–23, 36, 37,
   37n. 39, 38, 40, 51, 68, 79, 104

Schick, Allen, 63
Schlesinger, Arthur Meier, 68n. 27
Shapiro, Ian, 12
Shapiro, Robert Y., 4, 8, 9, 12n. 27, 23,
    30, 30n. 22, 31, 35, 52, 56, 77, 87, 88,
    89, 104n. 5, 106n. 7, 111, 114n. 4,
    124n. 14, 126, 161, 162, 178, 186
Shepsle, Kenneth A., 22
Shotts, Kenneth, 105, 112, 112n. 2, 116n.
    8, 157, 158n. 1
Shugart, Matthew Soberg, 190
Shull, Steven A., 34, 34n. 30
Sigelman, Lee, 132
Simon, Dennis M., 7n. 20
Sinclair, Barbara, 22
Skidmore, David, 137
Skocpol, Theda, 52
Skowronek, Stephen, 7n. 21, 13n. 30, 14,
    16n. 5, 38n. 41, 114, 132
Smith, Hedrick, 151n. 69
Smith, Renee M., 7n. 21, 13nn. 30, 33,
    16n. 5
Sniderman, Paul M., 115n. 5
Snyder, James M., 22
Sobel, Joel, 32
Sobel, Richard, 31, 35
Sperlich, Peter, 97
Stigler, George J., 104n. 2
Stimson, James A., 9, 77, 89, 106n. 7,
    111, 124, 161, 166n. 10
Stokes, Susan, 162n. 2, 163n. 4, 190n. 4
Stroh, Patrick, 23
Stuckey, Mary E., 140
Su, Tsai-Tsu, 60
Sullivan, Terry, 7nn. 20, 21, 11n. 25, 34,
    70n. 31

Tabellini, Guido, 115
Tetlock, Philip E., 115n. 5
Thomas, Martin, 127, 163
Tirole, Jean, 104n. 5, 115n. 6
Truman, David, 10
Tucker, Richard, 174n. 19
Tulis, Jeffrey K., 7n. 21, 8, 13nn. 30, 31,
    16n. 5, 39, 40, 52, 80, 101–2, 103n. 1,
    109

Volden, Craig, 6n. 18, 11n. 25, 25n. 16,
    60, 67–68n. 26

Waldman, Michael, 83
Waldron, Jeremy, xi
Wayman, Frank W., 22
Wayne, Stephen J., 13
Weingast, Barry R., 22
Weissberg, Robert, 9, 103n. 1, 109
White, Joseph, 60n. 16, 63
Wildavsky, Aaron, 7n. 19, 34, 63, 97,
    97n. 10
Wilson, James Q., 104n. 2
Wlezien, Christopher, 12n. 27, 62n. 19
Wood, B. Dan, 35n. 32, 95
Wright, Gerald C., 127, 161, 163, 167
Wright, John R., 22

Yao, Dennis, 8

Zaller, John R., 11, 30–31, 111, 127, 161,
    163
Zukman, Jill, 146n. 45, 148n. 51

Subject Index

Afghanistan, Soviet invasion of, 139
alternative political systems, 188–91
amendments, significance of, 57–58
analytical narratives, 131–32
Anderson, Martin, 153
Anti-Federalist Papers, 3–4
appeals, xii, 3–5; cost of, 16, 23, 29–30, 121; involvement of the mass public, xii–xiv, 4–5, 101–3, 186; scholarship on, 6–8, 10–11, 12–13, 23, 30–31, 36–39, 40, 41, 51–52, 79–80, 83, 186–87. *See also* domestic policy appeals; foreign policy appeals; Public Appeals Theory
approval ratings, 37, 77–78, 86–89, 132, 159; popularity of initiative and, 58–59; term of presidency and, 167–68, 176–77. *See also* personal popularity
Aristotle, xi, 188
arms reduction example, 31–33

Baker, Howard H., Jr., 154
Baker, James, 20
bargaining, presidential-congressional, 14, 22, 25, 60, 69, 70, 73, 108, 115, 138, 146, 156
blame-game politics, 155–56, 170, 178
Bosnia appeal of Bill Clinton, 20, 41, 42, 46–48. *See also* Clinton, Bill
budget: Budget Act of 1990, 142–43; Budget and Accounting Act of 1921, 59–60, 165; budgetary data, 59–61, 79, 89–90, 163–65, 181–82; discretionary spending, 60–61; impact of

budget share on likelihood of an appeal, 67, 71, 73, 91, 93; presidential budgetary success, 45–46, 48. *See also* Carter, Jimmy: reduction of humanitarian assistance proposal
Burford, Ann Gorsuch, 153
Bush, George Herbert Walker, 74, 177; approval ratings, 87, 140, 143, 145; campaign against Clinton, 144–45, 147–50; economy and, 140–50; pandering, 142–43, 145–50; policy leadership, 140–47; unemployment benefits policy, 105, 131, 140–50, 156; vetoes bills, 131, 141–42, 144–49
Bush, George W., 1–3

Cable Television Consumer Protection and Competition Act of 1992, 148–49
California state senators, 127n. 17
Calio, Nicholas, 141
Carnahan, Jean, 2–3
Carter, Jimmy, 74; budgetary concerns, 136–39; crisis of confidence speech, 53; economy and, 135–39; Iranian hostage crisis, 139; Panama Canal Treaties speech, 85; pandering, 136–40; policy leadership, 133–35; public approval ratings, 135, 136; public interest reputation, 133–34; reduction of humanitarian assistance proposal, 105, 108, 131, 133–40; Soviet invasion of Afghanistan, 139
Chambliss, Saxby, 2–3
cheap talk games, 31–32
Cleland, Max, 2

Clinton, Bill, 13, 77; Bosnia appeal, 20, 41, 42, 46–48; Brady Bill appeal, 55; campaign against Bush, 144–45, 147–50; health care initiative, 52, 53, 126; humanitarian aid initiative, 84; lack of responsiveness, 177–78; second term, 168, 179

committees, congressional, 8, 22, 37–38

common space (CS) scores, 169

communist containment, 134

competence of president, 183, 187–88; policy competence, 115–16

Conditional Pandering Theory, 105, 128–29, 131; action, 117; actors and interests, 114–15; behavior, 117; conceptual background, 112–17; pandering vs. concurrence, 106–7; policy competence, 115–16; policy congruence, 106–7, 123; policy incentives, 117–21; policy leadership, 152–53; policy resolution, 116; popularity/unpopularity of president, 127; predictions, 158–63; propositions, 121–23; related literature, 123–28; term of presidency and, 158–59; voters' beliefs, 116. *See also* policy pandering

Conditional Pandering Theory Popularity prediction, 168, 173, 176, 178

conflict, scope of, 10

Congress: effect of appeals on, 5, 20, 103; filibuster and, 67n. 26; Homeland Security Department and, 1–3; preferred outcomes, 21–23, 26–29; presidential veto and, 6, 8, 16, 67n. 26, 131, 141–42, 144–49, 191; responsiveness, 22–23, 38–39, 186n. 1; veto and, 16, 24–28, 147. *See also* veto

Congressional Budget Office (CBO), 143

Conservative Political Action Conference, 154

Constitution, 3–4

Constitutional Convention, 4n. 15

Contract with America, 126

Council of Economic Advisors, 150

Country Report on Human Rights Practices, 139

Crafting of Public Opinion perspective, 87–88, 125–26

credit-claiming/grandstanding, presidential, 5, 42, 51, 72, 76, 80, 92, 98, 101, 186

current opinion, 21, 25, 29, 31, 34, 42, 49, 112, 136, 177, 183, 185–88; definition, xiii, 5, 5n. 17; domestic policy appeals and, 36, 44–46; foreign policy appeals and, 88, 96, 101; pandering and, 105–6, 109, 111–12, 121n. 12, 122–23, 126–28. *See also* Latent Opinion; policy congruence

Daschle, Tom, 2

Defense Department, 1, 90

demagoguery, fear of, xi, 4, 101–2, 128, 187–88

Dole, Bob, 48, 146, 154

domestic policy appeals, 16–17, 51–53, 133, 185; effect on citizens' policy preferences, 51, 54, 56, 78n. 39, 78–79, 114; effect on salience of issues, 68, 71, 73, 75, 77; Influence over Domestic Affairs prediction, 43, 46, 51, 59, 65–66, 75–76; legislative influence, position popularity and, 35–39; noncompulsory primetime addresses, 53–59, 80; Popularity of Domestic Positions prediction, 37–38, 51, 59, 65, 70; public concern and, 68–69, 71, 73, 75; salience of issue and, 68, 71, 73, 75; Sincerity of Policy Debate prediction, 51, 59, 65, 70, 72, 76; targeted address and, 69–70, 71, 73, 75; testing of theories, 59–78; unpopular initiatives and, 52, 57, 72, 74, 86, 185–86

Dominici, Pete, 154

Downey, Thomas J., 143, 144

drawdown authority, 90, 91, 92, 93, 98; use as instrumental variable, 90, 91, 91n. 2, 92, 93, 98

Dynamic Representation, 124, 161–62, 177, 178

Education Department appeal of Ronald Reagan, 19–20, 41, 44–46

Eisenhower, Dwight D., 13, 52, 74, 87

Electoral Cycle, 127–28, 159, 161–63, 172, 176–77, 179

electoral incentives, 119–20, 121–22, 136–37, 152, 153, 179, 181, 183, 189

Electoral Proximity Hypothesis, 159–63, 168, 174–75, 178
Energy Department appeal of Ronald Reagan, 19–20, 41, 44–46
Environmental Protection Agency, Reagan and, 153
executive orders, 6, 25n. 17, 48, 191. *See also* unilateral action

Family and Medical Leave Act of 1992, 148–49
Federalist Papers, 3, 4, 12, 104, 187
Federal Reserve, 150
filibuster, 67n. 26
fixed-effects models, 174n. 18
Ford, Gerald, 84, 87
Foreign Assistance Act of 1961, 90
foreign policy appeals, 6, 16–17, 83–84, 100–102, 185; citizens' lack of knowledge, 31–32, 35; effect on citizens' policy preferences, 31–32, 86–87, 96, 114; effect on salience of issues, 91, 95; Influence over Foreign Affairs prediction, 40, 47, 83, 88–98, 100; noncompulsory primetime addresses, 84, 85–100; Popularity of Foreign Positions prediction, 40, 83–84, 86, 88, 90, 94, 98–100; public concern and, 91, 93, 95–97; Sincerity of Policy Debate prediction, 84, 90, 91–98, 100; targeted address and, 91, 93; testing, 89–100; unpopular initiatives and, 86–89, 94, 185–86
Frank, Barney, 1

Gephardt, Richard, 140
Gingrich, Newt, 48
going public, 7–8, 26, 33, 39–40, 60, 80, 88, 90, 99, 101, 185
Gore, Al, 140
Goss, Porter, 20
gross domestic product, and relationship to public appeals, 70, 71, 75, 91, 93
Gulf War, 140

Hamilton, Alexander, 4, 104
Harper, Ed, 152
Hepburn Act of 1906, 52
Homeland Security, Department of, 1–3
Huffington, Arianna, 103

humanitarian assistance proposals: Carter, 105, 108, 131, 133–40; Clinton, 84

ideology: ideological congruence of Congress and mass opinion, 170, 178; ideological congruence of president and mass opinion, 169–70, 177–78; ideological differences among citizens, 105, 107, 126; relationship to unified government, 76–77
impeachment, threat of, 179–80, 182
inflation, 137–38
Influence over Domestic Affairs prediction, 43, 46, 51, 59, 65–66, 75–76
Influence over Foreign Affairs prediction, 40, 47, 83, 88–98, 100
informational asymmetry, 105, 107, 112–14, 144; policy competence, 115–16; policy expertise, 30–34, 108–9, 187. *See also* policy information
instrumental variables, 64–65, 98; Budget Share, 67; Unified Government, 67–68
interest groups, 22, 38, 103–4
interest rates, 150
interim term, 190–91
Intermediate Range Nuclear Forces (INF) Treaty, 84, 87
involvement of the mass public, 34, 104, 185; definition, 4–5; societal welfare and, xii–xiv, 5, 8, 101–3, 156, 186
Iranian hostage crisis, 139

Jefferson, Thomas, 4n. 15
Jefford, James, 2n. 6
Johnson, Lyndon B., 53, 74, 87

Kennedy, John F., 55, 74, 85, 87

Labor, Department of, 145
Lack of Substantive Responsiveness perspective, 125–26, 161–62, 173, 177, 178
Latent Opinion, xiii(n.3), 10, 111, 116, 127, 161–63, 172, 177. *See also* current opinion
Latin American presidents, 162n. 2, 163n. 4, 189–90
Lewinsky scandal, 180

Madison, James, 3, 4, 12
media, 7, 23n. 14, 25, 29; coverage of presidential activities, 23n. 14, 35n.

media (*continued*)
   32; historical context, 12–13; prior
   salience, 68, 71, 73, 75, 91, 93, 95. *See
   also* television
Medicare, 151
Meese, Edwin, III, 153
Michel, Robert H., 146
Mill, John Stuart, xi, 187
Mitchell, George, 142
model-driven history, 132
modern presidency, 13

National Security Council, 83
Need-based Popularity perspective,
   124–25, 161, 162, 173
Nixon, Richard, 14, 55, 74, 77, 97, 177;
   second term, 168, 179

Office of Management and Budget
   (OMB), 143
O'Neill, Thomas P. (Tip), Jr., 20, 43
opinion dikes, 10
organizational capacity, 115

pandering, as term, 104n. 5, 104–5. *See
   also* policy pandering
parties, xiv, 13, 22, 163n. 4
party activists, 162n. 3
Perot, Ross, 143, 149nn. 57, 58
personal popularity, 6–7, 11, 30–31, 73,
   118–19, 136, 166–67; domestic policy
   and, 69, 71, 73, 74, 75; foreign policy
   and, 91, 93, 96; policy congruence
   and, 124–25, 157, 159–63; policy
   pandering and, 111–12, 118–21, 127,
   144; public appeals and, 37, 69, 74.
   See also approval ratings
plebiscitary activities. *See* involvement of
   the mass public
policy approval, 55–57, 62–63, 70–74,
   86–87, 89, 91–92n. 3, 93–94. *See also*
   position popularity
policy competence, 115–16
policy concurrence, 105–7, 157
policy congruence: electoral proximity
   and, 159–61, 172–74; personal popularity and, 124–25, 157, 159–63; in
   relation to policy pandering,
   106–7, 112, 123, 127, 128–29, 157,
   170

policy expertise, 31–32, 108–9, 113, 115,
   117, 187. *See also* policy information
policy information, 32–33, 109, 112–15,
   120. *See also* policy competence; policy expertise
policy leadership, 105, 106n. 7, 120,
   121–22, 131, 133, 140, 142–43,
   152–53, 157
policy pandering, 104–5, 128, 131; belief
   that voters are misinformed, 106, 111,
   112, 127; concurrence and, 105–7;
   electoral cycle and, 122; policy expertise and, 108–9; policy leadership and,
   105, 121–22; popularity/unpopularity
   of president, 111–12, 118–21, 127,
   144. *See also* Conditional Pandering
   Theory
policy resolution, 116
political systems, alternative, 188–91
Politics (Aristotle), xi
Popularity of Domestic Positions prediction, 37–38, 51, 59, 65, 70
Popularity of Foreign Positions prediction, 40, 83–84, 86, 88, 90, 94,
   98–100
position popularity, 35–39, 60, 86,
   164–65, 186. *See also* policy approval
presidential appeal. *See* appeals; domestic
   policy appeals; foreign policy appeals
presidential budgetary success: domestic
   policy, 63–68, 72–76, 76n. 35; foreign
   policy, 91, 97, 98
presidential speeches: noncompulsory
   primetime addresses, 52, 53–54, 62,
   84; State of the Union addresses, 9,
   15–16, 151, 154, 171
presidents, xi–xii; command of public
   attention, 13, 23n. 14, 25, 28–29, 30n.
   21, 35n. 32, 113; desire for favorable
   historical legacy, 114, 118–20, 158,
   178, 181; (in)competence and unre-
   sponsiveness, 187–88; motivations,
   21–23, 107–8, 114, 118, 133, 167,
   180; personal qualities, 70, 75, 105,
   107–8, 135, 171; policy competence,
   115–16; silence on unpopular positions, 37–38, 60, 86, 164–65, 186. *See
   also* involvement of the mass public;
   term of presidency
priority, 69, 71, 73, 75, 79, 91, 93

prior media salience, 68, 71, 73, 75, 91, 93, 95

public appeal. *See* appeals; domestic policy appeals; foreign policy appeals; Public Appeals Theory

Public Appeals Theory, 16, 20–21, 48–49; actions, 24–25; altering citizens' policy preferences, 23, 30–34; basic assumptions, 21–25; basic results, 26–29; behavior, 25; costly appeals, 29–30; examples, 41–49; foreign vs. domestic policy, 34–35; legislative influence, position popularity and domestic policy, 35–39; sincerity of policy debate, 40–41; testable hypotheses, 34–41; variation across administrations, 56–57. *See also* domestic policy appeals; foreign policy appeals

public concern, 68–69, 71, 73, 75, 91, 93, 95–97, 171

pull incentives, 22

Putnam, Adam, 1–2

radio, 15

random-effects probit model, 174, 176

rational choice theory, xiii, 11–12, 131

Reagan, Ronald, 7, 52, 74; blame-game politics, 155–56; contingency tax proposal, 105, 131, 150–56; defense spending initiative, 84, 87, 90; domestic policy appeals, 19–20, 41–46; Education Department initiative, 19–20, 41, 44–46; Energy Department initiative, 19–20, 41, 44–46; income tax initiative, 20, 41–42; Nicaraguan Contras speech, 85; pandering to conservatives, 154; policy leadership, 152–53; second term, 168, 179; State of the Union addresses, 151, 154

representation, archetypal perspectives of, 10–11

Rockefeller, Jay, IV, 140

Rohrabacher, Dana, 20

roll-call votes, 9, 64, 124–25, 169

Roosevelt, Franklin D., 13n. 33, 15–16

Roosevelt, Theodore, 13n. 33, 52

Roth, William V., Jr., 44

salience of issue, public, 22–23, 105; appeals, 91, 93, 95, 105; domestic policy success, 68, 71, 73, 75; foreign policy success, 39, 91, 93, 95; policy congruence and, 178, 180; success, vs. influence, 6, 8n. 22, 35–36n. 34, 43, 46, 57–58n. 11, 78, 88. *See also* prior media salience; public concern

simultaneous equations models, 64–65

Sincerity of Policy Debate prediction, 40–41; domestic policy appeals and, 51, 59, 65, 70, 72, 76; foreign policy appeals and, 84, 90, 91–98, 100

single presidential term, limit of, 189–90

societal welfare, 103–5, 113, 122, 126, 131, 144; involvement of the mass public and, xii–xiv, 5, 8, 101–3, 156, 186; term of presidency and, 185–86

Soviet Union, invasion of Afghanistan, 139

spatial modeling, 16, 65

speechwriting, 83

Talent, Jim, 2–3

targeted address, 69–70, 71, 73, 75, 91, 93

tax policy: contingency tax proposal of Ronald Reagan, 105, 131, 150–56; income tax initiative of Ronald Reagan, 20, 41–42

television: historical context and, 13; importance of for public relations, 2, 7, 29, 96. *See also* media

term limits, 189–90

term of presidency, 116–17, 125; alternative political systems, 189–91; approval ratings and, 167–68, 176–77; first half vs. second half, 159, 167–68, 173, 175–77; first-term presidents, 114, 158–59, 168, 174–80; limit of one term, 189–90; second-term presidents, 118, 158, 167–68, 178–82; societal welfare and, 185–86

Tocqueville, Alexis de, xi

transitions, presidential, 191

Truman, Harry, 1

tyranny of the majority, 104n. 3

unemployment benefits policy: George H. W. Bush and, 141–44; HR 3575, 142; HR 4095, 143; HR 5260, 143–44; S 1722, 141–42

unified government: domestic policy
appeals and, 67–68, 74, 76–77; foreign
policy appeals and, 91, 93, 97–98; relationship to ideological convergence
between President and Congress,
76–77; use as instrumental variable,
67–68, 91n. 2
unilateral action, 6n. 18, 25n. 17, 48,
83, 90, 92, 97. *See also* executive
orders

veto, 6, 8, 16, 24–28, 32–34, 37n. 38,
67n. 26, 191; Bush, George H. W.

and, 131, 141–42, 144–49; as pre-
ferred outcome, 26–28
Vietnam aid proposals, 84, 87
Vietnam War, 97, 98
Volcker, Paul, 140

war, 91, 92, 93, 98
Watergate, 180
Watt, James, 153
Wellford, Harrison, 191
Wilson, Woodrow, 13n. 33